The Enforcement and Setting Aside of Contracts

THE ENFORCEMENT AND SETTING ASIDE OF CONTRACTS

Dr Albert Keating BL

CLARUS PRESS

Published by
Clarus Press Ltd,
Griffith Campus,
South Circular Road,
Dublin 8.
www.claruspress.ie

Typeset by
Gough Typesetting Services,
Dublin

Printed by
CPI Antony Rowe,
Chippenham,
Wiltshire

ISBN
978-1-911611-49-3

A catalogue record for this book is available from the British Library

To Vera

PREFACE

The principles relating to the enforcement and setting aside of contracts analysed in Parts I – IV of the book may be presented in logical and numerical order as follows:

A. The Enforcement of Contracts [1]

1. A contract relating to the sale of land or interest in land may be enforced by specific performance.
    1.1 A contract for the sale of land or interest in land for enforcement by specific performance must be evidenced in writing in compliance with the Statute of Frauds (Ireland) 1695.
        1.1.1 A contract for the sale of land or interest in land which is not evidenced in writing may not be enforced by specific performance.
        1.1.2 A contract for the sale of land or interests in land may be enforced by specific performance notwithstanding the absence of evidence of the contract in writing on grounds of part performance and where it is shown that the Statute of Frauds is being used as a vehicle of frauds and where the contract in question has been substantially performed.
        1.1.3 A contract enforceable by specific performance may not be enforced on grounds of hardship.
        1.1.4 A building contract for renovations and repairs may not be enforced by specific performance where supervision of the court is required.
        1.1.5 A contract of loan may not be enforced by specific performance.
        1.1.6 A contract brought to a pre-mature determination by frustration may not be enforced by specific performance.
        1.1.7 An illegal contract may not be enforced by specific performance.
    1.2 A testamentary contract may be enforced by specific performance.
        1.2.1 A testamentary contract may be entered into where an owner of land promises to leave his or her land to another person in consideration of his or her work on

[1] See Part I – Chapters 1 – 5.

the land for meagre or no remuneration, and as such may be enforced by specific performance.

1.3 A *Pallant v Morgan* – type arrangement may be enforced by specific performance.

1.3.1 A *Pallant v Morgan* – type arrangement not evidenced in writing in compliance with the Statute of Frauds may not be enforced by specific performance.

1.3.2 A *Pallant v Morgan* – type arrangement may be enforced by what is known as a *Pallant v Morgan* – type equity.

1.4 A collateral contract may be used to enforce a promise given prior to the main contract and but for which this main contract would not have been made.

1.4.1 The consideration of a collateral contract, and as such rendering it legally binding, is the making of some other contact called the main contract, albeit a collateral contract is an independent contract in its own right, and may be enforced as such.

1.4.2 A written contract between parties will be presumed to contain the entirety of the terms agreed between them,

1.4.3 However, where a collateral contract is found or construed to exist between the parties to the main written contract by reference to pre-contractual documents, it may have the effect of altering the terms of the written contract, and may be enforced as such.

1.4.4 The pre-contractual documents may show that the party seeking to enforce the collateral contract had been induced to enter the main written contract by representations or statements.

1.4.5 The pre-contractual documents may provide the necessary "cogent evidence" for enforcing the collateral contract.

1.5 Estoppel principles include the principle of promissory estoppel and estoppel by convention.

1.5.1 The enforcement of a contract by specific performance may be defended by reliance on the principle of promissory estoppel.

1.5.2 A contract found to exist by virtue of assumptions may be enforced by estoppel by convention.

B. Setting Aside Contracts [2]

2. A contract may be set aside on grounds of equitable common mistake.

---

[2] See Part II – Chapters 6 – 9.

2.1.1 A contract may be rectified, instead of being set aside, where a subsequent record of the contract does not truly reflect the terms of the contract entered into by parties.

2.2 A contract entered into on foot of a misrepresentation may be rescinded.

2.2.1 A contract may be set aside by rescission once the prerequisites for establishing same are satisfied.

2.3 A contract may be set aside on grounds of undue influence.

2.3.1 A presumption of undue influence may arise out of a fiduciary relationship between contractual parties.

2.3.2 A presumption of undue influence may be rebutted by showing that independent legal advice was sought and followed.

2.4 A contract may be set aside on grounds of non est factum.

2.4.1 The Morris criteria may be applied when determining issues of non est factum.

2.5 A contract may be set aside on grounds of improvident transaction.

2.5.1 The Gilligan criteria may be applied when determining issues relating to improvident transactions.

C. The Enforcement of Debts and Guarantees by Summary Judgment [3]

3. The payment of money due on a contract of loan may be sought by summary proceedings.

3.1.1 The payment of a debt due on a loan may be enforced by summary judgment by notice of motion and grounding affidavits.

3.1.2 The payment of a debt may not be enforced by summary judgment where an arguable defence is established.

3.1.3 An arguable defence may remitted for plenary hearing.

3.1.4 An arguable defence will have to be substantiated at plenary hearing of the issue.

D. Discovery of Documents [4]

4. In relation to A, B and C above, the court may order discovery of documents where it is satisfied that the documents sought are both relevant and necessary for the fair disposal of the case or to save costs.

4.1 In order to discover particular categories of documents it must be shown that they are necessary for disposing fairly of the cause or matter, but the applicant does not have to prove that

[3] See Part III – Chapters 10 – 13.

[4] See Part IV – Chapter 14.

they are in any sense "absolutely necessary" to the cause or matter.

4.2 The primary principles are relevance and of necessity.[5]

4.3 The proportionality test may be viewed as a refinement of the concept of "necessity".[6]

4.4 "Necessity" means that the disclosure of the documents concerned may be necessary for the fair and just resolution of the proceedings and potentially for saving costs.

4.5 If it cannot be demonstrated that documents are relevant, then there could be no basis for requiring that they be discovered.

4.6 The fact that confidentiality (as opposed to privilege) does not provide a legitimate basis for refusing to require disclosure of documents should they prove necessary to the proper administration of justice. But they do provide a warrant for the court adopting appropriate measures to respect the importance of confidentiality by ensuring that it is only displaced when the production of confidential documentation proves truly necessary to the just resolution of proceedings.[7]

E. Interrogatories[8]

5. In relation to A, B and C above, interrogatories may be served not only in relation to facts directly in issue, but also in respect of facts the existence or non-existence of which is relevant to the existence or non-existence of facts directly in issue.

5.1 Instead of applying for discovery of documents "more efficient methods of disclosure should first be pursued", to seek the same information, such as by the delivery of interrogatories.

5.2 The right to serve interrogatories is not confined to facts which are in the peculiar knowledge of the other party. Rather, they may also be used for the purpose of obtaining an admission from the other side.

5.3 Interrogatories will only be allowed where they are necessary either for disposing fairly of the cause or matter or for saving costs.

5.4 Interrogatories will not be allowed where what is being sought

---

5 *Tobin v Minister for Defence* [2019] IESC 57, paras 6-7; see *Ryanair plc. v Aer Rianta cpt* [2003] 4 IR 264, 277; see *Compagnie Financiere et Commerciale du Pacifique v Peruvian Guano* (1882) 11 QBD 55; *Framus Ltd. v CRH plc* [2004] 2 IR 20 at 36.

6 See *Tobin v Minister for Defence* [2019] IESC 57; *Dome Telecom Ltd v Eircom Ltd.* [2007] IESC 59; *Astrazeneca AB and Ors. v Pinewood Laboratories Ltd. & Ors.* [2011] IEHC 159; *Persona Digital Telephony Limited & Anor v Minister for Public Enterprise & Ors.* [2017] IESC 27 and *SPV Osus Ltd v HSBC Institutional Trust Services (Ireland) Limited & Ors.* [2018] IESC 44.

7 See *Tobin v Minister for Defence* [2019] IESC 57, para 7.12.

8 See Part IV – Chapter 15.

is not an answer in respect of a factual matter, but rather relates to the interpretation of the contents of a document.[9]

F. Injunctions[10]

6. In relation to A above, the status quo of parties to an action on a contract sought to be specifically enforced may be maintained by an application for an interlocutory or mandatory interlocutory injunction.
   6.1 Where it is established that there is a fair or bona fide or serious question to be tried, the court may then consider the question of adequacy of damages.
   6.2 The courts by exercising its discretionary powers may award damages in lieu of equitable relief for injunctions.
   6.3 Where the court decides to grant an injunction to the plaintiff it may also require him or her to give an undertaking as to damages for any loss incurred by the defendant before the hearing of the action.
   6.4 A plaintiff may make an ex parte application to the court seeking a mareva injunction for the purpose of restraining the defendant from disposing of his or her funds before the hearing of an action on a contract between them.

G. Principles Applicable to Costs of Entire Proceedings[11]

7. In relation to A, B and C above, the general discretion of the Court in connection with the ordering of costs is preserved.
   7.1 In considering the awarding of costs of any action, the court should 'have regard to' the provisions of s 169(1) of the Legal Services Regulations Act 2015.
   7.2 In a case where the party seeking costs has been "entirely successful in those proceedings", the party so succeeding "is entitled" to an award of costs against the unsuccessful party unless the court orders otherwise.
   7.3 In determining whether to "order otherwise" the court should have regard to the "nature and circumstances of the case" and "the conduct of the proceedings by the parties".
   7.4 Further, the matters to which the court shall have regard in deciding whether to so order otherwise include the conduct of the parties before and during the proceedings, and whether it was reasonable for a party to raise, pursue or contest one or more issues.
   7.5 The court, in the exercise of its discretion may also make

---

9 *Allied Irish Bank plc v Doran* [2020] IEHC 210.

10 See Part IV – Chapter 16.

11 See Part IV – Chapter 17.

an order that where a party is "partially successful" in the proceedings, it should recover costs relating to the successful element or elements of the proceedings.

7.6 Even where a party has not been "entirely successful" the court should still have regard to the matters referred to in s 169(1)(a)-(g) when deciding whether to award costs pursuant to Ord 99, r 2(3) of the Rules of the Superior Courts (Costs) 2019.

7.7 In the exercise of its discretion, the court may order the payment of a portion of a party's costs, or costs from or until a specified date pursuant to s 168(2)(a)) of the Legal Services Regulations Act 2015.[12]

H. Principles Applicable to Costs in Interlocutory Applications [13]

8. In relation to interlocutory applications involving A, B, C, D and F above, a judge who has heard a motion is often better placed than the trial judge to consider the justice of where costs of that motion should lie.

8.1 The effect of Ord 90, r 1(4A) of the Rules of the Superior Courts (Costs) 2008 is that a court is required to adjudicate upon and make a costs order in respect of an interlocutory application, rather than reserve the costs.

8.2 Order 99, r 2(3) of the Rules of the Superior Courts (Costs) 2019 has identical provisions to the former Ord 99, r 1(4A) of the Rules of the Superior Courts (Costs) 2008. [14]

8.3 The court retains a wide discretion in deciding what costs order to make.

8.4 Options include making (a) an order awarding all or part of the costs to one party, (b) no order as to costs, or (c) the costs of the application costs in the cause.

8.5 Costs may only be reserved where it is not possible justly to adjudicate upon the costs of the interlocutory application.

8.6 Important factors in determining how to deal with the costs of an interlocutory application include (a) whether an application was required to be brought, (b) the success, or degree of success, of a party on the application, (c) whether the party bringing the application gave the opposing party an adequate opportunity to deal with the subject matter of the motion prior to its issue, and (d) whether the opposing party acted reasonably in refusing to deal with the particular matter on a

---

12 *Chubb European Group SE v The Health Insurance Authority* [2020] IECA 183.

13 See Part IV– Chapter 18.

14 *Paddy Burke (Builders) Limited (in liquidation and in receivership) v Tullyvaraga Management Company Limited* [2020] IEHC 199; *Crowley v Promontoria (Oyster) DAC* [2020] IEHC 365.

consensual basis.

8.7 In the case of interlocutory injunction applications, the diversity of outcomes following which the court may be asked to determine where the burden of costs should lie will inevitably bear on the court's determination.

8.8 Another factor is the inherent nature of an interlocutory injunction which is to preserve the status quo.

Thus, the law relating to the enforcement of contract is comprised of substantive principles such as specific performance and defence mechanisms such as promissory estoppel. The law relating to setting aside contracts is also comprised of substantive principles such as undue influence and misrepresentation. In an application for summary judgment of a debt owing and due as established in summary proceedings the plaintiff may apply for enforcement of the debt by way of summary judgment under Ord 37 of the Rules of the Superior Courts. However, where the defendant can show that he or she has an arguable defence based on such substantive principles as misrepresentation, undue influence or consideration, the court may remit the issue to plenary hearing where the application of such substantive principles may be debated. There are also adjunctive principles at play such as principles of discovery of documents, interrogatories, injunctions and costs. The principles of discovery of documents, interrogatories and injunctions may come into play as adjunctive principles to the substantive principles such as specific performance, undue influence or misrepresentation. The principles relating to costs may become an issue dependent upon the outcome of proceedings involving the application of the foregoing substantive or adjunctive principles.

In relation to judicial application of principles, where it is decided by a judge that a case may be justified by the application of a principle, the next step for him or her is to ensure that the correct principle is chosen to suit the circumstances of the case. It is for a subsequent judge to decide "whether or not it is a right principle, and, if not, he may himself lay down the true principle." [15] A judge may re-affirm an established principle instead of applying a newly formulated principle. In *Great Peace Shipping Ltd v Tsavliris Salvage (International) Ltd* [16] Lord Philips M.R., did not apply the concept and principle of equitable common mistake formulated by Denning L.J., but instead applied the legal doctrine of common mistake as formulated by the House of Lords in *Bell v Lever Brothers*, [17] and stated that the decision in *Bell* did not allow for the intervention of equity. Equity neither gave a party a right to rescind a contract nor conferred on the court

[15] See *Osborne v Rowlett* (1880) 13 Ch.D. 774, 785.

[16] [2002] 4 All ER 689, para 160.

[17] [1932] AC 161.

a discretion to set aside a contract. Lord Philips MR stated that it was "impossible to reconcile *Solle v Butcher* with *Bell v Lever Brothers*." [18] A judge may summarise a series of pertinent and applicable principles in relation to a particular aspect of substantive or procedural law. In *Tobin v Minister for Defence* [19] Clarke CJ summarised and applied substantive and procedural principles relating to the discovery of documents. In *Harrisrange Ltd. v Duncan* [20] McKechnie J formulated a series of substantive principles of summary judgment. In *Ulster Bank Ireland Ltd v Beades* [21] McKechnie J, made various commentaries on the litigation process involved in applying for summary judgment. In *Bank of Scotland plc v McDermott* [22] Barrett J, identified the key features of the power of inherent jurisdiction of the courts.

In relation to judicial formulation of new concepts, a judge may formulate a new principle that "both fits and justifies some complex part of the legal practices". [23] In *K v K*,[24] McDonald J, instead of applying the established principle of proprietary estoppel, formulated a new concept of testamentary contract based on a promise made by the deceased during her lifetime to the plaintiff, and that there was "ongoing consideration given by the plaintiff for the promise which his mother made to him." In *Solle v Butcher* [25] Denning LJ, formulated a new concept of common equitable mistake, and stated that the court had equitable jurisdiction to intervene where the parties have concluded a contract that was binding in law under a common misapprehension of a fundamental nature as to material facts or their respective rights, and where such is established a contract may be set aside. The principle of equitable common mistake was subsequently adopted by Costello J (as he then was) in *O'Neill v Ryan*. [26] In *Irish Pensions Trust v Central Remedial Clinic*, [27] Kelly J referred, though *obiter*, to the judgment of Costello J in *O'Neill v Ryan* with apparent approval of his approach to the question of shared common mistake based on the decision of Denning LJ in *Solle v Butcher*.

The author is extremely grateful to David McCartney and staff at Clarus

---

18 [2002] 4 All ER 689, para 157.

19 See *Tobin v Minister for Defence* [2019] IESC 57, paras 6-7.

20 [2003] 4 IR 1, 7; *Aer Rianta c.p.t. v Ryanair Ltd* [2001] 4 IR 607 at 623; see *Allied Irish Banks plc v Farrell* [2014] IEHC 395 at paras 32 to 34.

21 [2019] IESC 83.

22 [2017] IEHC 77; see *Allied Irish Banks PLC v Forde and O'Driscoll* [2020] IECA 133.

23 R. Dworkin, *Law's Empire* (Oxford: Hart Publishing, 2006) at p.228; see also, Albert Keating, "A Concept of Interpretative Methodology" (2017) 35 ILT 139.

24 [2018] IEHC 615, para 77.

25 [1950] 1 KB 671.

26 [1991] ILRM 672; see *Irish Pensions Trust v Central Remedial Clinic*, High Court, Kelly J, 18 March 2005; *Intrum Justitia BV v Legal and Trade Financial Services Ltd*, High Court, O'Sullivan J, 10 June 2005.

27 Unreported, High Court, Kelly J, 18 March, 2005.

Press for their assistance, efficiency and availability during the course of writing *The Enforcement and Setting Aside of Contracts*.

Albert Keating
26 February 2021

TABLE OF CONTENTS

TABLE OF CASES

TABLE OF LEGISLATION

PRE UNION IRISH STATUTES

IRISH LEGISLATION

STATUTORY INSTRUMENTS

Part I

THE ENFORCEMENT OF CONTRACTS

Chapter 1

THE ENFORCEMENT OF CONTRACTS BY SPECIFIC PERFORMANCE

Introduction

A contract for the sale of land or interest in land which is evidenced in writing by a note or memorandum may be enforced by specific performance.[1] The Statute of Frauds (Ireland) 1695 prescribes that a contract for the sale of land or any interest in land must be evidenced in writing by a note or memorandum to be enforceable. Therefore, a contract for the sale of land or interest in land may be enforced by specific performance where it is evidenced in writing in accordance with the provisions of the Statute of Frauds. Where a contract for the sale of land or interest in land is not evidenced in writing it may not be enforced by specific performance, unless the party seeking the enforcement of the contract can show that he or she has substantially performed his or her obligations under the contract, and in such circumstances, the court by exercising its discretionary powers may enforce the contract by applying the principle of part performance. The Statute of Frauds may not be used as a vehicle of frauds, and where it is shown that a contractual party purports to take advantage of a contract not being in writing in circumstances that would render it unconscionable for him or her to do so, the court may apply the principle of part performance to prevent a fraud from taking place, and enforce the contract by specific performance. The principle of part performance was formulated to prevent frauds, and the court will decide "whether the plaintiff has an equity arising from part performance which is so affixed upon the conscience of the defendant that it amounts to a fraud on his part to take advantage of the fact that the contract is not in writing".[2] **1–01**

Where it is shown that a contractual party would suffer hardship should the contract be enforced against him or her, the court may refuse specific **1–02**

[1] See *Donegan v Kenny* [2020] IECA 90.

[2] *Lowry v Reid* [1927] NI 142, 154–55; Albert Keating, *Equity in Practice* (Clarus Press 2020).

performance of it.[3] Where a defendant can show that it would be unfair to enforce a contract on grounds of *laches* or delay in bringing an action, the court may refuse specific performance.[4] The type of contract entered by parties may also determine whether it is capable of enforcement by specific performance. A building contract or contract for the repair or renovation of a building, which requires on-going supervision of the court, may not be enforced by specific performance. However, in exceptional cases, the court may intervene and decree specific performance of a building contract where the particulars of the contract are clearly set out.[5] Contracts of loan or guarantees relating to such loans will not be enforced by specific performance. In *Duggan v Irish Allied Building Society*,[6] Finlay P, when referring to contracts of loan, stated that a court could not and should not grant a specific performance of a contract to advance money. A contract that is deemed impossible to perform or is a frustrated contract or one that is illegal will not be enforced by specific performance.[7] In *Leggett v Crowley*[8] O'Connor J, when referring to illegal contracts involving contracts for the sale of land, and the burden of proof in establishing the illegality, stated that:

> The burden of proving an illegal contract lies with the party alleging the illegality. This is clear from the case of *Whelan v Kavanagh* [2001] IEHC 14, (unreported, High Court, 29th January, 2001), where Herbert J. stated that: "... a party who has executed a contract required by law to be evidenced in writing and which is regular and lawful on its face, and whose execution of that contract has been witnessed by his or her solicitor should not lightly be permitted to impugn that contract, particularly to his or her own advantage, by pleading illegality as a defence to a claim for specific performance. The onus of proving such alleged illegality lies firmly with the party raising it and the burden of proof is the same as in all civil actions."

1–03 The court, by exercising its discretionary powers, may award damages *in lieu* of specific performance, and indeed, may further award damages in addition to specific performance under s 2 of the Chancery Amendment Act 1858 (known as Lord Cairns' Act).[9] Where the court decides that damages *in lieu* of specific performance of the contract would be an adequate remedy,

---

3 See *Smelter Corporation of Ireland Ltd v O'Driscoll* [1977] IR 305; *Aranbel Ltd v Darcy* [2010] IEHC 272; *Leggett v Crowley* [2020] IECA 3.

4 See *Fitzsimons v Value Homes Ltd* [2006] IEHC 144; *White v McCooey* [1976–77] ILRM 72.

5 See *Fitzsimons v Value Homes Ltd* [2006] IEHC 144, paras 1.1–6; *Rushbrooke v O'Sullivan* [1908] 1 IR 232; *Wolverhampton Corporation v Emmons* [1901] 1 KB 515.

6 Unreported, High Court, Finlay P, 4 March 1976.

7 See *Collins v Gleeson* [2011] IEHC 200; *McGuill v Aer Lingus Teoranta*, unreported, High Court, McWilliam J, 3 October 1983; *Neville & Sons Ltd v Guardian Builders Ltd* [1995] 1 ILRM 1. *Quinn v Irish Bank Resolution Corporation Limited* [2012] IEHC 36; *Leggett v Crowley* [2019] IEHC 182.

8 [2019] IEHC 182, para 40.

9 See *Worth v Tyler* [1974] 1 Ch 30.

the rules for awarding and assessing damages for breach of contract will come into play. The general rule is that damages for breach of contract may be assessed at the date of the breach.[10] It may be added, however, that any alternative claim by a plaintiff, say, for damages for breach of contract is a separate and distinct common law remedy.[11] A claim for damages for breach of contract must be pleaded in the action. In *McGrath v Stewart*[12] Laffoy J, when referring to this aspect, stated:

> As regards the argument advanced on behalf of Mr. McGrath and the second Respondent, that they are entitled to damages at common law for breach of contract, I consider that, as no such claim was made or pleaded in the High Court or considered by the trial judge, they cannot pursue such a claim on the appeal.

The Enforcement of Contracts by Specific Performance

The following contracts may be enforced by specific performance: **1–04**

(i) Contracts for the Sale of Land or Interests in Land

A contract for the sale of land or an interest in land must comply with the provisions of s 2 of the Statute of Frauds (Ireland) 1695 in order to be enforceable. Section 2 of the Statute of Frauds provides that: **1–05**

> No action shall be brought whereby to charge … any person … upon any contract of sale of lands, tenements or hereditaments, or any interest in or concerning them … unless the agreement upon which such action shall be brought, or some note or memorandum thereof, shall be in writing, and signed by the party to be charged therewith, or some other person thereunto by him lawfully authorised.[13]

A party seeking the enforcement of a contract for the sale of land or an interest in land by specific performance must first show that the contract was evidenced a note or memorandum in writing.[14] Where no such evidence exists the contract will be unenforceable, though not void. In *Steadman v Steadman*[15] Simon LJ, when commenting on the effect of the statute of frauds on contracts for the sale of land, stated that: "The Statute of Frauds did not make such contracts void, but merely unenforceable, and, if the statute was to be relied on as a defence, it had to be specifically pleaded." **1–06**

---

10 See *Duffy v Ridley Properties Limited* [2008] 4 IR 282.

11 [2016] IESC 52, para 31; see *Collins v Gleeson* [2011] IEHC 200.

12 [2016] IESC 52, para 39; see *Duggan v Allied Irish Building Society*, unreported, High Court, Finlay J, 4 March 1976; *Collins v Gleeson* [2011] IEHC 200.

13 *Liberty Asset Management Ltd v Gannon* [2009] IEHC 468.

14 Statute of Frauds (Ireland) 1695, s 2; Albert Keating, *Equity in Practice* (Clarus Press 2020).

15 [1976] AC 536, 558; see *Mackie v Wilde (No 2)* [1998] 2 IR 578.

1–07 In *Mulhall v Haren*[16] Keane J, when considering what constitutes a sufficient note or memorandum to satisfy the provisions of the Statute of Frauds, stated:

> 1. A memorandum or note cannot satisfy the Statute of Frauds if, when it is read alone or with other documents which can properly be read with it, it does not contain a recognition, express or implied, of the existence of the oral contract sought to be enforced.

1–08 Where the note or memorandum also includes the expression "subject to contract" Keane J stated that:

> 2. A letter, which expressly states that a transaction is "subject to contract" cannot be a sufficient note or memorandum, since the use of those words is normally inconsistent with the existence of a concluded contract.

1–09 He added:

> 3. In applying the two foregoing principles, it is immaterial whether the writing relied on itself contains the words "subject to contract" or is part of a chain of correspondence initiated by a letter which makes it clear that any oral agreement already arrived at is "subject to contract".

1–10 However, in *Boyle v Lee*[17] Finlay CJ stated:

> In my view, the very definite statement that a note or memorandum of a contract made orally is not sufficient to satisfy the Statue of Frauds unless it directly, or by very necessary implication recognises not only the terms to be enforced, but also the existence of a concluded contract between the parties, and the corresponding principle that no such note or memorandum which contains any term or expression such as 'subject to contract' can be sufficient, even if it can be established by oral evidence that such a term or expression did not form part of the originally orally concluded agreement, achieves that certainty. The existence of such a rule or provision would not, in my view, allow for the "exceptional cases" mentioned by Keane J. in the decision in *Mulhall v Haren* [1981] I.R. 364.

(ii) Contracts for the Sale of Land or Interests in Land Substantially Performed

1–11 A court exercising equitable jurisdiction will not entertain a suit for specific performance of a contract for the sale or lease of land which fails to satisfy the provisions of the Statute of Frauds (Ireland) 1695. However, a court will not allow the Statute of Frauds to be used as a vehicle of fraud and, where such happens, it may apply the principle of part performance where it is shown that the plaintiff has substantially performed his or her obligations under the contract to the knowledge of the defendant. In *Steadman v Steadman*[18]

---

16 [1981] IR 364.

17 [1992] 1 IR 555, 574.

18 [1976] AC 536, 558; see *Mackie v Wilde (No 2)* [1998] 2 IR 578.

Simon LJ, when commenting on the Statute of Frauds and unconscionable dealings, stated that:

> … almost from the moment of passing of the Statute of Frauds, it was appreciated that it was being used for a variant of unconscionable dealing, which the statute itself was designed to remedy. A party to an oral contract for the disposition of an interest in land could, despite performance of the reciprocal terms by the other party, by virtue of the statute disclaim liability for his own performance on the ground that the contract had not been in writing. Common law was helpless. But equity, with its purpose of vindicating good faith and with its remedies of injunction and specific performance, could deal with the situation.

The principle of part performance is a "purely" equitable one, and was formulated to prevent fraud.[19] The question in each case is "whether the plaintiff has an equity arising from part performance which is so affixed upon the conscience of the defendant that it amounts to a fraud on his part to take advantage of the fact that the contract is not in writing".[20] **1–12**

The equity arises out of the plaintiff's acts of part performance of the contract. A court of equity may be prepared to decree specific performance of a contract founded on the doctrine of part performance where it is shown that: **1–13**

(i) There was an agreed and concluded contract between the parties;
(ii) The plaintiff acted in such a way that showed an intention to perform that contract;
(iii) The defendant induced such acts or stood by while they were being performed; and
(iv) It would be unconscionable and a breach of good faith to allow the defendant to rely on the terms of the Statute of Frauds (Ireland) 1695, s 2, to prevent performance of the contract.[21]

The rationale of the equitable principle of part performance was explained by Simon LJ in *Steadman v Steadman*[22] in the following passage: **1–14**

> Where, therefore, a party to a contract unenforceable under the Statute of Frauds stood by while the other party acted to his detriment in performance of his own contractual obligations, the first party would be precluded by the Court of Chancery from claiming exoneration, on the ground that the contract was unenforceable, from performance of his reciprocal obligations; and the court would, if required, decree specific performance of the contract. Equity would not, as it was put, allow the Statute of Frauds "to be used as an engine of fraud". This became known as the doctrine of part performance – the "part" performance being that of that party who had, to the knowledge of the other party, acted to his detriment in carrying

[19] See *Lowry v Reid* [1927] NI 142, 154–55.
[20] See *Lowry v Reid* [1927] NI 142, 154–55.
[21] See *Mackie v Wilde* [1998] 2 IR 578, 587.
[22] [1976] AC 536, 558.

out irremediably his own obligations (or some significant part of them) under the otherwise unenforceable contract.[23]

1–15 In his judgment in *Mackie v Wilde (No 2)*[24] Barron J, when considering the prerequisites of the principle of part performance, stated:

> It must not be forgotten that ultimately the court is seeking to ensure that a defendant is not, in relying upon the Statute, breaking faith with the plaintiff, not solely by refusing to perform the oral contract, but in the manner contemplated from the passage from the judgment of Simon LJ to which I have referred.
>
> The doctrine is based upon principles of equity. There are three things to be considered:
> (1) the acts on the part of the plaintiff said to have been in part performance or of concluded agreement;
> (2) the involvement of the defendant with respect to such acts;
> (3) the oral agreement itself.
>
> It is obvious that these considerations only relate to a contract of a type which the courts will decree ought to be specifically performed. Each of the three elements is essential. In my view, it does not matter in which order they are considered. Ultimately, what is essential is that:
> (1) there was a concluded oral contract;
> (2) that the plaintiff acted in such a way that showed an intention to perform that contract;
> (3) that the defendant induced such acts or stood by while they were being performed; and
> (4) it would be unconscionable and a breach of good faith to allow the defendant to rely upon the terms of the Statute of Frauds to prevent performance of the contract.

1–16 In *Liberty Asset Management Ltd v Gannon*,[25] Laffoy J, when considering whether it was necessary to plead part performance in the statement of claim, stated that: "In my view, the plaintiff is not precluded from relying on the equitable doctrine of part performance merely because it has not spelt out in the statement of claim or the reply its reliance on it."

Discretionary Enforcement of Contracts

(i) On Grounds of Hardship

1–17 The court, by exercising its equitable and discretionary powers, may refuse to make a decree of specific performance where it has the effect of causing

---

23 See *Mackie v Wilde* [1998] 2 IR 578, 587.

24 [1998] 2 IR 578, 586.

25 [2009] IEHC 468; see *Mackie v Wilde* [1998] 2 IR 578, 587; *JLT Financial Services Limited formerly known as Liberty Asset Management Limited v Gannon* [2017] IESC 70.

hardship to the defendant, or where it would be unfair in the circumstances. It is well established that the discretion of the court to order specific performance may not be exercised if the contract entered into between the parties is not fundamentally equal and fair, for instance, where the defendant was under a misapprehension as to the true facts, and would cause hardship to him or her, and be unjust for the court to decree specific performance of the contract.[26] In *Roberts v O'Neill*,[27] McCarthy J, when referring to the judgment of Budd J in *Lavan v Walsh*,[28] stated that:

> The court, it is well established, will not enforce the specific performance of the contract the result of which would be to impose hardship on either of the parties to it. It is conceded, however, that the question of hardship of a contract is generally to be judged at the time it is entered into. Change of circumstances taking place later, making the contract less beneficial to one party, are immaterial as a rule unless it is brought about by the action of the other party.

He added that: "To permit, as an ordinary rule, a defence of subsequent hardship, would be adding a further hazard to the already trouble strewn area of the law of contracts for the sale of land." **1–18**

The circumstances of a case will determine whether sufficient grounds of hardship are present to deny a plaintiff of specific performance of a contract. In *Leggett v Crowley*[29] the decision of the High Court was appealed on the grounds that performance of the contract was impossible by virtue of the boundary dispute that existed in relation to the property and/or that specific performance should be refused because of the alleged hardship which the appellant, his partner and his father would suffer if the contract was to be completed. The appellant argued that the trial judge erred in ordering specific performance of the contract because this would entail extinguishing the interest of the neighbouring landowner in the lands or compelling the neighbouring landowner to concur in the conveyance. Costello J found that this argument was misconceived: **1–19**

> In these proceedings, the appellant is the vendor and, therefore, he always contemplated the sale of his family home when he entered into a contract for the sale of the property. Furthermore, he will obviously obtain a reduction of his liabilities when the proceeds of sale are used to repay a portion of these liabilities.

In her judgment, the trial judge was correct in holding that it was not appropriate to refuse to order specific performance of the contract on the **1–20**

[26] See *Smelter Corporation of Ireland Ltd v O'Driscoll* [1977] IR 305.

[27] Unreported, Supreme Court, 8 December 1982; see also *Smelter Corporation of Ireland Ltd v O'Driscoll* [1977] IR 305.

[28] [1964] IR 87, 102.

[29] [2020] IECA 3.

asserted grounds of hardship, "and so this second ground of appeal likewise fails". She concluded:

> The fact that there may be a dormant boundary dispute affecting the property for sale does not mean that specific performance of the contract should not be ordered on the grounds of impossibility. The appellant had not established as a matter of fact that the sale, by him, of his family home to the respondent would result in hardship such that a decree of specific performance of the contract should not be ordered. Similarly, no case was established that the appellant's father would suffer a hardship arising from the sale of the family home such that an award of specific performance of the contract should be refused. The appellant has not established that the trial judge erred in law by making an order for specific performance of the contract of 25 February 2014, rather than awarding damages in lieu of specific performance. Accordingly, I would refuse the appeal and affirm the order of the High Court.

(ii) Equity like Nature does Nothing in Vain

1–21 As equity does not act in vain, a court will be reluctant to make a decree of specific performance of a contract against a defendant where there is no reasonable prospect of compliance with the decree by the defendant. In *Aranbel Ltd v Darcy*[30] Clarke J stated that:

> As the term implies, an order for specific performance is an order which requires the relevant defendant to complete the contract which is the subject of the proceedings in question. Specific performance is an equitable remedy. It has often been said that equity will not act in vain. A court should, therefore, be reluctant to make an equitable order where there is no reasonable prospect of the order concerned being complied with. I should add one qualification to that statement. There obviously may be cases where persons may simply decline to obey an order of the court. The fact that a party might be most unlikely to obey a court order could not, in my view, be a reason for the court not making the order in the first place. However, where it is clear on the evidence that a party would not, in fact, be able to comply with a court order, then a court should be most reluctant to make such an order.

1–22 He also stated:

> There would, in an ordinary case, be little point in making an order for specific performance against a vendor who did not have title although, in an appropriate case, (see *Mount Kennett Investment Ltd v O'Mara* [2007] IEHC 420) a court may make an order for specific performance where it is satisfied that the vendor concerned has it within its power to cure any problem with its title.

(iii) On Grounds of *Laches*

1–23 The court may in its discretion refuse specific performance on grounds of *laches*. As a plaintiff must act expeditiously when pursuing specific

---

[30] [2010] IEHC 272, paras 2.1–2.2.

performance of the contract, any delay or *laches* may result in depriving him or her of a remedy in equity. [31] In *Fitzsimons v Value Homes Ltd*[32] Clarke J stated:

> If a party not guilty of delay wishes to seek specific performance against a delaying party it seems to me that the innocent party can apply as soon as the delay occurs because it is settled that the remedy of specific performance (unlike many other remedies relating to failure to perform contracts in respect of land) does not depend on a breach of contract but upon the equitable duty to perform the contract *Marks v Lilley* (1959) 1 WLR 749 at 753 (per Vaisey J.).

In *McGrath v Stewart*[33] Laffoy J, when referring to the equitable doctrine of *laches* and a claim for damages at common law for breach of contract, stated that: **1–24**

> ... while the two systems of law (that is say, common law and equity) work evermore closely together and draw mutual inspiration from each other, the two systems "are not yet fused". In consequence, the doctrine of *laches* has, as such, no application to a claim at common law for damages for breach of contract where that claim is not otherwise barred by the Statute of Limitations.

Contracts Incapable of Enforcement by Specific Performance

(i) Building Contracts

The subject matter of a valid and enforceable contract may determine whether a decree of specific performance is an appropriate remedy in the circumstances. It appears that a building contract may not be enforced by specific performance because such contract would require on-going supervision by the court of construction works involving the repair or renovation of buildings. There are, however, exceptions where the court may intervene and decree specific performance of the contract, for instance, where the particulars of the work are clearly set out in the contract.[34] In relation to building or repair contracts, in *Wolverhampton Corporation v Emmons*[35] Romer LJ stated that: **1–25**

> There is no doubt as a general rule the court will not enforce specific performance of a building contract, but an exception from the rule has been recognised. It

[31] See *Fitzsimons v Value Homes Ltd* [2006] IEHC 144; *White v McCooey* [1976–77] ILRM 72.

[32] [2006] IEHC 144, paras 1.1–6.

[33] [2016] IESC 52, para 34.

[34] See *Fitzsimons v Value Homes Ltd* [2006] IEHC 144, paras 1.1–6; *Rushbrooke v O'Sullivan* [1908] 1 IR 232; *Wolverhampton Corporation v Emmons* [1901] 1 KB 515.

[35] [1901] 1 KB 515, 524.

> has, I think, for some time been held that, in order to bring himself within that exception, a plaintiff must establish three things. The first is that the building work, of which he seeks to enforce the performance, is defined by the contract; that is to say, that the particulars of the work are so far definitely ascertained that the court can sufficiently see what is the exact nature of the work of which it is asked to order performance. The second is that the plaintiff has a substantial interest in having the contract performed, which is of such a nature that he cannot be adequately compensated for.

1–26 In *Rushbrooke v O'Sullivan*[36] Meredith MR stated:

> … but it is now fairly settled that, subject to certain exceptions, the court will not specifically enforce contracts to build or repair, both because specific performance is "decreed only where the party wants the thing is specie, and cannot have it any other way," and because such contracts are for the most part so uncertain that the court would be unable to enforce its own judgment.

1–27 However, the court will grant specific performance of a building contract in exceptional circumstances similar to those found to exist in *Fitzsimons v Value Homes Ltd*.[37] The action in that case concerned a contract for the building and sale of what is known as affordable housing.

1–28 Clarke J stated that:

> Therefore it seems to me that Ms. Fitzsimons is, in principle, entitled to specific performance. There is ample evidence to support her contention that she is ready and willing to close the sale. However for the reasons indicated above it does not seem to me that it would be equitable to permit her to obtain a decree of specific performance at a purchase price other than one that reflected the variation agreement. However, again for the reasons set out above, it seems to me that the variation agreement must be reflected in full and that while, on the one hand, there was an agreement that the purchase price should be increased by €20,000 there was also a clear commitment on the part of Value Homes to complete by November 2003. It is now some 30 months later and it must inevitably be the case that Ms. Fitzsimons has suffered loss by reason of the failure of Value Homes to complete within the extended time frame provided for in the variation agreement. In those circumstances it seems to me that it would equally be inequitable for Value Homes to insist on obtaining the aspect of the variation agreement favourable to them (that is to say the uplift in the purchase price) without also making provision for the losses suffered by Ms. Fitzsimons by virtue of the failure of Value Homes to comply with its part of the bargain contained in the variation agreement. In those circumstances it seems to me that the uplift agreed must be abated by the extent of any losses suffered by Ms. Fitzsimons.[38]

1–29 Clarke J concluded:

> Subject, therefore, to the calculation of the amount of the abatement, as of the

---

[36] [1908] 1 IR 232.

[37] [2006] IEHC 144.

[38] *Fitzsimons v Value Homes Ltd* [2006] IEHC 144, para 5.2.

date of assessment, I would propose making a decree of specific performance in a sum calculated having regard to that abatement.[39]

(ii) Lending Contracts

It is well established that lending contracts are incapable of enforcement by specific performance. In *Gorringe v The Land Improvement Society*[40] Porter MR stated as follows: **1–30**

> As a general proposition it is correct to say that a mere agreement to lend money even upon security will not be specifically performed. If money is lent, the lender may call it in again and therefore specific performance will be futile. Money compensation in such a case affords an adequate and indeed the best remedy and goes nearer to complete restitutio in integrum than the enforcement of a loan which the lender might straightaway proceed to require back leaving the borrower in no better position after the interference of the court.[41]

(iii) Grounds of Frustration

A decree of specific performance of a contract may not be granted by the court where it is shown that the contract was prematurely brought to an end by the common law doctrine of frustration owing to unforeseen and intervening circumstances making the contract impossible to perform. In *McGuill v Aer Lingus Teoranta*[42] McWilliam J identified the applicable principles of frustration as follows: **1–31**

> 1. A party may bind himself by an absolute contract to perform something which subsequently becomes impossible.
> 2. Frustration occurs when, without default of either party, a contractual obligation has become incapable of being performed.
> 3. The circumstances alleged to occasion frustration should be strictly scrutinised and the doctrine is not to be lightly applied.
> 4. Where the circumstances alleged to cause the frustration have arisen from the act or default of one of the parties, that party cannot rely on the doctrine.
> 5. All the circumstances of the contract should also be strictly scrutinised.
> 6. The event must be an unexpected event.
> 7. If one party anticipated or should have anticipated the possibility of the event which is alleged to cause the frustration and did not incorporate a clause in the contract to deal with it, he should not be permitted to rely on the happening of the event as causing frustration.

---

39 *Fitzsimons v Value Homes Ltd* [2006] IEHC 144, para 6.3.

40 [1899] 1 IR 142.

41 See *Gorringe v The Land Improvement Society* [1899] 1 IR 142; *Duggan v Irish Allied Building Society*, unreported, High Court, Finlay P, 1 March 1976; *Tola Capital Management LLC v Linders (No 1)* [2014] IEHC 316.

42 Unreported, High Court, McWilliam J, 3 October 1983; see *Neville & Sons Ltd v Guardian Builders Ltd* [1995] 1 ILRM 1; *Collins v Gleeson* [2011] IEHC 200; *Leggett v Crowley* [2019] IEHC 182.

(iv) Grounds of Illegality

1–32 The court may refuse a decree of specific performance where the contract sought to be enforced is fundamentally illegal or contrary to public policy. In relation to contracts contrary to public policy, principles of public policy may be applied regardless of such considerations as justice or fairness, as, for instance, the principle *ex dolo malo non oritur actio*.[43] In *Holman v Johnson*[44] Lord Mansfield CJ stated that:

> The principle of public policy is this; *ex dolo malo non oritur actio*. No court will lend its aid to a man who founds his cause of action upon an immoral or an illegal act. If, from the plaintiffs own stating or otherwise, the cause of action appears to arise *ex turpi causa*, or the transgression of a positive law of this country, there the court says he has no right to be assisted. It is upon that ground the court goes; not for the sake of the defendant, but because they will not lend their aid to such a plaintiff. So if the plaintiff and defendant were to change sides, and the defendant was to bring his action against the plaintiff, the latter would then have the advantage of it; for where both are equally in fault, *potior est condition defendentis*.

1–33 In *Euro-Diam v Bathurst*[45] Kerr LJ found that the illegality defence rests ultimately on the principle of public policy that courts will not assist a party who has been guilty of illegal (or grossly immoral) conduct of which the courts should take notice. The test is thus whether it would be an affront to public conscience to grant relief to a plaintiff because thereby encouragement would be offered to similar acts. Kerr LJ in that case, identified the main situations in which the illegality defence would prima facie succeed. These are: where the plaintiff seeks to, or is forced to, found a claim on an illegal contract or to plead its illegality in order to support that claim; where the grant of relief would enable the plaintiff to benefit from criminal conduct; and where absent these situations the court should not be drawn into the enforcement of that which affronts the public conscience generally.

1–34 In *Leggett v Crowley*[46] O'Connor J, when addressing the question of the burden of proof in relation to illegal contracts, stated that:

> The burden of proving an illegal contract lies with the party alleging the illegality. This is clear from the case of *Whelan v Kavanagh* [2001] IEHC 14, (unreported, High Court, 29th January, 2001), where Herbert J. stated that: "... a party who has executed a contract required by law to be evidenced in writing and which is regular and lawful on its face, and whose execution of that contract has been witnessed by his or her solicitor should not lightly be permitted to impugn that contract, particularly to his or her own advantage, by pleading illegality as a defence to a claim for specific performance. The onus of proving such alleged

---

[43] *Quinn v Irish Bank Resolution Corporation Limited* [2012] IEHC 36.
[44] (1775) 1 Cowp 341, 343.
[45] [1990] 1 QB 1, 35.
[46] [2019] IEHC 182, paras 40–42.

> illegality lies firmly with the party raising it and the burden of proof is the same as in all civil actions." (pp. 11–12)
>
> Murphy J. reiterated in *Kavanagh v Caulfield* [2002] IEHC 67, (unreported, High Court, 19th June, 2002) that it was "… clear that the onus of proving illegality of a contract is, in this case, on the Defendant. The Defendant must prove an illegal intention on the part of the Plaintiff." (para. 7.1).

O'Connor J concluded: **1–35**

> This Court, applying the relevant standard of proof (balance of probabilities), has already found that the defendant did not agree to cash payments in addition to the final contract price of €460,000, (the balance of the 10% deposit, after accounting for the earlier booking deposit of €10,000 given to the auctioneer, was paid by an AIB bank draft dated 17th January, 2014, and forwarded to Greenes by letter from the plaintiff's solicitor dated 24th January, 2014). The defendant, therefore, cannot rely on illegality as a ground of defence.

Damages *In Lieu* of Specific Performance

Section 2 of the Chancery Amendment Act 1858 provides that: **1–36**

> In all cases in which the Court of Chancery has jurisdiction to entertain an application for an injunction against a breach of any covenant, contract, or agreement, or against the commission or continuance of any wrongful act, or for the specific performance of any covenant, contract or agreement, it shall be lawful for the same court, if it shall think fit, to award damages to the party injured either in addition to or in substitution for such injunction or specific performance, and such damages may be assessed in such manner as the Court shall direct.

In *Worth v Tyler*[47] McGarry J, and when referring to s 2 of the 1858 Act, stated: **1–37**

> Of the wording of the section, the power "to award damages to the party injured … in substitution for such … specific performance" at least envisages that the damages awarded will in fact constitute a true substitute for specific performance. Furthermore, the section is speaking of the time when the Court is making its decision to award damages in substitution for specific performance, so that it is at that moment that the damages must be a substitute. The fact that a different amount of damages would have been a substitute if the order had been made at the time of the breach must surely be irrelevant … a choice between the inadequate and the equivalent seems to me to be no real choice at all.

He concluded: **1–38**

> In my judgment, therefore, if under Lord Cairns' Act (i.e. the Chancery Amendment Act 1858) damages are awarded in substitution for a specific performance, the Court has jurisdiction to award such damages as will put the plaintiff into as good

---

[47] [1974] 1 Ch 30, 58.

a position as if the contract had been performed, even if to do so means awarding damages assessed by reference to a period subsequent to date of the breach.[48]

1–39 The court in exercising its discretion may decide to award damages *in lieu* of specific performance of the contract. If an award of damages would adequately compensate a contractual party the court may not decree specific performance of the contract.[49] The jurisdiction to award damages *in lieu* of specific performance was first conferred by s 2 of the Chancery Amendment Act 1858, also known as Lord Cairns' Act. Under s 2 of the 1858 Act the court has jurisdiction to entertain an application for the specific performance of any covenant, contract, or agreement, and "it shall be lawful for the same court, if it shall think fit, to award damages to the party injured, either in addition to or in substitution for such injunction or specific performance; and such damages may be assessed in such manner as the court shall direct". In *Holohan v Ardmayle Estates*[50] Walsh J, when referring to the issue of assessing damages, stated:

> The present claim, however, as in all actions for specific performance, is grounded upon the submission that the contract is in being and that it is to be enforced. I take the view, therefore, that when the facts of the case are such that the trial judge is of opinion that he could make an order for specific performance but in his discretion does not do so but awards damages in lieu thereof, he must take into account in assessing the damages not merely such items as the loss of bargain and other loss which flows from that breach but the out of pocket expenses and other money laid out by the plaintiff which would naturally include any part of the purchase money already paid.

1–40 The general rule is that damages for breach of contract should be assessed at the date of the breach.[51] The Supreme Court in *Duffy v Ridley Properties Limited*[52] held that damages *in lieu* of specific performance could only be granted where the court would have had jurisdiction to grant a degree of specific performance, and then went on to hold that whilst the general rule as to damages in breach of contract was that such damages were to be assessed as of the date of breach that it was open to a court in awarding damages *in lieu* of specific performance to fix a date other than the date of breach or the date of judgment. In *Duffy v Ridley Properties Ltd* Finnegan J identified the general common law rule as to damages as follows:

> The general common law rule as to damages for breach of contract is that where a party sustains a loss by reason for breach of contract, he is, so far as money can do it, to be placed in the same situation with regard to damages, as if the contract

---

48 [1974] 1 Ch 30, 60.

49 See *O'Connor v McCarthy* [1982] ILRM 201; *Malhotra v Choudhury* [1980] 1 Ch 52; *Worth v Tyler* [1974] Ch 33; *McGrath v Stewart* [2016] IESC 52.

50 Unreported, Supreme Court, 1 May 1967; see *McGrath v Stewart* [2016] IESC 52.

51 See *Duffy v Ridley Properties Limited* [2008] 4 IR 282.

52 [2008] 4 IR 282, 311.

had been performed. The general rule accordingly was that damage should be assessed as of the date of the breach.

In *Collins v Gleeson*[53] Feeney J, when referring to the quantum of damages, stated that: **1–41**

> [T]o award specific performance and that as of the date of closing the plaintiff was ready, willing and able to proceed. In the light of the election made by the plaintiff, to seek damages rather than specific performance, the Court will proceed to award damages to the plaintiff being satisfied that it is both within jurisdiction and equitable to award damages to the plaintiff. In assessing the quantum of damages the Court has considered it equitable to do so as of the date upon which the plaintiff elected for damages in lieu of the specific performance.

When calculating damages, he stated: **1–42**

> On the facts of this case a true substitute for specific performance of the contract and a process of assessing damages that would result in the plaintiff being placed in the same position as if the contract were completed can be achieved by a calculation made by reference to the agreed contract price as opposed to the market value of the lands as of the date of election. The plaintiff has lost the benefit of the contract price but has retained the lands which are worth less than the value provided for in the contract. By carrying out a calculation where the value of the lands, as of the date of election, is deducted from the contract price a figure is identified for damages, as of that date, that places the plaintiff in the same position as if the contract was completed and which puts the plaintiff in as good a position as if the contract were completed.

[53] [2011] IEHC 200, para 7.

Chapter 2

THE ENFORCEMENT OF TESTAMENTARY AND PRE-TESTAMENTARY CONTRACTS

Introduction

A contract whereby an owner of land promises to leave his or her land by will to another person in consideration of that person working on the owner's land for meagre or no wages creates a testamentary contract between the parties, and where the owner of land fails to fulfil his or her promise, the person to whom it was made may seek specific performance of the testamentary contract against the estate of the owner of the land. In *K v K*,[1] a testamentary contract was deemed to exist between the plaintiff and his mother under which she agreed to devise the lands to him by her will. McDonald J found that a testamentary contract existed between the plaintiff and his mother based on the following promise she made to him during her lifetime: **2–01**

> Well, the promise was made by my father and uncle down the years that I was getting part of the lands. When my father passed away in '96, he died suddenly, and she was left all the land, so she made a promise to me after my father died that I was to get the land from the [village] up to the yard at C ... She was anxious about probate and things like that after his passing so she said to me one day at home in the kitchen ... that I'm leaving you the land from [the village] up to the yard in C... which is 90 acres.

Equity may intervene and impose a constructive trust where it is shown that a pre-testamentary agreement was entered into by two testators to make mutual wills benefitting one another, and where the surviving testator refuses to comply with the terms of the pre-testamentary agreement. In *Darragh v Darragh*[2] McDonald J stated that: **2–02**

> Where there is evidence of an agreement as to mutual wills, a trust will come into effect on the death of the first testator to die (at least where the agreement is to the effect that neither testator will revoke or alter his or her respective will). In

1 [2018] IEHC 615, para 77.

2 [2018] IEHC 427, para 67; see Albert Keating, *Equity in Practice* (Clarus Press 2020); Albert Keating, *Will Trust and Equitable Property Rights* (Clarus Press 2019); Albert Keating, *The Law of Wills* Second Edition (Clarus Press 2018); Albert Keating, *Keating on Probate* (6th edn, Round Hall 2019).

> such circumstances, an immediate equitable obligation arises by operation of law for the benefit of the persons who had been intended by the testators to benefit under the wills in question.

2–03 Where a pre-testamentary contract to make mutual wills is found to exist it may be enforced by the imposition of a constructive trust. Where the surviving testator purports to contravene the terms of the pre-testamentary agreement to make mutual wills, equity may intervene to impose a constructive trust on the surviving testator compelling him or her to comply with the terms of the pre-testamentary agreement. It appears that the onus of proof in such cases rests on the party alleging the existence of the pre-testamentary agreement to make mutual wills. The onus may easily be discharged where it is shown that the testators declared in their wills that their wills were made and based on a pre-testamentary agreement to make mutual wills.

Testamentary Contracts

2–04 In *K v K*,[3] McDonald J found that where an owner of land promises to leave his or her land to another person by will in return for work done and/or services rendered by that person on the owner's land, such promise creates a testamentary contract between the owner and the other person, and is one that may be enforced against a deceased owner's estate by specific performance. In *K v K* a testamentary contract was found to exist on the basis of a promise made by the deceased during her lifetime to her son, the plaintiff. McDonald J, when considering the circumstances of the case, stated:

> I have considered whether a promise of this kind could be said to be supported by consideration given that, at the time the promise was made, the plaintiff had already left school at fifteen and had already done many years' work on the farm. It might be suggested that, in the circumstances, any consideration was purely past. However, in my view, it would be wrong to suggest that all of the consideration was past. It seems to me that the promise was, in fact, supported by fresh consideration moving from the plaintiff because the plaintiff remained involved in the farm and continued to work very long hours on the farm. In addition, he contributed his lorry to the sand and gravel business which was clearly a key part of the deceased's plans to generate income to pay off the bank. It is clear even from the evidence of the defendant that the sale of the lorry (which had been used to carry animals) was instrumental in allowing a new lorry to be purchased for the purposes of commencing a business in sand and gravel on the family farm. In my view, there was therefore ongoing consideration given by the plaintiff for the promise which his mother made to him.

[3] [2018] IEHC 615, para 77.

He referred to the Supreme Court decision in *McCarron v McCarron*,[4] and stated: **2–05**

> It will be seen from the decision of the Supreme Court in that case that a relatively general conversation may be sufficient (depending on the circumstances), to give rise to an enforceable contract. An important underlying factor in that case was that it was impossible to explain how a person in the claimant's position would have been prepared to work long hours on the farm of a stranger without any form of remuneration whatsoever. It might be said that this factor is absent in the present case in that the plaintiff here was the eldest son of the deceased. However, in contrast to the *McCarron* case, the interaction between the plaintiff and the deceased here (as recorded in para. 77 above) was much more detailed and specific.

At para 111, he continued: **2–06**

> I therefore propose to make an order for the specific performance of the testamentary contract described above. That order will require the defendant, as personal representative of the deceased, to transfer to the plaintiff the 90 acres that were identified during the course of the court hearing which run from the village to the yard at C. That is the extent of what was promised to the plaintiff under the testamentary contract.

McDonald J, when considering the issue of satisfying the equity in the case, stated: **2–07**

> In these circumstances, I believe that the only appropriate way in which to satisfy the equity of the plaintiff in this case is to make a declaration, in the alternative to the order for specific performance proposed in para. 111 above, that the plaintiff is entitled to the 90 acres described in para. 111 above in satisfaction of the equity arising in respect of his parallel proprietary estoppel claim. In circumstances where I propose to make an order in the terms of para. 111, in satisfaction of the plaintiff's claim for specific performance of the testamentary contract, I do not believe that it is necessary to make any further order for the transfer of the lands in satisfaction of the equity which I have just described.[5]

He concluded: **2–08**

> It seems to me that the promise made by the deceased here was intended to have legal effect. It is clear that this was not a vague or hastily made promise. The promise was in very definite terms. In all of the circumstances, I have come to the conclusion that an enforceable promise was made by the deceased to the plaintiff in the terms set out in para. 77 above which gave rise to a testamentary contract.[6]

As McDonald J based his judgment on the existence of a testamentary contract he stated: **2–09**

---

4 Unreported, Supreme Court, 13 February 1997; see *Coyle v Finnegan* [2013] IEHC 463.

5 [2018] IEHC 615, paras 121–26.

6 [2018] IEHC 615, para 127.

> In light of the conclusion which I have reached in relation to the testamentary contract, it is not strictly necessary that I should form any view in relation to the alternative claim based on estoppel.

Pre-Testamentary Contracts

2–10 Where testators agree to enter into a pre-testamentary contract to make mutual wills, equity may intervene and impose a constructive trust to prevent a surviving testator from revoking the mutual will. The prevention of fraud is also one of the reasons why equity intervenes for the purposes of imposing a constructive trust in the case of agreements by testators to make mutual wills.[7] A mutual will, like all other wills, is ambulatory and revocable during the lifetime of the testators who make such a will on foot of an agreement to do so, but unlike other wills, it may cease to be revocable by a surviving testator through the intervention of equity, especially where the surviving testator also receives a benefit under the deceased testator's will. In other words, a mutual will may become irrevocable on the death of one of the testators. Equity may intervene because:

> [H]e, that dies first, does by his death carry the agreement on his part into execution. If the other refuses, he is guilty of fraud, can never unbind himself, and become a trustee of course. For no man shall deceive another to his prejudice. By engaging to do something that is in his power, he is made a trustee for the performance, and transmit that trust to those that claim under him.[8]

2–11 The death of one of the testators activates the constructive trust founded on the pre-testamentary agreement, and equity may enforce it.

2–12 The surviving testator is not precluded from making a new will *simpliciter*, but he or she may be precluded from making a new will which revokes the terms of the earlier mutual will made by him or her and the deceased testator. The mutual will continues to be irrevocable. Even should a surviving testator disclaim a beneficial interest under the mutual will he or she may, nevertheless, continue to be bound by the constructive trust created by the pre-testamentary agreement, and which becomes operative on the death of the first testator. In *Re Hagger*[9] Clauson J stated:

> *Dufour v Pereira* (1769) 1 Dick. 419; 21 E.R. 332 decides that where there is a joint will such as this, on the death of the testator who first dies the position as regards that part of the property which belongs to the survivor is that the survivor will be treated in this court as holding the property on trust to apply it so as to carry into effect the provisions of the joint will.

---

7 *Dufour v Pereira* (1789) 1 Dick 419; *Birmingham v Renfrew* (1937) 57 CLR 666; see also *Re Hagger* [1972] 3 All ER 620.

8 *Dufour v Pereira* (n 7).

9 (n 7).

In *Re Hagger* a husband and wife made a joint will where they both agreed that neither of them would revoke the will without the consent of the other. The wife was the first to die. One of the remaindermen named in the will died during the husband's lifetime. A question arose as to whether the deceased remainderman became entitled to a vested interest on the death of the wife. Clauson J felt that he was bound to hold that: **2–13**

> [F]rom the death of the wife the husband held the property, according to the tenor of the will, subject to the trusts thereby imposed upon it, at all events if he took advantage of the provisions of the will.[10]

So far as the husband's interest in the property was concerned, the will operated as a trust from the date of the wife's death. Accordingly there was no lapse by reason of the remainderman's death during the husband's lifetime. **2–14**

In *Darragh v Darragh*[11] McDonald J stated that: **2–15**

> It is a legally necessary condition of mutual wills that there is clear and satisfactory evidence of a contract between two testators. However, the argument resting on the alleged insufficiency or uncertainty of the terms of this contract is misconceived. The case for the existence of mutual wills does not involve making a contractual claim for specific performance or other relief. The claimant in a mutual wills case is not even a party to the contract and does not have to establish that he was.
>
> The obligation on the surviving testator is equitable. It is in the nature of a trust of the property affected, so the constructive trust label is attached to it. The equitable obligation is imposed for the benefit of third parties, who were intended by the parties to benefit from it. It arises by operation of law on the death of the first testator to die so as to bind the conscience of the surviving testator in relation to the property affected.[12]

He went on to state: **2–16**

> It will be seen, therefore, that in cases where there is evidence of an agreement by two testators to execute mutual wills for the benefit of named beneficiaries on the basis that such wills would not be revocable, an immediate constructive trust will arise in favour of those beneficiaries upon the death of the first of the testators to die. Thus, if there was evidence in the present case of the existence of an agreement as to mutual wills (expressed to be irrevocable without the consent of both parties), and if the survivor (in this case the Defendant) were to deny the existence of any trust in favour of the beneficiaries, that would give rise to an entitlement on the part of the beneficiaries (including the Plaintiffs here) to bring

10 (n 7) 622.
11 [2018] IEHC 427; see *Olins v Walters* [2009] Ch 212; Albert Keating, *Equity in Practice* (Clarus Press 2020); Albert Keating, *The Law of Wills* (2nd edn, Clarus Press 2018).
12 [2018] IEHC 427, paras 36–37; see *Olins v Walters* [2009] Ch 212; Albert Keating, *Equity in Practice* (Clarus Press 2020); Albert Keating, *The Law of Wills* (2nd edn, Clarus Press 2018).

proceedings seeking appropriate declaratory and other relief as to the existence of a constructive trust and for orders that the survivor (in this case the Defendant) should comply with the terms of that trust and not revoke or alter the terms of her Will in the future.[13]

Commentaries on Testamentary and Pre-Testamentary Contracts

2–17 In *K v K*,[14] McDonald J stated that a testamentary contract may be enforced by specific performance. At para 111, he stated:

> I therefore propose to make an order for the specific performance of the testamentary contract described above. That order will require the defendant, as personal representative of the deceased, to transfer to the plaintiff the 90 acres that were identified during the course of the court hearing which run from the village to the yard at C. That is the extent of what was promised to the plaintiff under the testamentary contract.

2–18 However, it appears that the circumstances that give rise to a testamentary contract may also be sufficient to give rise to a claim based on proprietary estoppel, or indeed, a remedial constructive trust which may be enforced or imposed on the estate of the deceased owner of land where he or she reneged on a promise to leave the land to the person who had worked the land for paltry or no wage, and as such may also be pleaded in the alternative to one based on the existence of a testamentary contract or vice versa.[15] Further, in relation to use of the word testamentary in describing the contract, the word testamentary denotes a type of instrument in the nature of a will which in order to be valid must be in writing and executed in compliance with s 78 of the Succession Act 1965, and in the absence of writing and due execution such instrument may not be described as testamentary. Perhaps, a more appropriate description of the contract in *K v K* is that of a pre-testamentary contract with similar effect to the decision arrived at in that case, and further allowing for alternative claims in proprietary estoppel or remedial constructive trust.

2–19 A pre-testamentary contract to make mutual wills may be enforced by the

---

[13] [2018] IEHC 427, paras 69–70; see *Olins v Walters* [2009] Ch 212; Albert Keating, *Equity in Practice* (Clarus Press 2020); Albert Keating, *The Law of Wills* (2nd edn, Clarus Press 2018).

[14] [2018] IEHC 615, para 111.

[15] See *Thorner v Major* [2009] UKHL 18; *Finnegan v Hand* [2016] IEHC 255; Albert Keating, *Equity in Practice* (Clarus Press 2020); Albert Keating, "The Primacy of a Proprietary Estoppel or Remedial Constructive Trust" (2013) 18(1) CPLJ 9; Albert Keating, "The Recognition of Services as a Detriment for Proprietary Estoppel" (2014) 19(1) CPLJ 2.

imposition of a constructive trust. In *Darragh v Darragh*[16] McDonald J stated that:

> It will be seen, therefore, that in cases where there is evidence of an agreement by two testators to execute mutual wills for the benefit of named beneficiaries on the basis that such wills would not be revocable, an immediate constructive trust will arise in favour of those beneficiaries upon the death of the first of the testators to die.

The fact that testators make contemporaneous and similar wills only does **2–20** not render them mutual wills. An essential prerequisite for the concept of mutual wills to apply is the irrevocability of the mutual intentions, and that this must be made clear by the agreement entered into by the testators not to change their intentions on the death of the first of them.[17] Evidence may have to be adduced from the surrounding circumstances to show that they intended their wills to be irrevocable, but once this is established a constructive trust may be found to exist by operation of law.[18] But there must be evidence of the agreement between the testators not to change their intentions, and although the making of mutual wills by testators may be a relevant factor to be taken into account when deciding on the question of intention, that factor alone will not be sufficient for the concept to apply.[19]

In the event of the surviving testator marrying again, or entering into a **2–21** new civil partnership, the mutual will made by him or her may be subject to s 85(1) of the Succession act 1965 (the 1965 Act) which provides that a subsequent marriage or civil partnership will automatically revoke any pre-existing will by a testator, unless that will was made in contemplation of marriage or civil partnership which includes mutual wills. However, while a will may be revoked under s 85(1) of the 1965 Act, it appears that the terms of the pre-existing testamentary agreement by testators to make mutual wills continues to subsist and be enforceable by equity by the imposition of a constructive trust by the executors of the deceased testator. It also appears that even should the surviving testator divorce his or her new spouse or civil partner, and then go on to remarry again or enter into a new civil partnership, the original pre-testamentary agreement to make mutual wills with his or her deceased spouse or civil partner will continue to subsist, and remain binding and enforceable by equity imposing a constructive trust. The same might be said where the surviving testator purports to revoke his or her mutual will

---

16 [2018] IEHC 427; see *Olins v Walters* [2009] Ch 212; Albert Keating, *Equity in Practice* (Clarus Press 2020); Albert Keating, *The Law of Wills* (2nd edn, Clarus Press 2018).

17 *Re Goodchild* [1996] 1 WLR 1216.

18 *Re Oldham* [1925] Ch. 75; *Re Cleaver* [1986] 1 WLR 939; *Re Goodchild* [1996] 1 WLR 1216.

19 *Re Cleaver* [1986] 1 WLR 939; see *Gray v Perpetual Trustee Co Ltd* [1928] AC 391.

by any of the other methods of revocation under s 85(2) of the 1965 Act. It is the continued binding effect of the original pre-testamentary agreement between testators that makes mutual wills different from other wills, and further, by the intervention of equity imposing an overriding constructive trust on a surviving testator to comply with the terms of the pre-existing testamentary agreement to make mutual wills.

Chapter 3

PALLANT v MORGAN-TYPE ARRANGEMENTS AND EQUITY

Introduction

A *Pallant v Morgan*-type arrangement was described by Harman J as follows: **3–01**

> Thus where A. agreed with B. in effect that if B. would not try to buy a certain estate, A. would try to buy, and in case of success would cede a portion of the estate to B. at a certain price: and B. acted on his bargain and allowed A. to purchase: and A. having purchased refused to perform his part and set up the uncertainty of the part to be ceded: the court held that the defence could not avail and directed an inquiry to ascertain the portion to be given up and the price. It seems that if this could not have been ascertained, B. might have claimed the whole estate.[1]

Where a *Pallant v Morgan*-type arrangement is found to exist between contractual parties it may be enforced by equity because it would be "inequitable for a person who obtains a benefit (such as the withdrawal of a competitor from a bidding process) to retain the benefit without conceding the substance of the arrangement".[2] In *Shiel v McKeon*[3] Clarke J (as he then was) stated that "the *Pallant v Morgan* equity arises in circumstances where two persons may be engaged in a joint venture to purchase a property from a third party". **3–02**

In *Banner Homes plc v Luff Developments Limited and Another*[4] Chadwick LJ, when considering the nature of a *Pallant v Morgan*-type equity, stated: **3–03**

> A *Pallant v Morgan* equity may arise where the arrangement or understanding on which it is based precedes the acquisition of the relevant property by one party to that arrangement. It is the pre-acquisition arrangement which colours the subsequent acquisition by the defendant and leads to his being treated as a trustee if he seeks to act inconsistently with it. Where the arrangement or understanding is reached in relation to property already owned by one of the parties, he may (if the arrangement is of sufficient certainty to be enforced specifically) thereby constitute

---

1. *Pallant v Morgan* [1953] 1 Ch 43, 48; *Shiel v McKeon* [2006] IEHC 194, paras 3.6–3.7; Albert Keating, *Equity in Practice* (Clarus Press 2020).
2. *Pallant v Morgan* [1953] 1 Ch 43, 48; *Shiel v McKeon* [2006] IEHC 194, paras 3.6–3.7.
3. [2006] IEHC 194, paras 3.6–3.7; see *The MacGillicudy of the Reeks v Joy and Another* [1959] IR 189.
4. [2000] Ch 372, 397.

himself trustee on the basis that "equity looks on that as done which ought to be done", or an equity may arise under the principles developed in the proprietary estoppel cases. As I have sought to point out, the concepts of constructive trust and proprietary estoppel have much in common in this area.

3–04 Chadwick LJ also stated that:

> It is the existence of the advantage to the one, or detriment to the other, gained or suffered as a consequence of the arrangement or understanding, which leads to the conclusion that it would be inequitable or unconscionable to allow the acquiring party to retain the property for himself, in a manner inconsistent with the arrangement or understanding which enabled him to acquire it.

3–05 It may also be noted that in *McMahon v Kerry County Council*[5] Finlay P (as he then was) emphasised the part played by the notion of unconscionability in the application of all equitable principles:

> If a court applying equitable principles is truly to act as a court of conscience, then it seems to me unavoidable that it should consider not only conduct on the part of the plaintiff with particular regard to whether it is wrong and wilful but also conduct on the part of the defendant and furthermore the consequences and the justice of the consequences both from the point of view of the plaintiff and the defendant.

3–06 It may also be argued that *Pallant v Morgan*-type arrangements may be enforced by applying the equitable principles of proprietary estoppel or remedial constructive trusts. Chadwick LJ pointed out in *Banner Homes plc v Luff Developments Limited and Another*[6] that *Pallant* arrangements and equity arising out of them have much in common with concepts of constructive trust and proprietary estoppel.

Pallant v Morgan-Type Arrangements and Equity

3–07 A contract for the sale of land or interest in land may be enforceable if all of the elements necessary for the creation of contractual relations have been established and if there is a sufficient note or memorandum to satisfy the Statute of Frauds or a sufficient act of part performance. However, as Clarke J stated in *Shiel v McKeon*,[7] the principle behind the doctrine of part performance is that the Statute of Frauds cannot be used as an instrument of fraud, and that similarly a *Pallant v Morgan*-type equity "derives from the principle that it would be inequitable for a person who obtains a benefit

---

5 [1981] ILRM 419, 421.

6 [2000] Ch 372, 397.

7 [2006] IEHC 194, paras 3.6–3.7; see *The MacGillicudy of the Reeks v Joy and Another* [1959] IR 189.

(such as the withdrawal of a competitor from a bidding process) to retain the benefit without conceding the substance of the arrangement".

In *Pallant v Morgan*,[8] an agreement was reached between the agents of two neighbouring land owners in an auction room immediately before an auction. One agent agreed that he would refrain from bidding on the basis that there would be a division of the land according to a formula which left certain details to be agreed later. The parties subsequently failed to agree on those details and the aggrieved party claimed specific performance or alternatively a declaration of trust. In respect of the claim for specific performance the court held that the arrangements between the agents were not sufficiently precise (having left matters of some substance over for further agreement) to permit specific performance. There was, the court held, "too much left undecided". However, as equity also fastens onto the conscience of parties to such contract, transaction or arrangement, and where it is shown that the party relying on the absence of writing is using the Statute of Frauds as a vehicle of frauds to evade his or her obligations under the contract, transaction or arrangement, the court may, by applying the principle of part performance, enforce the contract, transaction or arrangement in circumstances where the party seeking specific performance has substantially performed his or her obligations under the contract, transaction or arrangement. **3–08**

Where a *Pallant v Morgan*-type arrangement cannot be enforced by specific performance because the arrangement is not evidenced in writing, the party seeking its enforcement may claim that the arrangement is enforceable under a *Pallant v Morgan*-type equity. However, a *Pallant v Morgan* equity must first be identified, and then established. In *Banner Homes plc v Luff Developments Limited and Another*[9] Chadwick LJ, when describing the concept of a *Pallant v Morgan*-type equity, stated that: **3–09**

> *Pallant v Morgan* [1953] Ch. 43 itself provides an illustration of this principle. There was nothing inequitable in allowing the defendant to retain for himself the lot (lot 15) in respect to which the plaintiff's agent had no instructions to bid. In many cases the advantage/detriment will be found in the agreement of the non-acquiring party to keep out of the market. That will usually be both to the advantage of the acquiring party – in that he can bid without competition from the non-acquiring party – and to the detriment of the non-acquiring party – in that he loses the opportunity to acquire the property for himself. But there may be advantage to the one without corresponding detriment to the other. Again, *Pallant v Morgan* provides an illustration. The plaintiff's agreement (through his agent) to keep out of the bidding gave an advantage to the defendant – in that he was able to obtain the property for a lower price than would otherwise have been possible; but the failure of the plaintiff's agent to bid did not, in fact, cause detriment to the plaintiff – because on the facts, the agent's instructions would not have permitted him to outbid the defendant. Nevertheless, the equity was invoked.

8 *Pallant v Morgan* [1953] 1 Ch 43, 48.
9 [2000] Ch 372, 397.

3–10 He went on to state:

> It is inequitable for the acquiring party to retain the property for himself in a manner consistent with the arrangement or understanding on which the non-acquiring party has acted. Those circumstances may arise where the non-acquiring party was never "in the market" for the whole of the property to be acquired; but (on the faith of an arrangement or understanding that he shall have a part of that property) provides support in relation to the acquisition of the whole which is of advantage to the acquiring party. They may arise where the assistance provided to the acquiring party (in pursuance of the arrangement or understanding) involves no detriment to the non-acquiring party; or where the non-acquiring party acts to his detriment (in pursuance of the arrangement or understanding) without the acquiring party obtaining any advantage therefrom.

3–11 Chadwick LJ also "advanced the following propositions" or prerequisites for a *Pallant v Morgan*-type equity to apply:

> (i) It is unnecessary that the arrangement or understanding should be contractually enforceable. Indeed, if there is an agreement which is enforceable as a contract, there is unlikely to be any need to invoke the *Pallant v Morgan* equity; equity can act through the remedy of specific performance and will recognise the existence of a corresponding trust.
> (ii) It is necessary that the pre-acquisition arrangement or understanding should contemplate that one party ("the acquiring party") will take steps to acquire the relevant property; and that, if he does so, the other party ("the non-acquiring party") will obtain some interest in that property.
> (iii) It is necessary that (whatever private reservations the acquiring party may have) he has not informed the non-acquiring party before the acquisition (or, perhaps more accurately, before it is too late for the parties to be restored to a position of no advantage/no detriment) that he no longer intends to honour the arrangement or understanding.
> (iv) It is necessary that, in reliance on the arrangement or understanding, the non-acquiring party should do (or omit to do) something which confers an advantage on the acquiring party in relation to the acquisition of the property; or is detrimental to the ability of the non-acquiring party to acquire the property on equal terms.
> (v) It is the existence of the advantage to the one, or detriment to the other, gained or suffered as a consequence of the arrangement or understanding, which leads to the conclusion that it would be inequitable or unconscionable to allow the acquiring party to retain the property for himself, in a manner inconsistent with the arrangement or understanding which enabled him to acquire it.
> (vi) It is inequitable for the acquiring party to retain the property for himself in a manner consistent with the arrangement or understanding on which the non-acquiring party has acted.

3–12 In *Shiel v McKeon*[10] Clarke J, when considering the application of a *Pallant v Morgan*-type equity, stated that:

[10] [2006] IEHC 194, paras 3.6–3.7; see *The MacGillicudy of the Reeks v Joy and Another* [1959] IR 189.

> the *Pallant v Morgan* equity arises in circumstances where two persons may be engaged in a joint venture to purchase a property from a third party. It has no application to the more straightforward case where one party is engaged with the other in negotiations for a direct sale of the property. In the latter case a contract will only be enforceable if all of the elements necessary for the creation of contractual relations have been established and if there is a sufficient note or memorandum to satisfy the Statute of Frauds or a sufficient act of part performance or where, as noted in *Banner Homes*, a proprietary estoppel arises. However the principle behind the doctrine of part performance is that the Statute of Frauds cannot be used as an instrument of fraud. Similarly the *Pallant v Morgan* equity derives from the principle that it would inequitable for a person who obtains a benefit (such as the withdrawal of a competitor from a bidding process) to retain the benefit without conceding the substance of the arrangement. I am therefore satisfied to follow *Pallant v Morgan and Banner Homes.*

In *Shiel v McKeon* the plaintiff and the defendant had an interest in purchasing a property. The property consisted of a house with surrounding garden backing onto a further plot of land which in turn backed onto the sea. The plaintiff owned a holiday home just across the road from the property. The defendant's family owned lands directly adjacent to the property. In a meeting between the parties the plaintiff contended that an arrangement was entered into whereby the defendant would purchase the property, would retain the rear portion for himself but would hold the front portion on trust for the plaintiff. The defendant denied that any such arrangement was entered into. Clarke J had to determine whether there was an arrangement between the parties as to the purchase of the property that made it inequitable for the defendant to retain the property in its entirety for himself. In his judgment Clarke J referred with approval to the judgment of Harman J in *Pallant v Morgan*[11] and that of Chadwick LJ in *Banner Homes plc v Luff Developments Limited and Another*,[12] and stated: **3–13**

> I see no reason not to follow the logic of the decisions in *Pallant v Morgan and Banner Homes* and hold that, independent of an entitlement to enforce a contract, there exists an equitable entitlement in the circumstances detailed in those authorities to the enforcement of an arrangement which may fall short, in some respects, from the requirements for the enforcement of a contract. As was pointed out in Banner Homes there would be no need for a *Pallant v Morgan* equity in circumstances where there was an enforceable contract because the aggrieved party could simply seek specific performance.

Clarke J referred to principle (3) in *Banner Homes plc v Luff Developments Limited and Another*[13] where Chadwick LJ stated: **3–14**

> (3) It is necessary that the pre-acquisition arrangement or understanding should contemplate that one party ("the acquiring party") will take steps to acquire the

[11] [1953] 1 Ch 43, 48.
[12] [2000] Ch 372, 397.
[13] [2000] Ch 372, 397.

> relevant property; and that, if he does so, the other party ("the non-acquiring party") will obtain some interest in that property. Further, it is necessary that (whatever private reservations the acquiring party may have) he has not informed the non-acquiring party before the acquisition (or, perhaps more accurately, before it is too late for the parties to be restored to a position of no advantage/no detriment) that he no longer intends to honour the arrangement or understanding.

3–15 At para 4.23 of his judgment he stated:

> I am also satisfied that Mr. McKeon was aware that his position was not secure until he had a formal legally enforceable contract signed by the vendor. It seems clear that he wished to keep, if at all possible, Mr. Shiel from becoming aware of the fact that he did not wish to go through with the arrangement until after he had secured a signed written agreement. While in fairness it should be noted that there was no suggestion that, if pressed, Mr. Shiel would not be told the true position, nonetheless it is clear that the desired position was that Mr. Shiel would not discover the true position until it would have been too late for Mr. Shiel to seek to do anything about it. That such a matter is a factor in determining whether a *Pallant v. Morgan* equity may be said to exist can be seen from item (3) in the passage from *Banner Homes* referred to at para. 3.3 above. Also that fact is only consistent with knowledge on the part of Mr. McKeon that it was likely that Mr. Shiel would refrain from any further attempt to bid on the property until such time as Mr. Shiel was told that all bets were off. It can only be to that end that it was decided to attempt to delay Mr. Shiel receiving that knowledge until after a signed contract was available to Mr. McKeon.

3–16 The "item (3)" referred to by Clarke J states that:

> It is necessary that the pre-acquisition arrangement or understanding should contemplate that one party ("the acquiring party") will take steps to acquire the relevant property; and that, if he does so, the other party ("the non-acquiring party") will obtain some interest in that property. Further, it is necessary that (whatever private reservations the acquiring party may have) he has not informed the non-acquiring party before the acquisition (or, perhaps more accurately, before it is too late for the parties to be restored to a position of no advantage/no detriment) that he no longer intends to honour the arrangement or understanding.

3–17 Clarke J concluded:

> In all those circumstances I am satisfied that equity does not require that Mr. McKeon comply with the terms of the informal arrangement. That arrangement was procured in circumstances where one party was, to the knowledge of the other party, unaware of a significant weakness in that party's position. While under no legal obligation to reveal that weakness, Mr. Shiel does not seek to enforce a legal entitlement. It seems to me that Mr. Shiel has lost his entitlement to resort to equity to pursue the matter by reason of his failure to disclose his weakened position at the meeting on Sunday 14th. While the parties were not, on any view, on equal terms prior to the meeting of the 14th the extent of that inequality was concealed by Mr. Shiel.

In all the circumstances of the case I therefore dismiss the plaintiff's claim.[14] **3–18**

ALTERNATIVE ENFORCEMENT OF *PALLANT V MORGAN*-TYPE ARRANGEMENTS BY PROPRIETARY ESTOPPEL OR CONSTRUCTIVE TRUSTS

In *Banner Homes plc v Luff Developments Limited and Another*[15] Chadwick LJ, when referring to *Pallant v Morgan*-type arrangements and *Pallant v Morgan*-type equity, proprietary estoppel and constructive trusts, stated that: "As I have sought to point out, the concepts of constructive trust and proprietary estoppel have much in common in this area." **3–19**

While the concept of proprietary estoppel may have much in common with a *Pallant v Morgan*-type arrangement and equity, where a proprietary estoppel is pursued as an alternative means of enforcement of such arrangement the principles governing the concept of a proprietary estoppel must first be established. In relation to the principles of proprietary estoppel, in *Owens v Duggan*[16] Hardiman J explained: **3–20**

> Where one person, A, has acted to his detriment on the faith of a belief which was known to and encouraged by another person, B, that he either, has or is going to be given a right in or over B's property, B cannot insist on his strict legal rights if to do so would be inconsistent with that belief.

In *Thorner v Major*,[17] the House of Lords found that a proprietary estoppel may be established once it is shown by the claimant that the representation or assurance was made to him or her by the owner of land, that he or she relied on the representation or assurance, and suffered a detriment in consequence of a reasonable reliance on it.[18] Further, the detriment occasioned by the claimant need not now take the form of a money expenditure on the land, as it is "sufficient if the party, to whom the assurance is given, acts on the faith of it, in such circumstances that it would be unjust and inequitable for the party making the assurance to go back on it".[19] In *Naylor v Maher*[20] O'Keeffe J referred with approval to the conditions necessary for establishing **3–21**

---

[14] *Shiel v McKeon* [2006] IEHC 194, 6.1–6.2.

[15] [2000] Ch 372, 397.

[16] Unreported, High Court, Hardiman J, 2 April 2004; see *Re Basham* [1986] 1 WLR 1498; *Prunty v Crowley* [2016] IEHC 293.

[17] [2009] UKHL 18.

[18] See *Thorner v Major* [2009] UKHL 18; Albert Keating, *Equity in Practice* (Clarus Press 2020); Albert Keating, "The Primacy of a Proprietary Estoppel or Remedial Constructive Trust" (2013) 18(1) CPLJ 9; Albert Keating, "The Recognition of Services as a Detriment for Proprietary Estoppel" (2014) 19(1) CPLJ 2.

[19] *Thorner v Major* [2009] UKHL 18.

[20] [2012] IEHC 408.

a proprietary estoppel in *Thorner v Major*,[21] and to the judgment of Murphy J in *McCarron v McCarron*,[22] regarding the nature of the detriment suffered by the claimant.

3–22 In *Banner Homes plc v Luff Developments Limited and Another*[23] Chadwick LJ also stated that the concept of constructive trust have much in common with a *Pallant v Morgan*-type arrangement and equity. Where a remedial constructive trust is relied on as an alternative to a *Pallant v Morgan*-type arrangement and equity the principles for establishing a remedial constructive trust must be satisfied. The circumstances giving rise to a proprietary estoppel may also be properly "regarded as giving rise to a species of constructive trust, which is the concept employed by a court of equity to prevent a person from relying on his legal rights where it would be unconscionable for him to do so".[24] In cases involving unconscionable behaviour which has future effect it appears that the imposition of a remedial constructive trust may be the more appropriate remedy rather than a proprietary estoppel which is primarily designed to afford immediate effect to a right to property. Where a claimant successfully establishes the existence of a remedial constructive trust over property he or she may acquire equitable rights to that property.

---

21 [2009] UKHL 18.

22 Unreported, Supreme Court, 13 February 1997; see *Owens v Duggan*, unreported, High Court, Hardiman J, 2 April 2004; *Prunty v Crowley* [2016] IEHC 293.

23 [2000] Ch 372, 397.

24 See *Finnegan v Hand* [2016] IEHC 255; *Thorner v Major* [2009] UKHL 18.

Chapter 4

THE PRINCIPLES OF ENFORCEMENT OF COLLATERAL CONTRACTS

Introduction

The purpose of a collateral contract is "to enforce a promise given prior to the main contract and but for which this main contract would not have been made".[1] Consideration is essential to the existence of every legally binding contract, and a collateral contract is no exception to this general rule. The consideration of a collateral contract, and as such rendering it legally binding, is the making of some other contract called the main contract, albeit a collateral contract is an independent contract in its own right, and may be enforced as such.[2] A written contract between parties will be presumed to contain the entirety of the terms agreed between them, however, where a collateral contract is found or construed to exist between the parties to the main written contract by reference to pre-contractual documents, it may have the effect of altering the terms of the written contract, and may be enforced as such. The pre-contractual documents may show that the party seeking to enforce the collateral contract had been induced to enter the main written contract by representations or statements.[3] The pre-contractual documents may provide the necessary "cogent evidence" for enforcing the collateral contract. In *Tennants Building Products Ltd v O'Connell*[4] Hogan J stated: **4–01**

> The effect of this case-law may be said to be that while the courts will permit a party to set up a collateral contract to vary the terms of a written contract, this can only be done by means of cogent evidence, often itself involving … written pre-contractual documents which, it can be shown, were intended to induce the other party into entering the contract.

The court may not, however, entertain or admit oral evidence which purports to vary the terms of the main written contract between the parties. Under the parol evidence rule a party to a contract may not be allowed to introduce new **4–02**

---

1 *Industrial Steel Plant Ltd v Smith* [1980] 1 NZLR 545, 555; *Allied Irish Banks Plc v Galvin Developments (Killarney) Limited* [2011] IEHC 314, para 97.

2 *Heilbut, Symons & Co v Buckelton* [1913] AC 30, 47.

3 See *City and Westminster Properties (1934) Ltd v Mudd* [1958] 2 All ER 733; *Allied Irish Banks Plc v Galvin Developments (Killarney) Limited* [2011] IEHC 314; *Tennants Building Products Limited v O'Connell* [2013] IEHC 197.

4 [2013] IEHC 197.

oral evidence which has the effect of contradicting or varying the terms of the written agreement between them. In *Ulster Bank v Deane*[5] McGovern J, when entertaining a claim for the enforcement of a collateral contract based on oral evidence only, stated:

> The defendants have offered no evidence other than verbal discussions which they say altered the terms of the facility letters, but such evidence is inadmissible, being in breach of the parol evidence rule and is a long way short of what was held to constitute a collateral agreement in the *City and Westminster Properties [1934] Ltd.* case.

4–03 On a procedural note, where a contractual party claims that the other party was in breach of a collateral contract such claim must be included in the pleadings; such claim will not be implied into the pleadings.[6]

The Concept of a Collateral Contract

4–04 The consideration for a collateral contract is the subsequent main contract between the parties, though the main contract and collateral contract exist independently of one another. In *Heilbut, Symons & Co v Buckelton*[7] Lord Moulton stated that: "It is evident, both on principle and authority, that there may be a contract the consideration for which is the making of some other contract." He added that: "It is collateral to the main contract, but each has an independent existence, and they do not differ in respect of their possession to the full the character and status of a contract."

4–05 Where the party alleging the existence of a collateral contract claims that he or she was induced to enter the main contract as a result of statements or representations made by the other party, and there are pre-contractual documents substantiating such a claim, the courts may enforce the collateral contract, and which may have the effect of altering the terms of the written main contract.[8] The evidence adduced in support of such claim will have to be convincing and "cogent".[9] Evidence of the circumstances surrounding the making of a contract may also be admitted to explain words used in it or identify matters forming the subject matter of it. In *ICDL GCC Foundation FZ–LLC v European Computer Driving Licence Foundation Ltd*[10] Fennelly J stated that:

---

5 [2012] IEHC 248, paras 9–12; see *Danske Bank v Shortt* [2020] IECA 137, paras 60–63.

6 See *Begley v Damesfield Ltd* [2020] IECA 171.

7 [1913] AC 30, 47; see *Webster v Higgins* [1948] 2 All ER 127.

8 See *City and Westminster Properties (1934) Ltd v Mudd* [1958] 2 All ER 733; *Allied Irish Banks Plc v Galvin Developments (Killarney) Limited* [2011] IEHC 314.

9 See *Tennants Building Products Limited v O'Connell* [2013] IEHC 197.

10 [2012] IESC 55.

> Evidence of the surrounding circumstances, but not of subjective intentions, may be admitted to explain the subject-matter and even what particular words used should be understood as referring to. Such evidence will not normally be allowed to alter the plain meaning of words.

In *Tennants Building Products Limited v O'Connell*[11] Hogan J, when considering the evidence of surrounding circumstances, stated: **4–06**

> In that respect, therefore, it is plain that evidence can be given of the surrounding circumstances which led up to the execution of the guarantee. If Mr. O'Connell could establish that he only executed that agreement on the express assurance of the plaintiff's agent that the guarantee was merely an empty formula designed to placate his head office, then in such circumstances he could obtain relief either for misrepresentation or by reason of the existence of a collateral contract or, for that matter, on the basis that the parties had not actually intended to create legal relations.

However, parol evidence may not be adduced for the purposes of contradicting or altering the terms of a written contract. The parol evidence rule provides that a party to a contract may not be allowed to introduce new oral evidence that has the effect of contradicting the terms of a written agreement between them. Thus, oral evidence of statements or representations inducing a contract, and argued as giving rise to a collateral contract, may not be adduced to alter the terms of the written main contract. It may be different where the main contract is a totally oral contract, and where the evidence adduced is credible and cogent. **4–07**

Public policy considerations may also be taken into account when applying the parol evidence rule. As stated by Hogan J in *Tennants Building Products Limited v O'Connell*[12]: **4–08**

> If the parol evidence rule were to be applied with remorseless and unbending logic, it might create a form of immunity for those who would carelessly, recklessly and perhaps even falsely misrepresent the terms of the written agreement, often to the disadvantage of the weaker party, thus undermining the very public policy on which the very existence of the parol evidence rule rests. While perfect consistency is impossible, the courts have nonetheless sought to strike a balance between the certainty of the written word on the one hand and guarding against the possible injustice which would be visited on those who entered into written agreements on the basis of an incorrect and even deliberately false representation on the other. This would be especially true where (as here) the written document has been prepared by one side for execution by the other.

---

[11] [2013] IEHC 197, paras 22–23.

[12] [2013] IEHC 197; see *Allied Irish Banks Plc v Galvin Developments (Killarney) Limited* [2011] IEHC 314.; *Macklin v Graecen & Co.* [1983] IR 61; *ICDL GCC Foundation FZ-LLC v European Computer Driving Licence Foundation Ltd* [2012] IESC 55; *Ulster Bank v Deane* [2012] IEHC 248; *Danske Bank v Shortt* [2020] IECA 137, para 30 – 33.

4–09 In *Danske Bank v Shortt*[13] Ni Raifeartaigh J made the following *obiter* comments in relation to the parol evidence rule and collateral contracts based on the authorities and arguments presented in the case:

> First, I would suggest that in some of the judgments described there may have been a degree of conflation as between the *admissibility of evidence* (the subject of the parol evidence rule) and the *weight of evidence* in support of an alleged collateral contract, and this may explain why it may sometimes have been stated (particularly in some of the banking cases referred to) that the parol evidence rule prevented the establishment of a collateral contract despite the fact that the judge went on to consider the evidence in support of the collateral contract, such evidence is, strictly speaking, a contradiction in terms because the parol evidence rule, is an admissibility rule, and would preclude the evidence being admitted in the first place.
>
> Secondly, I would venture to suggest that the position regarding collateral contracts and the parol evidence rule is simply this: that where a person seeks to establish a collateral contract, the parol evidence rule will not operate to prohibit the admission of oral evidence in support of the alleged contract. Whether one considers this an "exception" to the parol evidence rule or simply a situation where the parol evidence rule does not apply in the first place may, perhaps, be no more than a semantic exercise. However, it can result in a situation where the terms (or a term) of the written contract on the face of the document are not ultimately enforced by the court.
>
> Thirdly, a separate issue from the admissibility issue is whether the evidence is sufficiently cogent to establish a collateral contract; this is an issue concerning the weight of the evidence, and should be informed by the discussion in such a case as *Galvin* and *Tennants Building Products*.
>
> Fourthly, I find very interesting the *dicta* of Hogan J. in *Tennants Building Products*, suggesting an underlying rationale for cases where the parol rule has not been applied. It may ultimately provide a better explanation for decisions such as *Moroney*, *Black* and *Whelan*, than the explanation of a special "exception" to the parol evidence rule based on "consideration" in contracts.[14]

The Enforcement of Collateral Contracts

4–10 Where a collateral contract is found or construed to exist between the parties to the main written contract by reference to pre-contractual documents, such documents constituting the collateral contract may be construed as altering the terms of the main contract, and may be enforced as such. In *City and Westminster Properties (1934) Ltd v Mudd*[15] a tenant had signed a lease containing a covenant not to use or permit the use of the premises

13 [2020] IECA 137, paras 60–63.
14 See *Revenue Commissioners v Moroney* [1972] IR 372; *Black v Grealy*, unreported, High Court, Costello J, 10 November 1977; *Whelan v Kavanagh*, unreported, High Court, Herbert J, 29 January 2001.
15 [1958] 2 All ER 733.

except as the shop of the tenant for his business. The landlords knew that the tenant resided on the premises as well as using it for his business. A representative of the landlords orally informed the tenant that the landlords would not object to his residing on the premises if he would sign the lease in its original form. A collateral contract was found to exist between the parties regarding the matter of the tenant residing on the business premises, and was enforced as such. In *Ulster Bank v Deane*[16] McGovern J, when commenting on *Mudd*, stated:

> The pre-contractual documents also showed clearly that the tenant intended to use a business premises as a private dwelling. It was found that the tenant was induced to enter into a different lease which made no reference to this matter following assurances by the landlord that this clause would not be enforced. This was held to amount to a collateral contract which bound the landlord.

Statements and promises made by parties during the course of negotiating a contract may create a collateral contract where such statements and promises were intended to have contractual effect, and may be enforced as such. In *Allied Irish Banks Plc v Galvin Developments (Killarney) Limited*[17] Finlay Geoghegan J stated that: **4–11**

> It is clear that not every statement or promise made in the course of negotiations for a contract may give rise to a finding that a collateral contract exists. To be so treated, a statement must be intended to have contractual effect, see *Chitty on Contracts*, 29th Ed., para. 12-004 and cases referred to therein.

When referring to the facts of the case, she stated: **4–12**

> I have concluded on the facts found herein that there existed a collateral contract in the sense of a prior representation by AIB intended to have contractual effect that it would limit its recourse to the Galvin Brothers (and by subsequent agreed inclusion GDK) to 50% of the drawn debt of agreed facilities, which became a binding collateral contract when those parties entered into the agreements in March 2007 in relation to the facilities referred to in the letters of loan sanction and continued to subsist when the parties entered into the further agreements in September 2008 to extend the facilities already drawn down and make certain further borrowings.

In *Ulster Bank v Deane*[18] McGovern J, when commenting on *AIB v Galvin Developments (Killarney) Ltd*, stated that: **4–13**

> In the *AIB v Galvin Developments* case, Finlay Geoghegan J. held that the Heads of Terms were a representation by the bank that subject to conditions, it would make facilities available on the terms and conditions indicated. The two conditions were formal approval by the bank and the issuance of a formal letter of sanction.

[16] [2012] IEHC 248, paras 9–12.
[17] [2011] IEHC 314, para 98.
[18] [2012] IEHC 248, paras 9–12.

The representations were intended to induce the potential borrowers to continue in negotiations with the bank to obtain the facilities referred to therein. The bank knew that the terms set out in the Heads of Terms were fundamental as far as the defendants were concerned.

4–14 In *Ulster Bank v Deane*[19] McGovern J, when referring to *City and Westminster Properties (1934) Ltd v Mudd*[20] and *AIB v Galvin Developments (Killarney) Ltd*,[21] stated:

> In the plaintiff's application, Ms. Teresa Cole, the relationship manager in charge of the defendants' loan accounts, swore an affidavit stating there was no collateral or side agreement which overrode the facility letters. Mr. Norman Ginelly of the plaintiff Bank also swore an affidavit in which he specifically denied any collateral agreement. The defendants have offered no evidence other than verbal discussions which they say altered the terms of the facility letters, but such evidence is inadmissible, being in breach of the parol evidence rule and is a long way short of what was held to constitute a collateral agreement in the *City and Westminster Properties (1934) Ltd.* case.
>
> In *AIB v Galvin Developments*, the facts were also very different to this case. A collateral agreement was to be found in written Heads of Agreement drawn up by the Bank according to which the Bank agreed to limit its right of recourse to 50% of the drawn debt. But in the case before me, the defendants have been unable to point to any written document which purports to vary the terms of the facility letters or on foot of which they agreed to sign the facility letters.

4–15 He concluded:

> The facts of that case bear no resemblance to the case which I have to decide, and the defendants have simply not been able to point to any written document or any facts which go any way near to establishing a collateral agreement.

4–16 In *Tennants Building Products Limited v O'Connell*[22] Hogan J stated that:

> The parties to a written contract are presumed to have reduced the entirety of their agreement to writing and … to permit one party to introduce new oral evidence which in effect contradicts the terms of the written agreement would be destructive of legal certainty.

4–17 However:

> The effect of this case-law may be said to be that while the courts will permit a party to set up a collateral contract to vary the terms of a written contract, this can only be done by means of cogent evidence, often itself involving (as in *Mudd* and in *Galvin*) written pre-contractual documents which, it can be shown, were intended to induce the other party into entering the contract. By contrast,

[19] [2012] IEHC 248, paras 9–12.
[20] [1958] 2 All ER 733.
[21] [2011] IEHC 314.
[22] [2013] IEHC 197, para 19.

generalised assertions regarding verbal assurances given in the course of the contractual negotiations will often fall foul of the parol evidence rule for all the reasons offered by McGovern J. in *Deane*.

In *Tennants Building Products Limited v O'Connell* the defendant contended that he entered the contract between himself and the plaintiff following an assurance or representation given by the plaintiff that the guarantee between them would be not be unilaterally enforced without his consent, and that such assurance or representation established the existence of a collateral contract between him and the plaintiff. When applying the principles of collateral contracts to the facts of the case, Hogan J stated that: **4–18**

> It may first be noted that unlike cases such as *Mudd* and *Galvin*, Mr. O'Connell can adduce no *written evidence* of any kind to suggest that an assurance of this kind regarding the non-enforceability of the personal guarantee was ever in contemplation. While not fatal to an otherwise compelling case, the absence of such written pre-contractual documents of this kind must nevertheless be regarded objectively as weakening that case.
>
> Second, if the general background to the guarantee clearly shows that if Mr. O'Connell was reluctant to give such a guarantee, then by the same token Tennants were unwilling to supply Dry Lining without some further letter of comfort such as a personal guarantee. Mr. Peden acknowledged that the personal guarantee may well have been intended for the benefit of the London office, but he also stressed – correctly, in my view – that this was not the same thing as a commitment to the effect that the guarantee would never be activated.
>
> Third, with the exception of Mr. O'Connell's own evidence, no witness has actually stated in express terms that an assurance of this kind was given. Mr. Cullen denied that such was given and as I interpret Mr. Coffey's evidence he did not quite go so far as to say that Mr. O'Connell was given such an unequivocal commitment that the guarantee would never be used.
>
> Fourth, the contemporary record supplied by Mr. Cullen's email strongly suggests that Mr. O'Connell signed the personal guarantee without Mr. Cullen being physically present and that this occurred on 6th October, 2008. This is re-enforced by the fact that Tennants's date stamp on the personal guarantee suggests that it was received by post by them on Friday, 8th October, 2008.
>
> Fifth, I accept the evidence given by Mr. Peden that he did raise the issue of the personal guarantee with Mr. O'Connell at the meeting in April 2010 and that there was, in fact, no suggestion that the guarantee was not enforceable.

He concluded that: **4–19**

> A. The guarantee was signed and duly executed by Mr. O'Connell. It is, therefore, *prima facie* binding.
>
> B. If Mr. O'Connell could have shown by cogent evidence that it had been represented to him that the guarantee was not intended to be binding, it would

have been open to him to establish the existence of a collateral contract to this effect or even, indeed, that there was no intention to create legal relations. To do this, however, it is often in practice necessary to point to some documentary material or perhaps other unequivocal evidence which demonstrates the existence of such a representation.

C. Viewed objectively, the evidence does not support this claim, as there was, at most, pre-contractual representations that it was unlikely that the personal guarantee would have to be called upon. Critically, however, the email sent by Mr. Cullen to Ms. McCausland on 6th October, 2008, bears out the plaintiff's contention that the guarantee was signed by Mr. O'Connell on that day. This evidence accordingly undermines the defendant's contention that the guarantee was signed two days later at a meeting in Galway. It also further undermines the contention that at such a meeting there was a representation by Mr. Cullen to the effect the guarantee would not be enforced and that its execution was required simply for presentational reasons.

For these reasons, therefore, I find myself compelled to the conclusion that the guarantee binds the defendant. In these circumstances, I must accordingly give judgment for the plaintiff in the sum of €293,841.

4–20 However, where "cogent evidence" is adduced establishing the existence of a collateral contract between parties to the main contract such contract may be enforced. In *AIB Mortgage Bank v Hayes*[23] Gilligan J stated:

As, I think, Baker J. found in her judgment, it is clear from the undisputed evidence that the promise of a review after five years was a key factor in inducing the defendant/appellant to enter this contract of loan with AIB.

4–21 He went on to refer to the judgment of Hogan J in *Tennants Building Products Ltd v O'Connell* and stated:

As Hogan J. stated in *Tennants Building Products Ltd. v O'Connell* [2013] IEHC 197 following a review of the authorities on this point: "The effect of this case-law may be said to be that while the courts will permit a party to set up a collateral contract to vary the terms of a written contract, this can only be done by means of cogent evidence, often itself involving … written pre-contractual documents which, it can be shown, were intended to induce the other party into entering the contract."

In the present case, the documentation relied on by the High Court showed that the promise of the five year review was a critical factor in the defendant's decision, so that the "cogent evidence" required in *Tennants Building Products* is satisfied in the present case.

4–22 He concluded:

Accordingly, the judgment and order of the High Court of 27th May 2016, whereby judgment was entered against the defendants in the sum of €3,972,893.57 and the

[23] [2018] IECA 152, paras 10–11.

> orders for possession in respect of the 22 identified properties must be set aside and the appellants can proceed ahead with their counterclaim for damages for breach of contract, misrepresentation, negligence and breach of duty.

Procedural Fairness

A party claiming damages for breach of a collateral contract must state such claim in the pleadings otherwise the court may not be able to hear and consider such claim, and further, no such claim may be implied into the pleadings. In *Begley v Damesfield Ltd*[24] Donnelly J, when considering the issue of procedural fairness in a case where no claim of breach of collateral contract was set out in the pleadings, stated: **4–23**

> In my view, therefore, the question of whether a judge may grant relief in respect of a claim that was not made in the course of pleadings is a matter which goes to jurisdiction. It is a jurisdictional issue not least because it has at its heart the issue of procedural fairness.

And further: "In my view, there is no jurisdiction to proceed to a finding of breach of a collateral contract where that had not been pleaded." **4–24**

Donnelly J concluded: **4–25**

> In the course of this judgment, I have held that the trial judge made clear findings of a breach of a collateral contract on the part of the appellant. There was evidence before her which was sufficiently cogent to permit her to make that finding on the evidence. However, a breach of a collateral contract had never been pleaded, there was no application to amend the pleadings and there were no legal submissions at the end of the evidence squarely addressing the issue. In those circumstances, there was a procedural unfairness to the appellant of such significance that it is necessary to allow the appeal.

---

[24] [2020] IECA 171, paras 94–97.

Chapter 5

ESTOPPEL PRINCIPLES

Introduction

In *Doran v Thompson Ltd*[1] Griffin J defined the principle of promissory estoppel as follows: **5–01**

> Where one party has, by his words or conduct, made to the other a clear and unambiguous promise or assurance which was intended to affect the legal relations between them and to be acted on accordingly, and the other party has acted on it by altering his position to his detriment, it is well settled that the one who gave the promise or assurance cannot afterwards be allowed to revert to their previous legal relations as if no such promise or assurance had been made by him, and that he may be restrained in equity from acting inconsistently with such promise or assurance.

In *National Asset Loan Management Ltd v Downes*[2] Charleton J referred to the 32nd edition of *Snell's Principles of Equity* for a modern statement of the principle of promissory estoppel, as follows: **5–02**

> Where by his words or conduct one party to a transaction freely makes to the other a clear and unequivocal promise or assurance which is intended to affect the legal relations between them (whether contractual or otherwise) or was reasonably understood by the other party to have that effect, and, before it is withdrawn, the other party acts upon it, altering his or her position so that it would be inequitable to permit the first party to withdraw the promise, the party making the promise or assurance will not be permitted to act inconsistently with it.[3]

The principle of promissory estoppel is based on representations made by one contractual party to another which causes that party to rely on them and act on foot them to his or her detriment. The principle of promissory estoppel may be used as a defence mechanism or "shield" by a defendant against the enforcement of contractual terms by a plaintiff. The principle may also be used as a defence by a plaintiff in the event of a counterclaim being made by a defendant. In *Chartered Trust Ireland Ltd v Healy*,[4] Barron J stated that the "shield" aspect of the principle "does not prevent the plaintive from relying upon an estoppel as a defence to the defendant's counterclaim". **5–03**

---

1 [1978] IR 223, 230; see *Healy v Ulster Bank Ltd and Promontaria (Aran) Ltd* [2020] IECA 332.

2 [2014] IEHC 71.

3 (Sweet & Maxwell 2010) para12-009.

4 Unreported, High Court, Barron J, 10 December 1985.

5–04 The detriment suffered by the defendant must be pleaded and proved, and also be substantial enough, to ground a claim in promissory estoppel. Where a claim of promissory estoppel is established by the defendant, the next step is for the court to decide on how the equity is to be satisfied, and when doing so, the court may be guided by general equitable principles, such as proportionality and fairness. Also, the court is not confined to monetary considerations when deciding on how best a defendant might be compensated for the loss suffered by him or her.[5] It is also important to emphasise that promissory estoppel may be applied as a temporary measure to suspend the legal and contractual rights of the plaintiff, and not to totally abrogate them.[6] Therefore, a person who makes to another a clear and unambiguous representation of fact intending that other to act on it, if the representation turns out to be untrue, and if that other does act upon it to his prejudice, the representor is prevented or estopped from denying its truth.

5–05 Where contractual parties tacitly recognise and accept changed circumstances surrounding their contract as a result of a mistake, and yet they continue with the performance of their contract knowing of the mistake, it will be *assumed* that they have accepted the changed contractual circumstances following upon the mistake. Where one party later changes his or her mind, and insists on reverting to the position before the changed contractual circumstances, that party may be prevented by the court from doing so by the application of the equitable principle of estoppel by convention. The principle of estoppel by convention is based on assumptions, and not on representations, as in cases of proprietary and promissory estoppel.[7] The conduct of a party may also be taken account of by the court when applying estoppel by convention.[8] In *Johnson v Gore Wood and Co (No 1)*[9] Lord Goff observed that many circumstances capable of giving rise to an estoppel cannot be accommodated within a single formula, and that unconscionability provides the link between them.

The Application of the Principle of Promissory Estoppel

5–06 Where a defendant can show that he or she relied on clear and unambiguous representations made by the plaintiff in relation to terms of a contract,

---

[5] See *Daly v Minister for the Marine* [2001] 3 IR 513 at 529; see *Industrial Yarns Ltd v Leo Greene and Arthur Manley* [1984] ILRM 15, 23; *Naylor v Maher* [2018] IECA 32.

[6] See *Healy v Ulster Bank Ireland Ltd* [2018] IEHC 12.

[7] See *Courtney v McCarthy* [2008] 2 IR 376; *Amalgamated Investment and Property Co Ltd v Texas Commerce International Bank* [1982] 1 QB 84.

[8] See *McMahon v Kerry County Council* [1981] ILRM 419.

[9] [2002] AC 1.

and also that he or she had acted upon such representations to his or her detriment, the court may apply the principle of promissory estoppel, and refuse to enforce the contract.[10]

(i) The Principle of Promissory Estoppel

In *Central London Property Trust Ltd v High Trees House Ltd*[11] Denning J (as he then was) defined promissory estoppel as follows: **5–07**

> Where a contractual party makes a clear and unambiguous representation of fact to the other contractual party regarding their contract, and that latter party in fact acts on it, but thereafter the former party reneges on the terms of the representation, the latter party may rely on principle of promissory estoppel as a defence to any claim made against him or her on foot of the original contract.

In the *High Trees* case, Denning J also stated that a promise intended to be acted upon, and is in fact acted upon, is binding insofar as its terms properly apply. In *Combe v Combe*[12] Denning LJ (as he then was) stated that the principle of promissory estoppels never stood alone as giving rise to a cause of action in itself. The principle can never do away with the necessity of consideration when that is an essential part of the cause of action. The doctrine of consideration is too firmly established "to be overthrown by a side-wind". Birklett LJ added that principle may only be relied on as a "shield" and not a "sword", ie to defend an action and not to institute one based on it. **5–08**

In *Kenny v Kelly*,[13] Barron J, when referring to *Central London Property Trust Ltd v High Trees House Ltd*[14] and the principle of promissory estoppel, stated that: **5–09**

> In *Central London Property Trust Ltd v High Trees House Ltd*, the essence of promissory estoppel was said to be a promise intended to be binding, intended to be acted upon and in fact acted upon. In my view, the facts of the present case come within these principles. Each of the elements necessary to establish the estoppel is present.

---

10 See *The Revenue Commissioners v Moroney* [1972] IR 372; *National Asset Loan Management Ltd v Downes* [2014] IEHC 71; *Kenny v Kelly*, unreported, High Court, Barron J, 27 July 1988; *Flynn v Breccia* [2018] IECA 273; *Sheehan v Breccia* [2018] IECA 286; *Naylor v Maher* [2012] IEHC 408.

11 [1947] KB 130.

12 [1951] 1 All ER 767.

13 Unreported, High Court, Barron J, 27 July 1988.

14 [1947] KB 130.

(ii) Clear and Unambiguous Representations of Fact

5–10 In *Ryan v Connolly*[15] Keane CJ, when referring to the nature of representations for the application of the principle, stated:

> ... Griffin J. had pointed out that ... it was not necessary that the representation should be one "positively incapable of more than one possible interpretation". A party seeking to rely on the principle cannot, in other words, rely on a strained or fanciful interpretation of the words used, he must show that it was reasonable in the circumstances for him to construe the words used by the other party in a sense which would render it inequitable for that party to [resile from them].

5–11 In *The Revenue Commissioners v Moroney*,[16] Kenny J, when considering the scope of promissory estoppel, stated:

> In my view there is no reason why the principle of promissory estoppel should be confined to cases where the representation related to existing contractual rights. It includes cases where there is a representation by one person to another that rights which will come into existence under a contract to be entered into will not be enforced.

5–12 In *National Asset Loan Management Ltd v Downes*[17] Charleton J stated that the estoppel:

> is based either on representation or situations of behaviour that, reasonably construed, clearly withdraw or alter the strictures of legal obligations in such a way that it would be unfair to later enforce these.

5–13 The representee must also show that he or she was influenced by what was said or done by the representor. *In Industrial Yarns Ltd v Leo Greene and Arthur Manley*[18] Costello J stated:

> But to establish that an estoppel has arisen the representee must show that what was said or done by the representor influenced both the belief and conduct of the representee to his detriment.

(iii) A Party's Detriment

5–14 In *Daly v Minister for the Marine*[19] Fennelly J, speaking for the Supreme Court, stated that:

> It is the fact that it would be unconscionable for one party to be permitted to

---

[15] [2001] 1 IR 627, 632.
[16] [1972] IR 372, 381.
[17] [2014] IEHC 71.
[18] [1984] ILRM 15, 23; see *Re JR a Ward of Court* [1993] ILRM 657; *Tool Metal Manufacturing Co Ltd v Tungsten Electric Co Ltd* [1955] 2 All ER 657.
[19] [2001] 3 IR 513, 529; see *Industrial Yarns Ltd v Leo Greene and Arthur Manley* [1984] ILRM 15, 23.

> depart from a position, statement or representation, upon which the other party has acted to his detriment, which justifies the courts in intervening to restrain him from doing so. If the recipient of a promise or representation, is to be dispensed from any obligation to demonstrate reliance, the doctrine would be more than exceptionally generous. It would be a virtually ungovernable new force affecting potentially not only equity but the laws of contract and property and, as here, the exercise of administrative powers.

The detriment alleged to have been suffered must be pleaded and proved by the defendant. In *McGuinness v McGuinness*,[20] Kinlen J stated: **5–15**

> It must be pleaded and proved. It must be substantial although not necessarily confined to monetary considerations. It must be tested against the principle that it would be unjust or inequitable to allow the assurance to be disregarded.

In *Flynn v Breccia*[21] the estoppel issue arose out of the following circumstances, as *per* Hogan J: **5–16**

> In March 2014 the plaintiffs had begun a series of steps regarding the possible purchase of their loans from the National Asset Loan Management Ltd. ("NALM"), itself a subsidiary entity of the National Asset Management Agency ("NAMA"). To that end the plaintiffs both sought and received a redemption figure from NALM in respect of those loans. It is common case that this figure did not include a figure for surcharge interest. The plaintiffs contend that as a result they altered their position in reliance on this representation as to the appropriate redemption figure. In particular, they contend that they entered into arrangements to their detriment with third party capital venture fund with a view to purchasing these loans.

Hogan J stated: **5–17**

> On any view, therefore, these representations amount to a "clear and unambiguous promise or assurance which was intended to affect the legal relations between them and to be acted on accordingly": see *Doran v Thompson Ltd.* [1978] I.R. 223, 230, per Griffin J. As I just indicated, these requirements are satisfied in that:
> i. the NALM representations were clear and unambiguous;
> ii. they affected the legal relationships between the parties, because they indicated the figures necessary to redeem the loans, thus ending the relationship of debtor and creditor between these parties;
> iii. it was supplied in the understanding that it would be acted on by Mr. Flynn and Benray.
>
> The first limb of the test required to satisfy the requirements of estoppel by conduct is therefore fully satisfied.

Hogan J referred to the judgment of Griffin J in *Doran v Thompson Ltd*[22] for what was required in respect of the second limb of the test: **5–18**

---

[20] Unreported, High Court, Kinlen J, 19 March 2002; see *Healy v Ulster Bank Ireland Ltd* [2018] IEHC 12; *Bank of Scotland v Kennedy* [2013] IEHC 420, paras 11–16.

[21] See *Flynn v Breccia* [2018] IECA 273; *Sheehan v Breccia* [2018] IECA 286.

[22] [1978] IR 223, 230.

> … and the other party has acted on [the promise or assurance] to his detriment, it is well settled that the one who gave the promise or assurance cannot afterwards revert to their previous legal relation as if no such assurance or promise had been made by him, and that he may be restrained in equity from acting inconsistently with such promise or assurance.

5–19 Hogan J went on to state:

> The next question, therefore, is whether Mr. Flynn and Benray acted to their detriment on foot of these representations such that it would now be inequitable for Breccia as assignee of NALM to go back on these assurances.
>
> I turn now to the issue of whether Mr. Flynn and Benray relied to their detriment on the representation given by NALM as to the redemption figure. In essence, the argument here advanced by Breccia is that neither Mr. Flynn or Benray changed their position in reliance on these representations, since they were going to have to re-finance these loans in any event. Moreover, as the relevant witness for the plaintiffs on this issue was Mr. James Flynn (who is the son of Mr. John Flynn), Breccia submits that James Flynn cannot give evidence of what John Flynn had in his mind at the time he entered into the guarantee in question. It was further contended that as the Talos transaction had been agreed before 13 March 2014 (i.e. the date on which Mr. Hoey on behalf of NALM issued the spreadsheet containing the redemption figures), there was no detrimental reliance on these figures.[23]

5–20 He concluded:

> In my view, there was abundant evidence to sustain the inference drawn by Haughton J. to the effect that both Mr. John Flynn and Benray had relied to their detriment on the NALM representations. Neither of them had been given any reason to think that any other amount such as surcharge interest would be added to these redemption figures. It is clear from the terms of the letter of the 4 April 2014 from Matheson that NALM knew that these figures were being relied upon by Mr. Flynn and Benray for re-financing purposes. In any event Mr. Hoey gave unchallenged evidence along similar lines.[24]

(iv) Satisfying an Equity

5–21 In *Naylor v Maher*,[25] Peart J, when determining the appropriate method of satisfying an equity in a claim of promissory estoppel for the detriment suffered by the plaintiff, stated:

> The present case is a good example of where the court's consideration of how the plaintiff's claim in equity to the lands ought to be satisfied must embrace more than simply how much money the plaintiff has lost by making a decision to move back to the family farm, and remaining there in reliance upon the representations made to him. The detriment to him is not confined to a reduction of income or other purely monetary loss. He altered the course of his life. One cannot forecast how

[23] [2018] IECA 273, paras 28–31; see also *Sheehan v Breccia* [2018] IECA 286.
[24] [2018] IECA 273, para 35; see also *Sheehan v Breccia* [2018] IECA 286.
[25] [2018] IECA 32; see *K v K* [2018] IEHC 615.

> his life might have evolved had he remained working in Dublin or, indeed, in any other urban environment, but it is reasonable to presume that he would not have spent his life as a farmer. But there will be other cases where the circumstances presented may indicate that it is just that the particular equity found to exist would be justly satisfied by a pecuniary award.[26]

(v) The Temporary Nature of Promissory Estoppel

It also appears that the principle of promissory estoppel may be applied to suspend, and not permanently abrogate, a plaintiff's legal rights under a contract. The principle merely suspends legal rights until such time as reasonable notice to resume them has been given.[27] In *Healy v Ulster Bank Ireland Ltd*[28] Barrett J, when referring to the temporary nature of a promissory estoppel, stated that: **5–22**

> An aspect of the doctrine of promissory estoppel that is sometimes overlooked is the fact that the representation of forbearance giving rise to an estoppel will usually be temporary in nature. This was an aspect of matters considered by Laffoy J. in *Barge Inn, op. cit.*, paras.70–72.[29]

He went on to state: **5–23**

> In *Snell's Equity* (32nd Ed.) the editors deal with the effect of promissory estoppel and, in particular, the relief which can be afforded when it is established as follows (at para. 12–14): "The effect of the doctrine of promissory estoppel can be either temporary or permanent. But it is usually temporary. Where the promise or assurance is more than a temporary concession, [the promisor] will be entitled to withdraw the concession in accordance with its terms. Even where the promise or assurance cannot be construed as a temporary concession [the promisor] will usually be entitled to withdraw the promise on giving reasonable notice and the promise will only become final and irrevocable if [the promisee] cannot resume his or her former position. In this sense the doctrine of promissory estoppel has much in common with the principle of waiver of rights which permits a party to revoke any waiver upon reasonable notice to the other party."[30]

In *Tyrrell v Wright*[31] Whelan J, when considering the temporary effect of a promissory estoppel, stated that: "It is well established in our jurisprudence that the effect of estoppel is to suspend rather than extinguish the promisor's rights." **5–24**

In her judgment, Whelan J referred with apparent approval to *The Barge* **5–25**

---

26 [2018] IECA 32, paras 14–15.
27 See *Tool Metal Manufacturing Co Ltd v Tungsten Electric Co Ltd* [1955] 2 All ER 657.
28 [2018] IEHC 12; see *Ajayi v RT Briscoe (Nigeria) Limited* [1964] 1 WLR 1326, 1330.
29 [2018] IEHC 12, para 57.
30 [2018] IEHC 12, paras 7072.
31 [2018] IECA 295, paras 43–44.

Inn Limited v Quinn Hospitality (Ireland) Operations 3 Limited[32] where Laffoy J stated:

> … its effect is to suspend not to give up altogether a legal right, the right to resile from the promise being available where reasonable notice is given (per Clarke at p. 79). Applying the suspensory effect of the doctrine to the various circumstances which may arise is the most difficult aspect of the application of the doctrine. In the U.K. textbooks, the terminology used to describe the effect of the doctrine tends to be to describe it as being either temporary or permanent, depending on the factual circumstances.

5–26 In *Tyrrell v Wright* Whelan J concluded:

> I am satisfied that this ground of appeal as argued by Mr. Wright fails to meaningfully engage with the substance of the trial judge's legal analysis. Particularly the principle that the estoppel contended for was of a temporary nature only and could be withdrawn upon reasonable notice by Launceston or its agent was not addressed beyond a bare denial. There was clear evidence before the trial judge which entitled her to conclude that any concession had been effectively and validly withdrawn. No legal basis to interfere with that determination has been made out.[33]

The Application of the Principle of Estoppel by Convention

5–27 Where contractual parties tacitly recognise and accept changed circumstances surrounding their contract as a result of a mistake, and yet they continue with the performance of their contract knowing of the mistake, it will be *assumed* that they have accepted the changed contractual circumstances following upon the mistake, "neither of them will be allowed to go back on that assumption when it would be unfair or unjust to allow him to do so", by the application of the equitable principle of estoppel by convention.

(i) An Underlying Assumption

5–28 In *Amalgamated Investment and Property Co Ltd v Texas Commerce International Bank*[34] Lord Denning MR described the principle of estoppel by convention as follows:

> When the parties to a transaction proceed on the basis of an underlying assumption – either of fact or of law – whether due to misrepresentation or mistake makes no difference – on which they have conducted the dealings between them – neither

---

32 [2013] IEHC 387, para 70.

33 [2018] IECA 295, para 45.

34 [1982] 1 QB 84 at 22; see *Amalgamated Investment and Property Co Ltd v Texas Commerce International Bank* [1982] 1 QB 84; *Courtney v McCarthy* [2008] 2 IR 376.

> of them will be allowed to go back on that assumption when it would be unfair or unjust to allow him to do so. If one of them does seek to go back on it, the courts will give the other such remedy as the equity of the case demands.

In *Ulster Investment Bank Ltd v Rockrohan Estate Ltd*[35] Charleton J, when considering the nature of estoppel by convention, stated: **5–29**

> Estoppel can arise, however, through an assumption shared by those interacting. This does not necessarily always have to be written or spoken once the state of affairs is clear, and therefore obvious, and the parties act upon it. For estoppel to arise, it is essential that there is conduct which establishes an objective state of affairs, whereby the party to be estopped, who would otherwise be bound by the legal relations, is placed in circumstances whereby it is clearly understood that a new state of affairs governs the rights and obligations as between the parties. This requires some demonstrable action, behaviour or representation by the party who is to be bound by the altered state of affairs. It is insufficient, to establish estoppel, merely for the party later pleading that defence to conclude that matters must be so. There must, instead, be a foundation in the behaviour of the party who is to be estopped from asserting a legal entitlement, either pursuant to contract or otherwise.

Where an estoppel is used as a sword, he stated that: **5–30**

> The same applies where estoppel is used not as a shield but as a sword. It would be an unwarranted and dangerous extension of the doctrine of estoppel to permit it to be one-sided; which it would be if based on bare assumption. It has always been central to the equitable principle of estoppel that it derives either from representations or from situations of behaviour that, reasonably construed, clearly withdraw or alter the strictures of legal obligations in such a way that circumstances may later arise whereby it would be unfair to enforce these. Where the matter is one of representation, it should be relatively simple to identify the legal term supposedly set aside thereby, and where, and in what terms, the representation had been directed in this regard. Where, on the other hand, it is a matter of both parties proceeding on the basis of a clear common understanding, the mutual convention of the parties may suffice as a foundation for estoppel. Depending on the facts, estoppel may become operative in that situation, but only because of that common understanding.

(ii) A Clear Common Understanding Between Parties

A "clear common understanding" or an assumption between contractual parties must be shown to exist for the principle of estoppel by convention to apply. In *National Asset Loan Management Ltd v Downes*[36] Charleton J stated that: **5–31**

> What is needed in any form of estoppel is "a clear and unequivocal promise or assurance". While, perhaps, some authorities might take the approach that it is the unfairness of allowing the party with the legal rights to go back on their

[35] [2015] IESC 17, para 26.
[36] [2014] IEHC 71, para 23.

> stated position, there must still be a stated representation or underlying shared circumstance giving rise to the other party, at a minimum reasonably, concluding that relevant legal rights have been set aside. The proof of any such alleged representation through words or circumstances is on the party seeking to rely on it; here, the defendant.

5–32 And that:

> When it comes to an assumed state of affairs, an assumption on its own is not sufficient unless there is proof that the assumption is shared by both sides or is made by one and acquiesced in by the other. In the context of estoppel by convention, for an estoppel to operate, acquiescence requires knowledge of the state of affairs, and therefore effective consent to any representation based on conduct.

5–33 In *National Asset Loan Management Ltd v Downes*[37] Charleton J, having found that the case was based on an "empty assumption", stated:

> In no sense would it be reasonable to conclude on the evidence heard that a mutually binding and differing state of affairs had come into being and in alteration of the legal relationship between the parties. There is nothing to indicate to anyone that simply because one legal summons does not include a particular defendant that such defendant is released from his legal obligations. In addition, the defendant claims a lack of pursuit of him as an estoppel. This is entirely unconvincing as are the other pieces of happenstance pleaded in aid.

5–34 He went on to state that:

> Any representation in alteration of legal rights only estops the maker thereof. What is missing here is a representation from someone other than the defendant or his solicitor. In fact, that is entirely absent in this case. Any representation that was made arose from what the defendant had said his solicitor told him following, as he put it, a full review of the securities that were in place. That cannot give rise to an estoppel. The defendant is to be admired for the frankness of his evidence. In particular, the defendant made it clear that he assumed that such advice could not possibly have been given to him by his solicitor were it not the case that the solicitor had first checked with AIB Bank and received an assurance that established that advice as correct. That, again, and even at its height is not an estoppel. Any lawyer can review obligations under a set of securities and come to a conclusion that these are binding or are flawed in some way or have been altered by collateral obligations or, instead, are in full force and effect. The degree to which inventive argument can be constructed upon even the plainest of points, the extent to which even written contracts can be subject to argument in litigation and the widely differing interpretations of even a recorded telephone conversation that can be urged in litigation, illustrates that lawyers, like doctors, may differ. No one can rely on advice from their own lawyer as founding an estoppel. If a lawyer, as agent, receives a representation from the party to be estopped or his agent then that is a different matter; and that is what happened in *Courtney v McCarthy*.[38]

---

[37] [2014] IEHC 71, para 20.
[38] [2014] IEHC 71, paras 22–23.

In *Ulster Investment Bank Ltd v Rockrohan Estate Ltd*[39] Charleton J, when referring to the facts of the case and the common assumption between the parties, stated: 5–35

> Through the decades following the making of the order, the bank was engaged in protracted litigation, in circumstances where the parties knew that the rights of the bank had been the subject of an order which was being held in abeyance at the express and open request of Rockrohan, made in the public forum of a court hearing, pending an expectation of success by Rockrohan as against that bank and as against the State. There was a common assumption between these parties, reasonably held and based on unequivocal circumstances, that the parties would hold their hand as against each other until such time as that litigation had come to a practical conclusion one way or the other. Had it come to a conclusion as against the bank, both parties assumed, again reasonably, as Rockrohan had expressly and publicly represented, that the debt would be paid out of the profit from the litigation. Had it come to a conclusion, which it did, as against Rockrohan, then that would be the end of any excuse whereby it could be claimed that the bank should hold off on selling the property or in making an application to court, usually only made in the case of some form of difficulty or obstruction, that an order for possession for the purpose of sale was not appropriate.[40]

(iii) Unconscionable Conduct

Any unconscionable conduct by a party to a contract may also be taken account of by the court when deciding whether or not to apply the equitable principle of estoppel by convention.[41] In *Johnson v Gore Wood and Co (No 1)*[42] Lord Goff made the interesting observation that many circumstances capable of giving rise to an estoppel cannot be accommodated within a single formula, and that unconscionability provides the link between them. Therefore, all estoppels may be linked by the test of unconscionability apropos the conduct of the litigant parties to determine "whether it is wrong and wilful" and the consequences of such conduct, and "justice of the consequences". In *Johnson v Gore Wood and Co (N o1)* Lord Goff also stated that when, as the trial judge in that case, the principle of estoppel by convention had been urged upon him, but had hesitated to accept it. Instead, he based his decision in that case on a broader base of unconscionability. In his speech he accepted that certain circumstances may have the effect of enabling a party to enforce a cause of action by estoppel which, without the estoppel, would not exist. However, in his view it was not enough for that purpose that the estoppel may be characterised as an estoppel by convention, or that it could be said to be founded on a common assumption by the parties. He stated that he was reluctant to proceed on the basis of estoppel by 5–36

39 [2015] IESC 17, para 26.
40 [2015] IESC 17, para 24.
41 See *McMahon v Kerry County Council* [1981] ILRM 419.
42 [2002] AC 1; see *McMahon v Kerry County Council* [1981] ILRM 419; see *Prunty v Crowley* [2016] IEHC 293.

convention. He thought that the case could be the appropriate subject matter for an estoppel by representation, whether in the form of promissory estoppel or acquiescence. He further stated that many circumstances capable of giving rise to an estoppel cannot be accommodated within a single formula, "and that it is unconscionability which provides the link between them".

Part II

SETTING ASIDE CONTRACTS

Chapter 6

DOCTRINES OF COMMON MISTAKE AND RECTIFICATION

Introduction

A contract may be deemed void for common mistake at common law where the mistake relates to the existence of the subject matter of a contract, the ownership of the property forming the subject matter of a contract, and the quality of the subject matter of a contract. The House of Lords debated the legal doctrine of common mistake at length in *Bell v Lever Brother Ltd*,[1] and found that common mistake at common law which rendered a contract void was confined to circumstances where parties contracted under a common mistaken assumption in relation to the existence of the subject matter of the contract, or that the property forming the subject matter of the contract already belonged to the party purchasing it, or that there was a mistake as to the quality of the subject matter of the contract, and without such quality the subject matter was "essentially different from the thing as it was believed to be". **6–01**

A new concept of equitable common mistake was introduced by Denning LJ in *Solle v Butcher*.[2] In *Solle v Butcher*[3] Denning LJ, when considering the legal doctrine of common mistake, found that the court also had equitable jurisdiction to intervene where the parties have concluded a contract that was binding in law under a common misapprehension of a fundamental nature as to material facts or their respective rights, and where such is established the contract may be set aside. The concept of equitable common mistake was subsequently incorporated into Irish contract law by Costello J (as he then was) in *O'Neill v Ryan*.[4] In *Irish Pensions Trust v Central Remedial Clinic*,[5] Kelly J also referred, though *obiter*, to the judgment of Costello J in *O'Neill v Ryan* and the decision of Denning LJ in *Solle v Butcher*. **6–02**

A contract may be rectified by the court where a party to a contract claims **6–03**

---

1 [1932] AC 161.
2 [1950] 1 KB 671.
3 [1950] 1 KB 671.
4 [1991] ILRM 672; see *Irish Pensions Trust v Central Remedial Clinic*, High Court, Kelly J, 18 March 2005; *Intrum Justitia BV v Legal and Trade Financial Services Ltd*, High Court, O'Sullivan J, 10 June 2005.
5 Unreported, High Court, Kelly J, 18 March 2005.

that the subsequent written record of the contract does not truly reflect the terms of the contract originally agreed by the parties.[6] The application of the principle of rectification is dependent on the answer to the following two questions: first, did the parties enter into a binding contract and, secondly, did the subsequent written document reflect a true representation of the contractual provisions; an affirmative answer to these two questions is vital to the application of the principles. Where there is a clear discrepancy between the contract agreed by the parties and the subsequent written version of it, equity may intervene and apply the principle of rectification. The onus of proof, however, is a heavy one, and rests on the party who claims rectification of the erroneous subsequent written record of the contract.[7]

Doctrines of Common Mistake

(i) Common Law Mistake

6–04 In *Bell v Lever Brothers Ltd*[8] the House of Lords considered the circumstances in which mistake avoided a contract, and held that it did so where the parties contracted under the common mistaken assumption that the subject matter of the contract existed when, in fact, this was not the case (*res extincta*), or where unknown to the parties the buyer was already the owner of the property forming the subject matter of the contract (*res sua*). Mistake as to quality of the subject matter of a contract may not avoid a contract unless it is "essentially different from the thing as it was believed to be".[9] In *Bell v Lever Brother Ltd*, Lever had a controlling interest in another company called Niger and appointed Bell chairman and Snelling as vice-chairman of the board of Niger at salaries of £8,000 and £5,000 a year respectively. While acting as chairman and vice-chairman Bell and Snelling acted in breach of duty which would have justified their dismissal. Niger amalgamated with another company and Bell and Snelling were made redundant. The chairman of Lever being unaware of their breaches of duty paid Bell £30,000 and Snelling £20,000 on the termination of their employment contracts. When Lever and Niger discovered the breaches of duty by Bell and Snelling they brought an action claiming *inter alia* the recovery of the sums paid to them on foot of the termination of their employment contracts. The House of Lords held that Bell and Snelling owed no duty to disclose the breaches of duty to Lever and Niger, and as the identity of the subject matter was not

---

6 See *East v Pantiles (Plant Hire) Ltd* (1981) 263 EG 61; *Investors Compensation Scheme Ltd v Bromwich Building Society* [1998] 1 WLR 896; *Danske Bank A/S v Coyne* [2011] IEHC 234.

7 See *Boliden Tara Mines Ltd v Cosgrove* [2010] IESC 19; *Lansing Linde Ltd v Alber* [2000] PLR 15; *Whiteside v Whiteside* [1950] 1 Ch 65, 71; *Thomas Bates and Son Limited v Wyndham's Lingerie Limited* [1981] 1 WLR 505, 521.

8 [1932] AC 161.

9 [1932] AC 161, 218.

destroyed by mistake, it was not fundamental enough to render the contract void. In *Associated Japanese Bank (International) Ltd v Credit du Nord SA*,[10] under a sale and leaseback arrangement the plaintiffs bought precision engineering equipment from a Mr. Bennet and leased the same back to him. This transaction was guaranteed by the defendants. Later it was discovered that the equipment never existed, and Mr. Bennet disappeared without meeting his repayments. The plaintiffs sought to enforce the guarantee. The court held that as a matter of construction the guarantee was subject to condition precedent that the machines that were the subject matter of the lease were in existence. As a result, Steyn J held that the guarantee was void for common mistake. In *Western Potato Co-Operative Ltd v Durnan*,[11] the plaintiff contracted to supply seed potatoes to the defendant in order to grow eighty tons of potatoes which were then to be resold to the plaintiff, but as the seed potatoes were not capable of producing the crop because of physical defects in their genetic structure, both parties entered into the contract on the basis of a mistaken fact or assumption. Clarke J (as he then was) held that the contract was void for common mistake.

(ii) Equitable Mistake

In *Solle v Butcher*[12] Denning LJ stated that a court had an equitable power to set aside a contract where parties entered a contract under a "common misapprehension". He stated that: **6–05**

> A contract is also liable in equity to be set aside if the parties were under a common misapprehension either as to facts or as to their relative and respective rights, provided that the misapprehension was fundamental and that the party seeking to set it aside was not himself at fault.[13]

In *Solle v Butcher* the defendant agreed to let a flat to the plaintiff for £250 a year. The flat had previously been let at a rent of £140 a year. Substantial renovations had been carried out on the flat and both parties believed that the renovations so altered the nature of it as not to come within the provisions of the Rent Restriction Acts. However, they were mistaken in this belief. The defendant would have been able to charge the plaintiff an increased rent of £250 to reflect the work carried out on the flat had he complied with the requisites of the Rent Restriction Acts but he failed to do so, and as a result, he could not lawfully charge a rent higher than £140. It was held that the parties had concluded the lease under a common mistake of fact. The common mistake was on a matter of fundamental importance to the existence of the contract, and the defendant was entitled to rescind the lease. In *O'Neill* **6–06**

[10] [1988] 3 All ER 902.
[11] [1985] ILRM 5.
[12] [1950] 1 KB 671; see *Cooper v Phibbs* (1867) LR 2 HL 249.
[13] [1950] 1 KB 671, 693.

v Ryan[14] two actions between the plaintiff and defendants were allowed by the court to be heard together. As a result of settlement negotiations they decided to settle their actions. However, after the settlement agreement, the defendants claimed that the agreement related to the two actions, whereas the plaintiff claimed that it related to one of the actions only and decided to apply to the court for specific performance of the settlement agreement. The defendants in their defence claimed that the settlement agreement had been entered by mistake. Costello J, when considering the issue of mistake raised by the defendants, referred with apparent approval to *Solle v Butcher*, and stated that the court may in the exercise of equitable jurisdiction set aside a contract even though it was not avoided or nullified by the common shared mistake. A shared common mistake will not normally avoid a contract, but this did not mean an aggrieved party was left without a remedy. Costello J referred to *Solle v Butcher*, which showed that the court may in the exercise of equitable jurisdiction set aside a contract even though it is not avoided by the shared common mistake of the parties. Costello J went on, however, to grant specific performance of the settlement agreement to the plaintiff. In *Irish Pensions Trust v Central Remedial Clinic*,[15] Kelly J referred, though *obiter*, to the judgment of Costello J in *O'Neill v Ryan* with apparent approval of his approach to the question of shared common mistake based on the decision of Denning LJ in *Solle v Butcher*.

(iii) Great Peace

6–07 In *Great Peace Shipping Ltd v Tsavliris Salvage (International) Ltd*[16] the defendants entered into a contract to hire the plaintiffs' ship *Great Peace* to escort and standby their ship *Cape Providence*, which was sinking. However, another ship in the vicinity – *Nordfarer* – came to the assistance of the *Cape Providence* and rescued it. The defendants cancelled the contract with the plaintiffs and refused to pay a five-day cancellation fee agreed in the contract. Lord Philips MR held that:

> The parties entered into a binding contract for the hire of the *Great Peace*. That the contract gave the appellants an express right to cancel the contract subject to the obligation to pay the cancellation fee of five days hire. When they engaged the *Nordfarer* they cancelled the *Great Peace*. They became liable in consequence to pay the cancellation fee. There is no injustice in this result.[17]

6–08 In *Great Peace* Lord Philips MR stated that the legal doctrine of common mistake did not allow for the intervention of equity. Equity neither gave a

---

[14] [1991] ILRM 672; see *Irish Pensions Trust v Central Remedial Clinic*, Unreported, High Court, Kelly J, 18 March 2005; *Intrum Justitia BV v Legal and Trade Financial Services Ltd*, Unreported, High Court, O'Sullivan J, 10 June 2005.

[15] Unreported, High Court, Kelly J, 18 March 2005.

[16] [2002] 4 All ER 689.

[17] [2002] 4 All ER 689, para 166.

party a right to rescind a contract nor conferred on the court a discretion to set aside a contract. He also stated that it was "impossible to reconcile *Solle v Butcher* with *Bell v Lever Brothers*".[18] He added:

> If coherence is to be restored to this area of law, it can only be by declaring that there is not jurisdiction to grant rescission of a contract on the ground of common mistake where that contract is valid and enforceable on ordinary principles of contract law.

As a result of the decision in *Great Peace* it appears that the only grounds for avoiding or setting aside a contract for common mistakes by parties are those set down by the House of Lords in *Bell v Lever Brothers*, and thereby overruling the principles of equitable common mistake formulated by Denning LJ in *Solle v Butcher*. The decision in *Great Peace* is not, of course, binding on the Irish courts, although it may be referred to as a persuasive authority in a future Irish case involving issues of common mistake. Until then the reasoning of Denning LJ in *Solle v Butcher* continues to hold sway in Irish law concerning the setting aside of contracts on grounds of equitable common mistake.[19] **6–09**

Rectifying Mistakes

Where a party to a contract claims that the subsequent written record of the contract does not truly reflect the terms of the contract originally entered into by the parties, that party may seek the intervention of equity to rectify the mistake in the subsequent written record of the contract to reflect the terms of the contract originally agreed between the parties, and the enforcement thereof. In *O'Neill v Ryan*[20] Costello J stated that the court may grant relief by way of rectification where the parties have entered into a contract but where a mistake was made in giving effect to the parties common intentions in a written contract. The general principle is that where there is a common shared mistake in that the written contract fails to record the intention of both parties the court may order rectification of the contract. Rectification may also be granted when a party has entered into a written contract by mistake, if he or she establishes that the other party with knowledge of the mistake concluded that contract. The principle of rectification may be applied at the discretion of the court. In *Lansing Linde Ltd v Alber*[21] Rimer J, when discussing the discretionary nature of the remedy, stated that: **6–10**

[18] [2002] 4 All ER 689, para 157.

[19] See *O'Neill v Ryan* [1991] ILRM 672; *Irish Pensions Trust v Central Remedial Clinic*, High Court, Kelly J, 18 March 2005; *Intrum Justitia BV v Legal and Trade Financial Services Ltd*, High Court, O'Sullivan J, 10 June 2005.

[20] [1991] ILRM 672.

[21] [2000] PLR 15.

> Rectification is a discretionary equitable remedy which is available to correct the manner in which a transaction is recorded in a written instrument. It is not a remedy which is available to change the transaction itself. The need for the remedy is because it is a fact of life that sometimes mistakes arise in the drafting of documents which the signatories do not spot before they sign. The result is that they lend their names to a document which they believe and intend achieves effect X, whereas by mistake it in fact purports to achieve a different, and unintended effect, Y. Provided the requisite conditions are satisfied, the court has a discretion to correct the executed document so that it reflects the intention to achieve effect X. There is, however, a strong presumption that a signatory of a document intends to sign it in its executed form, since the purpose of singing it is to make the document do the legal job it purports to do; and of course the signatory has every opportunity to satisfy himself before he signs it that it is in a form which meets his needs, an opportunity which responsible signatories will usually take. The jurisdiction to rectify documents is, therefore, one which is "cautiously watched and jealously exercised".[22]

6–11 While the principle of rectification allows the court to use its discretion to amend the wording of contract which does not reflect the true intentions of the contractual parties, it may not alter the original contract agreed between the parties. In *Moorview Developments v First Active Plc*[23] Clarke J (as he then was) stated that:

> Rectification is a discretionary remedy which allows a court to amend the wording, but not affect the making, of a contract, where the wording does not reflect the intentions of the parties to the contract. The party seeking rectification must provide evidence of a common continuing intention in relation to the provisions of the contract agreed between the parties up to the point of execution of the formal contract.

6–12 The application of the equitable principle of rectification appears to be dependent on the answer to the following two questions: first, did the parties enter into a binding contract and, secondly, did the subsequent written document reflect a true representation of the contractual provisions; an affirmative answer to these two questions is vital to the application of the principles. Where there is a discrepancy between the contract agreed by the parties and the subsequent written version of it, equity may intervene and apply the principle of rectification.

The circumstances in which rectification is available was authoritatively considered by the Supreme Court in *Irish Life Assurance Co v Dublin Land Security*.[24] In that case Griffin J, speaking for the Supreme Court, adopted

[22] See *Whiteside v Whiteside* [1950] 1 Ch 65, 71; *Thomas Bates and Son Limited v Wyndham's Lingerie Limited* [1981] 1 WLR 505, 521.

[23] [2008] IEHC 214; [2009] 1 IR 274, para 9.9; see *Irish Life Assurance Co v Dublin Land Securities Ltd* [1989] IR 253.

[24] [1989] IR 253, 263; see *Boliden Tara Mines Ltd v Cosgrove* [2010] IESC 19.

the principles outlined by Lord Lowry LCJ in *Rooney McFarland v Carlin*[25] where he said:

> 1. There must be a concluded agreement antecedent to the instrument which is sought to be rectified; but
> 2. The antecedent agreement need not be binding in law (for example, it need not be under seal if made by a public authority or in writing and signed by the party if relating to a sale of land) nor need it be in writing: such incidents merely help to discharge the heavy burden of proof;
> 3. A complete antecedent concluded agreement is not required, so long as there was prior accord on a term of a proposed agreement, outwardly expressed and communicated between the parties as in *Joscelyne v Nissen* [1970] 2 Q.B. 86.

When applying the foregoing principles to the facts of the case in *Irish Life Assurance Co v Dublin Land Security*[26] Griffin J stated: **6–13**

> Applying those principles to the facts of this case, and bearing in mind the heavy burden of proof that lies on those seeking rectification, the question to be addressed is whether there was convincing proof, reflected in some outward expression of accord, that the contract in writing did not represent the common continuing intention of the parties on which the court can act, and whether the plaintiff can positively show what that common intention was in relation to the provisions which the appellants say were intended to exclude the vacant lands at Palmerstown.

In *Irish Pension Trust Ltd v Central Remedial Clinic*[27] Kelly J, referring to *Irish Life Assurance Co v Dublin Land Security*[28] and *Rooney McFarland v Carlin*,[29] stated, "Rectification permits the court to correct an instrument which has failed to record the actual intentions of the parties to an agreement. It is a discretionary equitable remedy." He added, **6–14**

> "All of these comments were of course made in the context of bilateral contracts."[30]

The court may not rectify the original or "actual" contract entered into by the parties; it is only the written record of the contract that may be rectified. In *Danske Bank A/S v Coyne*[31] Charleton J commented: **6–15**

> Rectification allows the court to correct or rectify a written instrument, usually as to one particular point, so that it accurately reflects the true agreement or contract of the parties. The jurisdiction of the court does not extend to rectifying the actual contract of the parties: it is only the written record of the contract that

25 [1981] NI 138, 146.
26 [1989] IR 253, 263; see *Boliden Tara Mines Ltd v Cosgrove* [2010] IESC 19.
27 [2005] IEHC 268.
28 [1989] IR 253, 263; see *Boliden Tara Mines Ltd v Cosgrove* [2010] IESC 19.
29 [1981] NI 138, 146.
30 See also *Danske Bank A/S v Coyne* [2011] IEHC 234; *Slattery v Friends First Life Assurance Company Ltd* [2015] IECA 149.
31 [2011] IEHC 234, para 19.

may be rectified. Once an agreement has been expressed between the parties, a misstatement in the contract may be rectified so that neither party may move away from what is established as the accord of the parties. The party seeking rectification bears a heavy burden of proof.

6–16 The purposive approach may be adopted by the courts when dealing with issues involving the construction of pension schemes and the application of the equitable principle of rectification. The construction of a pension scheme should be practicable and purposive rather than detached and literal, and the scheme should be construed so as to give reasonable and practical effect to it.

6–17 The onus of proof in cases involving the application of the principle of rectification is a heavy one, and rests on the party who claims rectification of the erroneous subsequent written record of the contract.[32] As regards the burden and standard of proof in cases of rectification, Griffin J in *Irish Life Assurance Co v Dublin Land Securities*[33] stated that there must be

> convincing proof, reflected in some outward expression of accord, which the contract in writing did not represent the common continuing intention of the parties on which the court can act.

6–18 There is, however, a greater burden on a party seeking rectification where it is shown that long negotiations had taken place between the parties, and where both of whom had taken legal advice during such negotiations. As regards evidence of rectification and standard of proof, Hardiman J in *Boliden Tara Mines Ltd v Cosgrove*[34] stated that:

> There is but one standard of proof (apart from criminal proceedings) which is the balance of probability, but in some cases that standard will be more easily met than in others. For example, a case where commercial parties have had their intentions expressed in a professionally drafted legal document, which document is later said not in fact to express the intentions of the parties', will naturally call for evidence which is clear, coherent and convincing if the onus of establishing on the balance of probability that the parties' intention was not correctly expressed is to be discharged. This is so obvious as to be almost a truism. The onus will, of course, be easier to discharge if the facts put forward are entirely uncontradicted notwithstanding that a representative of the class of persons interested in having the claim for rectification rejected was present and professionally represented, and did not cause the witnesses as to fact to be cross-examined.

6–19 The court may apply the principle of rectification where it is shown the parties have reached a contract, but that a mistake was made in giving effect to the common intention of the parties in a subsequent documentary record

---

32 See *Boliden Tara Mines Ltd v Cosgrove* [2010] IESC 19; *Lansing Linde Ltd v Alber* [2000] PLR 15; *Whiteside v Whiteside* [1950] 1 Ch 65, 71; *Thomas Bates and Son Limited v Wyndham's Lingerie Limited* [1981] 1 WLR 505, 521.

33 [1989] IR 253, 263; see *Boliden Tara Mines Ltd v Cosgrove* [2010] IESC 19.

34 [2010] IESC 19, para 52.

of the contract. However, two conditions must be satisfied before the court will correct a mistake: one, there must be a clear mistake, and two, it must be clear what the correction ought to be.[35] In *Danske Bank A/S v Coyne*[36] Charleton J, when applying the two foregoing conditions in the construction of a contract, stated:

> The purpose of the court in construing any contract is to get to as close as possible to the meaning which the parties intended. This exercise could never confine the court to reading the document without regard to its background. It is well established that the context within which an agreement is made will inform both the manner of performance of the contract and the parties by whom the obligations set out therein by written agreement are required to be performed.

When applying the principles of rectification, he concluded: **6–20**

> The situation in this case involved an agreement which when written down establishes clearly a shared or common mistake made by both parties. The agreement in writing was designed to give effect to a prior oral agreement, which was then evidenced by an exchange of correspondence. The principles of rectification apply to that situation as the same principles apply to a situation, which is not applicable here, where one party sees a mistake in a written agreement and, aware that the other party has not realised that mistake, signs that agreement knowing that it contains a mistake. In the circumstances of this case I would have been obliged, because of the common mistake of the parties, to order a rectification. Because of the misnomer principle, however, the application of the jurisdiction of the Court to rectify a written contract is not necessary.[37]

[35] See *East v Pantiles (Plant Hire) Ltd* (1981) 263 EG 61; *Investors Compensation Scheme Ltd v Bromwich Building Society* [1998] 1 WLR 896; *Danske Bank A/S v Coyne* [2011] IEHC 234.

[36] [2011] IEHC 234, para 13; see *Irish Pensions Trust Limited v Central Remedial Clinic* [2006] 2 IR 126, 150–51; *East v Pantiles (Plant Hire) Ltd* (1981) 263 EG 61; *Investors Compensation Scheme Ltd v Bromwich Building Society* [1998] 1 WLR 896; *Knockacummer Wind Farm Limited v Cremins* [2018] IECA 252.

[37] [2011] IEHC 234, paras 20–21; see *Irish Pension Trust Ltd v Central Remedial Clinic* [2005] IEHC 268.

Chapter 7

THE RIGHT TO RESCIND

Introduction

Where a statement is made before or at the time of making the contract regarding some existing or future fact or event which had the effect of inducing a party to enter a contract, the contract may be rescinded or set aside on grounds of misrepresentation.[1] A statement to qualify as a misrepresentation must also relate to existing or future facts surrounding the making of the contract. In *Harlequin Property (SVG) Ltd v O'Halloran*[2] McGovern J, in relation to the intention of the party making a statement inducing a contract by misrepresentation, stated that: 7–01

> A statement as to the future will often imply a statement as to present intention. A promissor generally represents by implication that he has, at the moment of making the promise, the intention of fulfilling the obligations that he is undertaking. If it can be shown that no such intention existed at that moment, he is guilty of a misrepresentation. But the mere fact that the intention which was represented to exist was not eventually carried into effect offers little evidence of the original non-existence of the intention.

In *Mulcahy v Mulcahy*,[3] Laffoy J referred to the speech of Lord Wilberforce in *British Airways Board v Taylor*[4] where he distinguished between a promise as to future action and a statement as to an existing fact, where he said: 7–02

> … the distinction in law between a promise as to future action, which may be broken or kept, and a statement as to existing fact, which may be true or false, is clear enough. There may be inherent in a promise an implied statement as to a fact, and where this is really the case, the court can attach appropriate consequences to any falsity in, or recklessness in the making of that statement. Everyone is familiar with the proposition that a statement of intention may itself be a statement of fact and so capable of being true or false. But this proposition should not be used as a general solvent to transform the one type of assurance with another; the distinction is a real one and requires to be respected …

In *Cecil v Bayat*[5] Hamblen J, referring to the same distinction between present and future facts, stated: 7–03

---

1 See *Anderson v Ryan* [1967] IR 34; *Kiely v Delaney* [2008] IEHC 69.
2 [2013] IEHC 362, para 84.
3 [2011] IEHC 186.
4 [1976] 1 ALL ER 65, 68.
5 [2010] VWHC 641 (Comm), para 26.

> A representation of intention is a statement of present intention. It is only because it speaks to the present that it can be regarded as a representation of fact. If it speaks to the future it would be a statement of future intention, not a representation of fact.

7–04 While the silence of a contractual party does not normally give rise to a misrepresentation, such stance may not relied on by a party to a contract of insurance, as a party seeking insurance cover is under a duty to make full disclosure of all facts within his or her knowledge that may affect the mind of a prudent insurer when deciding on whether or not to accept the risk or when fixing a premium. Contracts of insurance are known as contracts *uberrimae fidei* (of utmost good faith), and where a party is in breach of the duty to make full disclosure of information the insurer may rescind the contract of insurance. A contract may be rescinded in such circumstances where there is "very little said which ought not to have been said, and very little not said which ought to have been".[6]

7–05 However, the right to rescind or set aside a contract on grounds of misrepresentation is subject to the rule of *restitutio in integrum* which requires that a party be substantially restored to the position he or she occupied before the contract was entered into, and where such cannot be achieved the court may refuse to grant rescission of a contract. The right to rescind a contract may also be lost where a third party who is a bona fide purchaser for value acquires the goods. A delay or *laches* in bringing an action may also defeat the right to rescind. The remedy of damages *in lieu* of rescission appears to be available only, and limited to, those contracts governed by the Sale of Goods and Supply of Services Act 1980 (the 1980 Act). Under s 43 of the 1980 Act an award of damages *in lieu* of rescission may be made on grounds of misrepresentation in cases of contracts for the sale of goods, hire-purchase contracts, contracts for the letting of goods and contracts for the supply of services.

7–06 A party induced to enter into a contract by a fraudulent misrepresentation may also claim damages in the tort of deceit. In *Derry v Peek*[7] Lord Hershell, when formulating the concept of fraudulent misrepresentation, stated that:

> At law, a misrepresentation is made fraudulently if, when he makes it, the representor knows that the representation is untrue or is reckless as to whether it is true or not. A person who deceives another fraudulently and thereby causes loss is liable in damages for the tort of deceit.

---

6 *Davies v London & Provincial Marine Insurance Co* (1878) 8 ChD 469, 475.

7 [1889] 14 App Cas 337, 279; see *Harlequin Property (SVG) Ltd v O'Halloran* [2013] IEHC 362, para 81.

The Right to Rescind Contracts

Where it is shown that a party was induced to enter into it on foot of a misrepresentation made to him or her by the other contractual party before or at the time of making the contract, the contract may be rescinded or set aside by the court.[8] The court may, however, refuse to grant rescission of a contract on the following grounds: 7–07

(i) Where *Restitutio in Integrum* Cannot be Achieved

The right to rescind a contract is subject to rule of *restitutio in integrum*, which requires that a party be substantially restored to the position he or she occupied before the contract was entered into, and where such cannot be achieved the court may refuse to grant rescission of a contract.[9] In *Newbigging v Adam*[10] Bowen LJ stated that the representee is entitled to rescind the contract, and be placed *in statu quo ante*. There should be a giving back and a taking back by both representor and representee, including the giving and taking back of obligations the contract created, as well as the giving back and the taking back of the advantages.[11] Where the substantial identity of the property forming the subject matter of the contract remains the same, the plaintiff may be ordered by the court to restore the property, and to indemnify the defendant against any loss incurred for any deterioration in the condition of the property. 7–08

In *Marlan Homes Ltd v Walsh*[12] Clarke J (as he then was), when referring to the decision of Henchy J in *Northern Bank Finance Corporation Limited v Charlton*,[13] stated that: 7–09

> However, it is also clear from *Charlton* that rescission will only be granted where a true restoration to the original position can be attained or can be attained to such an extent that no injustice will be suffered. The purpose of this rule is to protect a defendant from being put in an unjustifiably worse position than he occupied before the contract was made. However, deterioration of the subject-matter does not destroy the right to rescind nor prevent true restoration to the original position. Being an equitable remedy, a court has full power to make all just allowances although it may not be able to restore the parties precisely to the state in which they were before they entered into the contract.

Clarke J, when referring to the facts of *Marlan*, stated: 7–10

---

8 See *Kiely v Delaney* [2008] IEHC 69.

9 See *Northern Bank Finance Corporation Limited v Charlton* [1979] IR 149, 197; *Kiely v Delaney* [2008] IEHC 69; *Marlan Homes Ltd v Walsh* [2009] IEHC 576.

10 (1888) 13 App Cas 308.

11 See *Redgrave v Hurd* (1881) 20 ChD 1.

12 [2009] IEHC 576, para 11.2.

13 [1979] IR 149, 197; see *Kiely v Delaney* [2008] IEHC 69; *Marlan Homes Ltd v Walsh* [2009] IEHC 576.

> Two questions, in reality, arise. The first is as to whether Marlan is, *prima facie*, entitled to rescission on the facts of this case. The second is as to whether there are any circumstances (such as an absence of an ability to restore the parties more or less to the position in which they were) that would debar rescission as being an appropriate remedy.

7–11 When addressing the first question, he stated:

> So far as the first question is concerned it seems to me that Marlan has met the required test. It was a fundamental term of the November Agreement that Marlan would be able to obtain effective security over all of the subject lands to enable it to raise finance for the purposes of carrying out the development which was at the heart of the contract between the parties. Any breach of contract on the part of Mr. Walsh and Mr. Wedick which prevented Marlan from being able to give effective security (in accordance with what had been agreed in the November Agreement) to a lender, must, necessarily, amount to a fundamental breach because it goes to the very heart and root of the contractual arrangements between the parties. Without finance Marlan could not comply with the other terms of the contract. To require Marlan to be content with damages for breach of contract in circumstances where it was deprived of the means (*i.e.* finance) of complying with the principal object of the contract would, in my view, be inequitable. It follows, therefore, that Marlan are *prima facie* entitled to rescission of the contract.

7–12 When addressing the second question, he stated:

> The second question which arises is as to whether there are any circumstances that ought to prevent, on the facts of this case, Marlan from being entitled to rescission. Two possible issues arise. The first concerns the question of whether it is now feasible to restore the parties to the position in which they were prior to the contract. The second, and at least to some extent connected, question concerns delay.

7–13 In relation to the first issue, of whether it is feasible to restore the parties to the position they were in prior to the contract, he stated:

> it seems to me to be clear that the parties can be restored to the position which they were in prior to the contract being entered into. On that basis Mr. Walsh and Mr. Wedick get their property back and Marlan gets its money back. The fact that the property may be less valuable than it was at the time of the contract is not, as Griffin J. pointed out in *Northern Bank Finance Corporation Ltd.*, a bar to rescission. Neither am I satisfied that any action has been taken in relation to the possible right of way in favour of NI Property Development Ltd which could affect the title of Mr. Walsh and Mr. Wedick. That leads, therefore, to the question of delay.[14]

7–14 In relation to the second issue of delay, he concluded that:

> In those circumstances and while in no way exonerating Marlan for any blame attaching to the delay which occurred between the early part of 2007 and the

[14] [2009] IEHC 576, paras 12.1–12.8.

> end of that year, it does not seem to me that it has been established that any such delay has, in fact, prevented *restitutio in integrum*. The onus, in my view, was on Mr. Walsh and Mr. Wedick to establish that fact if reliance was to be placed on it. It would be pure speculation on my part to predict the attitude which DCC might take still less what view a court might take should DCC suggest that the December Agreement is now at an end.
>
> In all the circumstances I am not, therefore, satisfied that there is any barrier to rescission.[15]

(ii) Where a Bona Fide Purchaser for Value Acquires the Goods

The right to rescind a contract may also be lost where a third party who is a bona fide purchaser for value acquires the goods. Section 23 of the Sale of Goods Act 1893 provides that: 7–15

> Where the seller of goods has a voidable title thereto, but his title has not been avoided at the time of the sale, the buyer acquires a good title to the goods, provided he buys them in good faith and without notice of the seller's defect of title.

In *Anderson v Ryan*[16] Henchy J stated that: "One looks then to see what title, if any, such person conveyed to the defendant. The answer is found in s.23 of the Act." When referring to the evidence and facts of the case, he stated: 7–16

> It is clear from the evidence that Mr. Davis had not avoided the title of the person who sold the car to the defendant at the time of that sale, and it has not been suggested that the defendant bought otherwise than in good faith and without notice of the seller's defect of title. I am satisfied, therefore, that the defendant acquired a good title to the car and that he in turn passed a good title to the plaintiff. It is unfortunate that the plaintiff has been deprived of a car of which he was the rightful owner, but the fault does not lie with the defendant.

He concluded that no liability attached to the defendant for the plaintiff's loss. 7–17

(iii) Laches

A delay or *laches* in bringing an action based on a misrepresentation may defeat a right to rescind a contract. In *Marlan Homes Ltd v Walsh*[17] Clarke J, when considering the question of delay and the equitable principle of rescission, stated that: 7–18

> Delay arises in two ways. First it is often said that delay defeats equity. A party who delays in exercising a claim to an equitable remedy may, thereby, lose that remedy. In that context it is necessary to analyse when the entitlement to equity first arose so as to determine the extent of any relevant delay and the consequences of it.

---

[15] [2009] IEHC 576, paras 12.8–12.9.
[16] [1967] IR 34.
[17] [2009] IEHC 576, para 12.5.

Damages *In Lieu* of Rescission

7–19 The remedy of damages *in lieu* of rescission appears to be available only, and limited to, those contracts governed by the Sale of Goods and Supply of Services Act 1980 (the 1980 Act). Part V of the 1980 Act allows for the award of damages *in lieu* of rescission on grounds of misrepresentation in the case of contracts coming within the ambit of its provisions, and such contracts include contracts for the sale of goods, hire-purchase contracts, contracts for the letting of goods and contracts for the supply of services.[18] Under s 44 of the 1980 Act where a person has entered into a contract after a misrepresentation has been made to him or her, and (a), the misrepresentation has become a term of the contract, or (b), the contract has been performed, or both, then if otherwise he or she would be entitled to rescind the contract without alleging fraud, he or she will be so entitled, subject to the provisions of Part V of the 1980 Act notwithstanding the matters mentioned in (a) and (b). It can be seen that s 44 of the 1980 Act removes certain of the bars to rescission for innocent misrepresentation. Section 45(1) of the 1980 Act provides that where a person has entered into a contract after a misrepresentation has been made to him or her by another party thereto, and as a result has suffered loss, then if the party making the misrepresentation would be liable to damages in respect thereof had the misrepresentation had been made fraudulently, that party may be so liable notwithstanding that the misrepresentation was not made fraudulently, unless he or she proves that he or she had reasonable grounds to believe and did believe up to the time the contract was entered into that the facts represented were true. Under s 45(2) where a person has entered into a contract after a misrepresentation has been made to him or her otherwise than fraudulently, and he or she would be entitled by reason of the misrepresentation to rescind the contract, then if it is claimed in any proceedings arising out of the contract that the contract ought to be or has been rescinded, the court may declare the contract subsisting and award damages in lieu of rescission, if of the opinion that it would be equitable to do so, having regard to the nature of the misrepresentation and the loss that would be caused by it if the contract were upheld, as well as loss that rescission would cause to the other party. Section 45(3) provides that damages may be awarded against a party under s 45(2) whether or not he or she is liable to damages under s 45(1), but where he or she is so liable any award under s 45(2) will be taken into account in assessing his or her liability under s 45(1). Section 46(1) of the 1980 Act deals with attempts by contractual parties to exclude or restrict liability for misrepresentation by contractual provisions, and provides that if any contract contains a provision which purports to exclude or restrict liability for misrepresentation, that provision may not be enforceable unless it is shown to fair and reasonable.

[18] s 43, Sale of Goods and Supply of Services Act 1980.

Damages for Fraudulent Misrepresentation

Where it is shown that the plaintiff was induced to enter into a contract by a fraudulent misrepresentation, he or she may be awarded damages in the tort of deceit. The elements of the tort of deceit are found in *Derry v Peek*.[19] In that case, Lord Hershell stated: 7–20

> I think the authorities establish the following propositions: first, in order to sustain an action of deceit, there must be proof of fraud, and nothing short of that will suffice. Secondly, fraud is proved when it is shewn that a false representation has been made (1) knowingly, or (2) without belief in its truth, or (3) recklessly, careless whether it be true or false. Although I have treated the second and third as distinct cases, I think the third is but an instance of the second, for one who makes a statement under such circumstances can have no real belief in the truth of what he states. To prevent a false statement being fraudulent, there must, I think, always be an honest belief in its truth. And this probably covers the whole ground, for one who knowingly alleges that which is false, has obviously no such honest belief. Thirdly, if fraud be proved, the motive of the person guilty of it is immaterial. It matters not that there was no intention to cheat or injure the person to whom the statement was made.[20]

In *McAleenan v AIG (Europe) Ltd*[21] Finlay Geoghegan J, when referring to the speech of Lord Hershell in *Derry v Peek*, stated: 7–21

> However, in accordance with the principles set out above, neither of the above findings precludes a finding of fraud in the making of the false statement if the untrue statement was made "recklessly", in the sense that the term was used in *Derry v Peek*, i.e. careless as to whether the statement be true or false. It is clear that "careless" for this purpose is not the same as when used in relation to the tort of negligence. The carelessness must be something greater to constitute recklessness for the purposes of fraud. As pointed out by Lord Herschell in the extract from his speech referred to above, a statement may be considered as made recklessly where the circumstances are such that the Court considers the maker can have no real belief in the truth of what he states. It appears to require an objective consideration by the Court as to whether the circumstances in which the plaintiff signed the Proposal Form (and, by doing so, made the representations or statements contained therein) were so careless as to whether the statements were true or false that the Court must conclude that she could have had no real belief in the truth of the statements contained in the Proposal Form.

In *Harlequin Property (SVG) Ltd v O'Halloran*[22] McGovern J, when considering the issue of fraudulent misrepresentation, stated that: 7–22

> At law, a misrepresentation is made fraudulently if, when he makes it, the representor knows that the representation is untrue or is reckless as to whether

---

19 [1889] 14 App Cas 337.
20 [1889] 14 App Cas 337, 279.
21 [2010] IEHC 128, para 123; see *Moore v Moore* [2018] IECA 118.
22 [2013] IEHC 362, para 81; see *Derry v Peek* [1889] 14 App Cas 337, 279.

it is true or not. A person who deceives another fraudulently and thereby causes loss is liable in damages for the tort of deceit.

Where a misrepresentation is made fraudulently the representor may also be liable for damages in the tort of deceit. The award of damages in such instances is not made *in lieu* of rescission, but rather in the tort of deceit. The rationale here appears to be that if a person deceives another fraudulently, and causes loss, he or she is liable in damages in the tort of deceit. Where a fraudulent misrepresentation is alleged the plaintiff must show that:

(i) the alleged representation consists of something said, written or done that amounts to a representation;
(ii) the defendant was the person who made the representation;
(iii) the plaintiff was the person to whom the representation was made;
(iv) the representation was both false and fraudulent;
(v) the representation was a material inducement to the claimant to act on it;
(vi) the plaintiff did in fact alter his position on foot of the representation;
(vii) the plaintiff thereby suffered damage.[23]

7–23 When referring to the facts of *Harlequin Property*, McGovern J stated:

> The plaintiffs sought damages (including exemplary damages) for fraud and/or fraudulent misrepresentation and a declaration that the plaintiffs and each of them were joint beneficial owners of a dwelling house which, the plaintiffs alleged, was purchased by the first defendant out of monies misappropriated from the plaintiffs. The second named defendant was the father of the first named defendant and the plaintiffs' claim against him was that he received money from the first named defendant from sums misappropriated by the first named defendant from the plaintiffs. The defendants submitted that a distinction must be drawn between actionable fraudulent misrepresentations which must necessarily relate to present facts or present intention, and statements of future fact or future intention which are said to be incapable of amounting to an actionable misrepresentation.

7–24 He went on:

> The plaintiffs argued that the position in this case was similar to that in *Edgington v Fitzmaurice* (1885) 29 Ch. D 459, where it was held that a prospectus was deceptive when it contained false statements of what the company intended to do with the investor's money once they had got it. In that case, a company issued a prospectus seeking subscriptions by way of debenture bonds, which were purportedly to be applied towards development and expansion of the trade of the company. In fact, the funds were put towards discharging existing liabilities. Furthermore, the plaintiff erroneously came to the belief that the debentures would incorporate a charge over the property of the company. The monies were advanced by the plaintiff and the company subsequently became insolvent. The court held that the representation as to the purpose for which the monies would

[23] *Northern Bank Finance v Charleton* [1979] IR 149; see *Harlequin Property (SVG) Ltd v O'Halloran* [2013] IEHC 362; *Mulcahy v Mulcahy* [2011] IEHC 186; *Moore v Moore* [2018] IECA 118.

be applied was capable of operating as a "*material misstatement of fact*" capable of giving rise to a tortious action in deceit.[24]

He concluded: **7–25**

> I am satisfied that the first named defendant, on numerous occasions, represented that Phase 1 of Buccament Bay project would be completed by 1st July, 2010. These representations were made by him at a time when he knew they were untrue or when he was reckless as to the truth of the statements. He knew that the plaintiffs were relying on those statements, and acting on his representations, they continued to employ the ICE Group and pour ever-increasing sums of money into the project. The first named defendant induced Harlequin to continue making payments on foot of his representations. There is convincing evidence that the first named defendant knew both of his own knowledge and from information he was receiving from other professionals employed by the ICE Group that Phase 1 could not be delivered by 1st July, 2010. The first named defendant persisted in ignoring all warnings which he received from such professionals and continued to press Harlequin for more and more funds.[25]

---

24 [2013] IEHC 362, para 85.
25 [2013] IEHC 362, para 90.

Chapter 8

PRESUMPTIONS OF UNDUE INFLUENCE

Introduction

A contract may be set aside on grounds of undue influence where it is shown that pressure, as opposed to persuasion, was exerted on a party to enter into a contract, or make a gift, or to sign a guarantee, and where a party did not freely consent to the transaction.[1] The onus of proof rests on the person alleging undue influence to show that it existed and was exerted by the other person to the transaction before or at the time of making it. Where, however, a defendant comes within a certain category of relationships to the plaintiff a presumption of undue influence may arise, and where such is the case, the onus of proof will rest on the defendant to rebut the presumption by showing that the plaintiff had freely consented to the transaction. In *Bourke v O'Donnell*[2] Hedigan J, when considering relationships and the presumption of undue influence, stated: **8–01**

> The law assumes that certain relationships of their very nature give rise to a presumption of undue influence and where this occurs the burden of proof shifts and the onus falls upon the party seeking to uphold a transaction to show the other party freely consented to it.

In *Danske Bank A/S trading as National Irish Bank Plc v Madden*, McGovern J, when referring to contracts procured by fraud or undue influence by a third party, stated: **8–02**

> I accept the contention of the plaintiff that where a party is seeking to set aside a contract on the basis that it was procured by the fraud or undue influence of a third party, it is necessary that the party seeking to enforce the contract had actual or constructive notice of the fraud or undue influence. The onus is on the defendant to establish that the plaintiff had actual or constructive knowledge of the fraud or undue influence.[3]

An action for undue influence may be defeated by a defendant relying on a defence of *laches*. *Laches* may arise where a plaintiff fails to bring an **8–03**

---

1 See *Carroll v Carroll* [1999] 4 IR 241; *Bourke v O'Donnell* [2010] IEHC 348.
2 [2010] IEHC 348, para 82.
3 [2009] IEHC 319, para 17.

action within a reasonable time of the cessation of the undue influence by the defendant.[4]

8–04 A contract may also be set aside where it is shown that a party was forced into a contract by duress. Where it is alleged that duress was present at the time of entering a contract, it must be shown that the consent of a party had been "so wrongfully obtained that it can properly be described as an illegitimate and significant cause of the party ostensibly contracting giving assent".[5]

Presumptions of Undue Influence

8–05 A presumption of undue influence may arise in certain categories of relationship between a plaintiff and defendant. However, it may be added that the categories of relationship are not exhaustive or completely defined.[6] The nature of the transaction entered into by the parties may also be taken into account especially where it is shown to be an improvident transaction.[7] Other factors, such as the age, position in life, state of health and other particular vulnerabilities of a plaintiff may also be taken into consideration in deciding on the application of the presumption of undue influence.[8] Where there is a blood relationship between the parties such relationship will not itself be sufficient to give rise to a presumption of influence.[9] Nor will the relationship of husband and wife.[10]

8–06 In *R (Proctor) v Hutton, re Founds Estate*[11] Lord Lowry LCJ, when referring to relationships that may give rise to a presumption of undue influence, stated:

> The relationships which raise the presumption are left unlimited by definition, wide open for identification on the facts and in all the circumstances of each particular case as it arises … it is a common but not a necessary feature of the relationship that the person on whose part undue influence is alleged assumed a responsibility for advising the donor even managing his property. There are certain relationships which are recognised as giving rise to the presumption, but there are also those which, upon a consideration of the particular facts, may raise the same presumption.

---

4 *Humphreys v Humphreys* [2004] EWHC 2201; *McCormack v Our Lady Queen of Peace Achill House of Prayer Ltd* [2018] IEHC 26.
5 *ACC Bank Plc v Dillon* [2012] IEHC 474.
6 See *R (Proctor) v Hutton, re Founds Estate* [1978] NI 139; *McGonigle v Black*, unreported, High Court, Barr J, 14 November 1988.
7 See *Bourke v O'Donnell* [2010] IEHC 348.
8 *Prendergast v Joyce* [2009] IEHC 199.
9 *Gregg v Kidd* [1956] IR 183.
10 *Irish Bank Resolution Corporation v Quinn* [2011] IEHC 470.
11 [1978] NI 139.

A similar view was expressed by Barr J in *McGonigle v Black*.[12] He stated that: **8–07**

> the categories of relationship to which the presumption applies are neither closed nor rigid. The presumption may be applied in the context of a friendship between the lonely and vulnerable donor of land, who could not cope well without support and had resorted to alcohol abuse, and a friend who lived nearby, who had frequent contact with him and provided him with some home comforts.

In *Bourke v O'Donnell*[13] Hedigan J, when considering the nature of the relationship between the parties to the transaction, and whether the presumption of undue influence arose, stated that: **8–08**

> In this case, it is clear there was a long-term relationship in existence between the plaintiff and the first and second defendants. It was a relationship in which the plaintiff was dependent to varying degrees at different times on these defendants. They called to see her – minded her house – had possession of her old age pension book. The nursing home notes show that they were the most frequent visitors to her in the nursing home. Although her nephew visited four/five times a year, these defendants were, in reality, her only link to the world outside the nursing home. She had been very seriously ill in the six months prior to the transaction. Her illness, as the defendants well knew, involved long periods of confusion and disorientation. She was a highly vulnerable, elderly lady. The transaction itself was wholly improvident. She was divesting herself of the large bulk of her assets for no return whatever. Taking all of these circumstances, including the fact of the transaction itself into account, it is clear, upon the basis of the law outlined above, that a presumption of undue influence arises. The first and second defendants chose not to give any evidence and consequently I find the presumption is unrebutted and the transaction will be set aside.[14]

The presumption arises from the "actual relationship" that exists between the parties. In *Prendergast v Joyce*[15] Gilligan J stated: **8–09**

> It is clear from the passages quoted that the presumption arises from the actual relationship between donor and donee at or shortly before the time of the impugned transaction, coupled with the circumstances of the parties relevant to the acquisition of a position of influence, including the age, position in life, state of health and other particular vulnerabilities of the donor. This is probably because these and other vulnerabilities can give rise to a degree of influence over the donor in a relationship where no such influence would arise if both parties were of the same capacity and in the same position to protect their interests.

In *Gregg v Kidd*[16] Budd J, when considering whether blood relationships gave rise to the presumption between parties, stated that: **8–10**

---

12 Unreported, High Court, Barr J, 14 November 1988.
13 [2010] IEHC 348, para 82.
14 [2010] IEHC 348, para 8.3.
15 [2009] IEHC 199.
16 [1956] IR 183, 195.

> While close family relationship creates a situation where influence is readily acquired, mere blood relationship is not sufficient of itself to call the principle into play; it must be shown that the actual relations between the parties give rise to a presumption of influence.

8–11 Whether a presumption of undue influence arose between husband and wife was considered by Kelly J in the case of *Irish Bank Resolution Corporation v Quinn*.[17] In his judgment he stated that:

> It was argued during the course of the hearing that there is at law a presumption of undue influence between husband and wife. There is not. That much is clear from case law going back to the middle of the eighteenth century. In Halsbury's *Laws of England* (4th Ed.) para. 40, vol. 18, one finds on this topic the following under the heading "*No presumption between husband and wife*" – "it is noticeable that the relation of husband and wife is not one which gives rise to the presumption that undue influence was exercised".[18]

Rebutting Presumptions

8–12 The presumption of undue influence may be rebutted by showing that a contractual party obtained independent legal advice before entering into the contract, and that he or she was acting independently and with the full appreciation of what he or she was doing.[19] The advice must also be such as a competent advisor would give if acting solely in the interests of the donor.[20] In relationships of solicitor and client, there has to be some "positive evidence" to rebut that presumption of undue influence.[21] However, the onus can be discharged by evidence showing that the contract or gift "was the independent and well understood act of a person in a position to exercise free judgment".[22]

8–13 In *Inche Noriah v Shaik Allie Bin Omar*[23] Lord Hailsham LC, when considering the question of rebuttal of the presumption and independent advice, stated:

> It is necessary for the donee to prove that the gift was the result of the free exercise

[17] [2011] IEHC 470; see *In Re Hunting Lodges Limited* [1985] ILRM 85; *Ulster Bank (Ireland) Ltd v De Kretser* [2017] IECA 119; *ACC Loan Management Ltd v Connolly* [2017] IECA 119.

[18] [2011] IEHC 470, paras 38–40.

[19] See *Inche Noriah v Shaik Allie Bin Omar* [1929] AC 127, 135–36; see *Carroll v Carroll* [1999] 4 IR 241; *Lancashire Loans Ltd v Black* [1934] 1 KB 380.

[20] *Prendergast v Joyce* [2009] IEHC 199.

[21] See *Danske Bank A/S trading as National Irish Bank Plc v Madden* [2009] IEHC 319.

[22] *MC (a Ward of Court) v C* [2013] IESC 36, para 17.

[23] [1929] AC 127, 135–36; see *Carroll v Carroll* [1999] 4 IR 241; *Lancashire Loans Ltd v Black* [1934] 1 KB 380.

> of independent will. The most obvious way to prove this is by establishing that the gift was made after the nature and effect of the transaction had been fully explained to the donor by some independent and qualified person so completely as to satisfy the Court that the donor was acting independently of any influence from the donee and with the full appreciation of what he was doing; and in cases where there are no other circumstances this may be the only means by which the donee can rebut the presumption.

Where a person receives advice it may not be sufficient to rebut the presumption. In *Prendergast v Joyce*[24] an elderly woman who was "very frail, depressed and severely anxious", as well as suffering from poor concentration and memory, opened a joint account with her nephew a few days after the death of her husband. She subsequently transferred significant amounts of money, which had previously been held in an account with her husband, into the account. In his judgment, Gilligan J, when considering the advice given to the donor by a bank manager, found that it did not suffice to rebut the presumption. He stated that: **8–14**

> The advice must also be such as a competent advisor would give if acting solely in the interests of the donor. In my view a person in such a position vis-à-vis [the aunt] would of necessity have cautioned her about the gravity of what she was doing. The evidence does not establish that this was done in the present case … I am not satisfied on the evidence that [she] received adequate independent expert advice to give her a full appreciation of what she was doing at the time she gave effect to the transfer.

However, the court does not require that there be "absolute disproof" of undue influence in order to rebut the presumption.[25] In *Carroll v Carroll*[26] Barron J, in relation to the issue of independent legal advice, stated that: **8–15**

> (1) a solicitor who acts for both parties cannot be independent of the donee in fact; and
>
> (2) to satisfy the court that the donor was acting independently of any influence from the donee and with the full appreciation of what he was doing it should be established that the gift was made after the nature and effect of the transaction had been fully explained to the donor by some independent and qualified person. Further, the advice must be given with knowledge of all relevant circumstances and must be such as a competent advisor would give if acting solely in the interests of the donor.

In *Danske Bank A/S trading as National Irish Bank Plc v Madden*[27] McGovern J, when considering the relationship of solicitor and client and the presumption of undue influence, stated that: **8–16**

[24] [2009] IEHC 199; see *Carroll v Carroll* [1999] 4 IR 241.
[25] *Prendergast v Joyce* [2009] IEHC 199.
[26] *Carroll v Carroll* [1999] 4 IR 241, 265; see *Gregg v Kidd* [1956] IR 183, 195.
[27] [2009] IEHC 319.

> The relationship of solicitor and client is one in which it has been held that undue influence will be presumed. It is necessary, therefore, to examine the evidence to see whether this presumption has been rebutted in the present case.
>
> There is no evidence to show that the defendant was either a vulnerable or dependent person. He was an established businessman and retained Mr. Byrne as his solicitor in the usual way. While they appear to have cooperated in at least one property transaction (which was not completed), I find no evidence that the advice being received by the defendant from Mr. Byrne was not *"independent legal advice"* as that expression is normally understood. The usual meaning of such advice is that it is advice obtained by the party himself from a lawyer retained by him and not advice coming from the legal advisor of a third party with whom he is entering into a legal relationship. There was no evidence of any conflict of interest on the part of Mr. Byrne in this transaction that was apparent, or ought to have been apparent, to the bank, in circumstances where he was advising the defendant with regard to the loan agreement. If there was an issue on the question of Mr. Byrne acting for the defendant in what was, in effect, the transfer of his interest in the property to the defendant, that was a matter between the defendant and his solicitor and did not concern the bank. Insofar as the issue of *"independent legal advice"* was relevant, it was in the context of ensuring that the defendant was not receiving legal advice from the bank's solicitors in relation to a loan being offered by the bank.
>
> Because there is a presumption of undue influence in the relationship of a solicitor and client, there has to be some positive evidence to rebut that presumption.[28]

8–17 In *MC (a Ward of Court) v C* [29] McMenamin J stated that:

> Once a relationship giving rise to a presumption of undue influence is established, and where it has been shown in evidence that a donee has received a substantial benefit, the law provides the onus then lies on the donee to establish that the gift or transaction resulted from the free exercise of the donor's will. That onus can be discharged by evidence showing the gift was the independent and well understood act of a person in a position to exercise free judgment.[30]

Laches

8–18 A claim of undue influence may fail on grounds of *laches*. The application of the equitable principle of *laches* was considered in *McCormack v Our Lady Queen of Peace Achill House of Prayer Ltd*[31] where the defendant applied for an order for the dismissal of proceedings by the plaintiff on grounds that the claim of undue influence was barred by the Statute of Limitations

---

28 [2009] IEHC 319, paras 13–15.

29 [2013] IESC 36; see *Reg (Proctor) v Hutton* [1978] NI 139; *Inche Noriah v Shaik Allie Bin Omar* [1929] AC 127; *Allcard v Skinner* [1887] 36 ChD 145.

30 [2013] IESC 36, para 17.

31 [2018] IEHC 26.

1957, as amended, and/or the equitable principle of *laches*. In her judgment Faherty J referred to *Humphreys v Humphreys*,[32] where Rimer J stated that:

> … once the complainant is no longer under the defendant's influence, a claim to set aside the transaction must be brought within a reasonable time. A failure to do so will be likely to attract a defence based on the equitable doctrine of laches …

In *McCormack* the plaintiff contended that the core issue in the case was unfairness or unconscionability in equity, and that delay of itself should not be sufficient to prevent him from obtaining relief. Faherty J refused the defendant relief on grounds of *laches*. **8–19**

Duress

A defendant may raise the defence of duress in an action on the contract in circumstances where the pressure exerted on him or her to enter the contract "can properly be described as an illegitimate and significant cause of the party ostensibly contracting giving assent".[33] In *ACC Bank Plc v Dillon*[34] Charleton J, when referring to the doctrine of duress, stated that: **8–20**

> Duress as a defence in contract law had a similar origin to that defence as an answer to a criminal charge. The threat of violence is no longer necessary to establish that a contract was entered into under duress. Nor is it necessary that consent to bargain is negatived; rather that consent must have been so wrongfully obtained that it can properly be described as an illegitimate and significant cause of the party ostensibly contracting giving assent.

When referring to the principles of the doctrine of duress, he stated: **8–21**

> It seems to me that principles such as the availability of an alternative course of action, a protest at the term agreed or bargain extracted, the availability of time and space to think and recourse to independent advice are items of evidence within which the illegitimacy of pressure may be analysed as constituting, or not amounting to, duress. The threat to do something unlawful, such as blackmail, will establish a sufficient degree of illegitimacy to enable the defence in most instances. This is notwithstanding that it can be the case that a threat to reveal a crime may be to adopt a lawful course of conduct. It is the failure to independently peruse that course from the point of view of public spirit and instead linking it to a commercial course of bargaining that is illegitimate. Even where a threat is wrong, it must be such as to wrongfully establish coercive effect on the mutuality which the law expects in the nature of the contract. Economic duress, far removed from the physical origins of the defence, can be sufficient as in *B& S Contracts and Design Ltd v Victor Green Publications Ltd* [1984] I.C.R. 419. There a contract to exhibit at a show was altered by a threat from the organiser to cancel seeking additional payment from the exhibitor because the organiser had been

[32] [2004] EWHC 2201, para 99.
[33] See *ACC Bank Plc v Dillon* [2012] IEHC 474.
[34] [2012] IEHC 474.

made subject to additional payment demands by its workforce. That particular case would also be an example of past consideration being insufficient to support a contract for the new exhibition charge.[35]

[35] [2012] IEHC 474, paras 5.2–5.3.

Chapter 9

THE MORRIS AND GILLIGAN CRITERIA

Introduction

Where a contractual party can establish in evidence that there was a radical and fundamental difference between the contract signed and that which was intended to be signed by him or her, and that he or she was not careless or negligent when signing the contract, the court may set aside the contract by applying the principle of *non est factum*.[1] Where *non est factum* is raised as a defence it is not enough for a contractual party to show that his or her mind "did not go with the pen" when signing the contract.[2] In *Saunders v Anglia Building Society*,[3] Lord Reid, when considering the essence of a plea of *non est factum*, stated: **9–01**

> Many people do frequently sign documents put before them for signature by their solicitor or other trusted advisors without making any inquiry as to their purpose or effect. But the essence of the plea *non est factum* is that the person signing believed that the document he signed had one character or one effect, whereas in fact, its character or effect was quite different. He could not have such a belief, unless he had taken steps or been given information which gave him some grounds for his belief.

The court, when deciding on whether or not to set aside the contract on grounds of *non est factum*, may apply the criteria formulated by Morris J (as he then was) in *Tedcastle McCormack and Co Ltd v McCrystal* when doing so.[4] The Morris criteria require that for the defence of *non est factum* to succeed a party must show: one, there was a radical or fundamental difference between what was signed and what it was thought was being signed; two, the mistake was as to the general character of the document as opposed to its legal effect; three, there was a lack of negligence, and four, the person concerned took all reasonable precautions in the circumstances to **9–02**

---

1 See *Tedcastle McCormack and Company Limited v McCrystal*, Unreported, High Court, Morris J, 15 March 1999; *Saunders v Anglia Building Society* [1971] AC 1004.

2 See *Howatson v Webb* [1907] 1 Ch 537; *Muskham Finance Ltd v Howard* [1963] 1 All ER 81; *Mercantile Credit Co Ltd v Hamblin* [1964] 3 All ER 592; *Foster v Mackinnon* (1889) LR 4 CP 704; *Carlisle and Cumberland Banking Co v Bragg* [1911] 1 KB 489; *Bank of Ireland v McManamy* [1916] 2 IR 161.

3 [1971] AC 1004, 1016.

4 Unreported, High Court, Morris J, 15 March 1999; see *Saunders v Anglia Building Society* [1971] AC 1004.

find out what the document was. There is also a heavy burden of proof placed on a contractual party seeking to rely on the defence of *non est factum*.[5] In *Saunders v Anglia Building Society*[6] Lord Reid, when referring to the burden of proof on the party relying on the defence of *non est factum*, stated:

> So there must be a heavy burden of proof on the person who seeks to invoke this remedy. He must prove all the circumstances necessary to justify its being granted to him, and that necessarily involves his proving that he took all reasonable precautions in the circumstances.

9–03 In the same case Lord Hudson stated:

> Want of care on the part of the person who signs a document which he afterwards seeks to disown is relevant. The burden of proving *non est factum* is on the party disowning his signature; this includes proof that he or she took care. There is no burden on the opposite party to prove want of care.

9–04 The court may set aside a contract on grounds that it was an improvident or unconscionable transaction by applying the Gilligan criteria when doing so. In *Prendergast v Joyce*[7] Gilligan J stated that a contract may be set aside as an improvident transaction where it is shown that: (i), one party was at a serious disadvantage to another by reason of poverty, ignorance, or otherwise; (ii), circumstances existed of which unfair advantage could be taken; and (iii), the transaction was at an undervalue; and (iv), there was a lack of independent legal advice. In other words, it must be shown that one party took advantage of the other party's inferior or weak bargaining power due to old age, ignorance or illness, that the property forming the subject matter of the transaction was sold below its market value, and that the disadvantaged party lacked independent legal advice at the time of entering into the transaction. In *Grealish v Murphy*[8] Gavan Duffy J stated that "equity comes to the rescue whenever the parties to a contract have not met on equal terms". There must be some "impropriety" in the conduct of the stronger party and in the conditions of the transaction.[9]

The Morris Criteria and Principle of *Non Est Factum*

9–05 In *Tedcastle McCormack and Company Limited v McCrystal* Morris J stated that in order to establish a defence of *non est factum* the following criteria must be satisfied:

---

5 See *Allied Irish Banks Plc v Higgins* [2015] IECA 2.
6 [1971] AC 1004, 1016.
7 [2009] IEHC 199; see *Carroll v Carroll* [1998] 2 ILRM 218, 230.
8 [1946] IR 35; see *Carroll v Carroll* [1998] 2 ILRM 218.
9 See *Alec Lobb (Garages) Ltd v Total Oil (Great Britain) Ltd* (1956) 99 CLR 362.

(a) That there was a radical or fundamental difference between what was signed and what it was thought was being signed;
(b) That the mistake was as to the general character of the document as opposed to its legal effect; and
(c) That there was a lack of negligence. That is, that the person concerned took all reasonable precautions in the circumstances to find out what the document was.

In *Tedcastle McCormack and Company Limited v McCrystal* the facts were essentially that the defendant was mentally and physically ill when he signed the document, and did not know the contents of document he signed. Morris J set aside the contract by applying the criteria formulated by him on grounds of *non est factum*. In *ADM Londis Plc v Gibson*,[10] Hedigan J, when applying the Morris criteria, stated that: "The law in relation to a claim of *non est factum* is set out in the judgment of Morris J. in *Tedcastle McCormack and Co. Ltd. v McCrystal* (High Court, 15th March, 1999.)". **9–06**

The Morris criteria may also be applied in actions involving contracts of guarantee. In *Allied Irish Banks Plc v Higgins*,[11] when referring to contracts of guarantee, the Court (Finlay Geoghegan, Peart and Mahon JJ) stated that: **9–07**

> Where the defence of *non est factum* is raised in cases involving the signing of guarantees the same principles as they are to other forms of contract: one, that there was a radical or fundamental difference between what was signed and what it was thought was being signed; two, that the mistake was as to the general character of the document as opposed to its legal effect; three, that there was a lack of negligence, and four, the person concerned took all reasonable precautions in the circumstances to find out what the document was.[12]

Morris J also stated that there is a heavy burden of proof imposed on a person seeking to rely on the defence of *non est factum* involving contracts of guarantee. **9–08**

However, a defence of *non est factum* which fails to satisfy the Morris criteria may not be sufficient to set aside the contract. In *ADM v Arman*[13] Clarke J (as he then was), when considering the defence of *non est factum* raised in the context of an application for summary judgment, stated: **9–09**

> On the facts of this case it is manifestly clear that the Defendants signed a document which is clearly, on its face, a guarantee. In those circumstances, even a cursory reading of the document would have brought to the Defendants' attention the fact that they were signing a guarantee. In those circumstances, it seems to

10 [2010] IEHC 432.
11 [2015] IECA 23.
12 See *Tedcastle McCormack and Company Limited v McCrystal*, unreported, High Court, Morris J, 15 March 1999; *Saunders v Anglia Building Society* [1971] AC 1004.
13 [2006] IEHC 309.

> me that the Defendants could not be said to have established any Defence under the non est factum doctrine. On that basis, it does not seem to me that that ground gives rise to any possible Defence or should lead to liberty to defend.

9–10 In *ADM Londis Plc v Gibson*,[14] Hedigan J, following the decision of Clarke J in *ADM v Arman Retail Ltd*,[15] stated that:

> The same applies here. There is no conceivable way that a person could sign the guarantee document relied on herein without knowing it was a guarantee. It says so repeatedly throughout and is headed "Guarantee". To sign such a document without discovering it was a guarantee, fails utterly the third test set out above even were the first two met by the defendants.

9–11 He added:

> The defendants in entering this contract of guarantee were acting as business people capable of contracting on their own without independent legal advice or any cooling off period. The guarantee was signed by both as directors of the company and they were free to contract or not as they wished. The fact that Mrs. Gibson's name did not appear in block letters opposite her admitted signature is of no substance.

9–12 In *Irish Bank Resolution Corporation Ltd v Quinn*[16] an application for summary judgment was made against the second defendant for a sum in excess of €3m. The claim was made on foot of a facility letter of 17 November 2006, a credit agreement of the same date and the then-prevailing general conditions for personal loans of the plaintiff. The amount of the facility was €3m, and the purpose was to provide the borrowers with a personal loan facility. The defendants were the borrowers and judgment had already been delivered against the first defendant. In his judgment, Kelly J stated:

> The first line of defence is that of *non est factum*. This is a defence which is only rarely invoked successfully. The law, both in England and in this jurisdiction on the topic is clear.

9–13 He referred to the Morris criteria in *Tedcastle McCormick and Company Limited v McCrystal*,[17] *Saunders v Anglia Building Society*[18] and his own decision in *Allied Irish Banks Plc v Higgins*,[19] and commented:

> Even the most cursory of glances at the documents which bear her signature would alert any but the illiterate to the fact that this was some form or borrowing

---

14 [2010] IEHC 432.
15 [2006] IEHC 195, para 3.
16 [2011] IEHC 470.
17 Unreported, High Court, Morris J, 15 March 1999.
18 [1971] AC 1004.
19 [2010] IEHC 219.

> transaction. But it would appear that even such information was lost on Mrs. Quinn because she apparently simply signed documents as part of a course of conduct without giving the matter a second thought. That is the height of the case which she makes. I am satisfied that it is one which falls far short of providing even a stateable defence on the basis of *non est factum*.[20]

He added: **9–14**

> Mrs. Quinn has been unable to demonstrate even arguably the existence of the first of the three ingredients set forth by Morris J. in the *Tedcastle McCormick* case. She has to be able to demonstrate an argument that there was a radical or fundamental difference between what she signed and what she thought she was signing. The truth is, she gave no thought to what she was signing and, therefore, could not know whether there was any difference between what she was signing and what she thought she was signing. To use the words of Lord Reid, "she could not have such a belief unless she had taken steps or being given information which gave some grounds for that belief".[21]

He concluded: **9–15**

> I am satisfied that under this line of defence of *non est factum* that it is very clear that Mrs. Quinn has no case. She has failed to adduce any evidence which would satisfy the existence of an arguable case in respect of two of the three ingredients of the defence of *non est factum* as demonstrated in the case law.[22]

The Gilligan Criteria and Improvident Transactions

In *Prendergast v Joyce*[23] Gilligan J formulated the following criteria for setting aside an improvident transaction: **9–16**

(i) one party was at a serious disadvantage to another by reason of poverty, ignorance, or otherwise;
(ii) that circumstances existed of which unfair advantage could be taken;
(iii) the transaction was at an undervalue; and
(iv) there was a lack of independent legal advice.

In *Prendergast v Joyce*[24] Gilligan J found that the donor was at a serious disadvantage to the donee owing to her mental impairment, the very recent loss of her husband and her advanced age. He regarded as unreal the proposition that her mental impairment was somehow absent at the time of the impugned transfer. Accordingly, the circumstances were such as to enable unfair advantage to be taken, whether or not such advantage was in **9–17**

[20] [2011] IEHC 470, para 34.
[21] [2011] IEHC 470, para 35.
[22] [2011] IEHC 470, para 37.
[23] [2009] IEHC 199; see *Carroll v Carroll* [1998] 2 ILRM 218, 230; *Fry v Lane* (1888) 40 Ch D 312.
[24] [2009] IEHC 199, paras 80–81.

fact taken. He held, citing *Carroll v Carroll*[25] as the authority on the matter, that the donee in fact took advantage of the donor's vulnerability. He went on to state:

> Having regard to her age, state of health, and shocked state very shortly after her husband's funeral, Monica Joyce was in my view unequal to protecting herself and was suffering an infirmity for the reasons as set out and did not have the benefit of independent advice such as to ensure she understood the nature and effect of the transfer.
>
> Accordingly I am satisfied that the transactions should be set aside for improvidence.

9–18 In *Grealish v Murphy*[26] Gavan Duffy J stated that "equity comes to the rescue whenever the parties to a contract have not met on equal terms", and in relation to vulnerable persons and improvident transactions he went on to state:

> The issue thus raised brings into play Lord Hatherley's cardinal principle (from which the exceptions are rare) that Equity comes to the rescue whenever the parties to a contract have not met on equal terms, see Lord Hatherley's judgment (dissenting on facts) in *O'Rorke v Bolingbroke*; the corollary is that the Court must inquire whether a grantor, shown to be unequal to protecting himself, has had the protection which was his due by reason of his infirmity, and the infirmity may take various forms. The deed here was in law a transaction for value ...; however tenuous the value may have proved to be in fact, and, of course, a Court must be very much slower to undo a transaction for value; but the fundamental principle to justify radical interference by the Court is the identical principle, whether value be shown or not, and the recorded examples run from gifts and voluntary settlements (including an abortive marriage settlement) to assignments for a money consideration. The principle has been applied to improvident grants, whether the particular disadvantage entailing the need for protection to the grantor were merely low station and surprise (though the grantor's rights were fully explained) ..., or youth and inexperience ..., or age and weak intellect, short of total incapacity, with no fiduciary relation and no "arts of inducement" to condemn the grantee ... Even the exuberant or ill-considered dispositions of feckless middle-aged women have had to yield to the same principle ...[27]

9–19 The court, when deciding whether or not to set aside a transaction on the grounds of improvidence, may take into account the vulnerability and state of health of a party to an improvident transaction. A contractual party's lack of understanding "of the overall ramifications of what he was doing" and his or her state of health may be sufficient grounds for setting aside an improvident transaction. In *Keating v Keating*[28] Laffoy J stated:

---

25 [1999] 4 IR 243, 258–59.

26 [1946] IR 35; see *Carroll v Carroll* [1998] 2 ILRM 218.

27 *Grealish v Murphy* [1946] IR 35, 49–50; see *Carroll v Carroll* [1999] 4 IR 243, 258–59.

28 [2009] IEHC 405.

> I have come to the conclusion that the plaintiff was seriously disadvantaged because of his lack of understanding of the overall ramifications of what he was doing after he contracted to sell the land to the first named defendant and his state of health was a contributory factor in relation to his inability to understand, or, alternatively, to do anything to reverse the situation. The second named defendant, with the approbation of the first named defendant, exploited the situation once the plaintiff was contractually bound to sell the land. Unfortunately, in the words of Gavan Duffy J. the plaintiff did not have "the protection which was his due by reason of his infirmity". Mr. Nolan allowed the Land Transfer to come to fruition on an irregular basis, in that the plaintiff had actually received almost half the purchase price, and had disposed of most of it, when the contract was signed. After the contract was signed, Mr. Nolan's focus was on the first named defendant getting title and vacant possession. In my view, given those circumstances, the plaintiff could not be said to have got independent legal advice. Aside from those circumstances, applying the principles set out by Barron J. in *Carroll v Carroll* (at p. 265), the plaintiff could not be said to have got the benefit of independent legal advice.

However, in *Blomley v Ryan*,[29] Fullagar J found that the circumstances that may seriously disadvantage a contractual party "can hardly be satisfactorily classified". He went on to state: **9–20**

> The circumstances adversely affecting a party, which may induce a court of equity either to refuse its aid or to set a transaction aside, are of great variety and can hardly be satisfactorily classified. Among them is poverty or need of any kind, sickness, age, sex, infirmity of body or mind, drunkenness, illiteracy or lack of education, lack of assistance or explanation where assistance or explanation is necessary. The common characteristic seems to be that they have the effect of placing one party at a serious disadvantage vis-a-vis the other.

In *Alec Lobb (Garages) Ltd v Total Oil (Great Britain) Ltd*[30] Peter Millett QC (as he then was), when considering the type of conduct of the stronger party in improvident transaction, stated that: **9–21**

> In short, there must, in my judgment, be some impropriety, both in the conduct of the stronger party and in the terms of the transaction itself ... which in the traditional phrase 'shocks the conscience of the court' and makes it against equity and good conscience of the stronger party to retain the benefit of a transaction he has unfairly obtained.

The value of the consideration passing between the parties may also be taken into account by the court when deciding whether or not to set aside the transaction. In *Noonan v O'Connell*[31] Lynch J set aside a gift of half share in the plaintiff's farm on the ground of improvidence. The court noted that the consideration of 50 pence could be disregarded as it did not constitute any real consideration for the purposes of determining whether the transfer **9–22**

---

[29] (1956) 99 CLR 362, 405.

[30] [1983] 1 WLR 87, 94–95.

[31] Unreported, High Court, Lynch J, 10 April 1987.

was improvident, and that although the plaintiff and defendant might have agreed that the defendant should support the plaintiff and carry out work for him, there was no mention of this in the deed. Accordingly, the court in effect treated the transfer as a gift and set it aside for improvidence. In *McGuirk v Branigan*[32] a gift of much of the plaintiff's garden was set aside as improvident. While the agreement provided for some consideration, there was no evidence that it had been paid, and Morris J attributed its inclusion in the agreement as a mere device to evade special requirements in a conveyance for natural love and affection. Accordingly, the transfer set aside was in fact a gift. The court may also consider the factors that rendered a donor vulnerable, and whether the donee had in fact taken advantage of or exploited the donor's vulnerability.

9–23 Thus, a transaction may be set aside by the court as improvident where it is shown that one of the contractual parties was seriously ill or elderly or ignorant, and was taken advantage of at the time the transaction was entered into, and who did not receive independent legal advice, and further that there was a serious inequality of bargaining powers between the parties.[33] The onus of proof rests on the party seeking to set aside the transaction set aside to show that the transaction was improvident by applying the Gilligan criteria to the circumstances of the case.

[32] Unreported, High Court, Morris J, 9 November 1992.

[33] See *Grealish v Murphy* [1946] IR 35, 49–50; *McGuirk v Branigan*, Unreported, High Court, Morris J, 9 November 1992; *Carroll v Carroll* [1998] 2 ILRM 218; *Prendergast v Joyce* [2009] IEHC 199; *Secured Property Loans Ltd v Floyd* [2011] IEHC 189.

PART III

THE ENFORCEMENT OF DEBTS AND GUARANTEES BY SUMMARY JUDGMENT AND ARGUABLE DEFENCES

Chapter 10

APPLICATIONS FOR SUMMARY JUDGMENT FOR ENFORCEMENT OF DEBTS, GUARANTEES AND ACCOUNT TAKEN

Introduction

Under Ord 2, r 1 of the Rules of the Superior Courts (RSC) a plaintiff may seek the recovery of a debt owing and due to him or her by the defendant or guarantee relating to such debt by way of summary summons. Order 4, r 4 of the RSC provides that the special indorsement of claim in a summary summons shall state specifically and with all necessary particulars the relief claimed and grounds thereof. A defendant to a summary summons is therefore entitled to have necessary particulars to enable him "to satisfy his mind whether he ought to pay or resist".[1] The payment of debts and guarantees relating to them may be enforced by seeking summary judgment of them under Ord 37 of the RSC. An application for summary judgment under Ord 37 of the RSC may be commenced by the plaintiff serving a notice of motion supported by a grounding affidavit on the defendant which may be joined and met by a replying affidavit from the defendant. In fact, there may be a plethora of affidavits exchanged between the parties before the hearing of the application for summary judgment.[2] The court, on hearing the application, may grant an order of summary judgment to the plaintiff, or dismiss the action, or remit any arguable defence raised by the defendant to plenary hearing.[3] **10–01**

An application to have an account taken may also be commenced by summary summons. Under Ord 2, r 1 of the RSC procedure by summary summons may be adopted in claims in which "the plaintiff in the first **10–02**

---

1 *Bank of Ireland Mortgage Bank v O'Malley* [2019] IESC 84; see *The Governor and Company of the Bank of Ireland v Ward* [2020] IEHC 257; *Allied Irish Bank Plc v O'Driscoll* [2020] IEHC 253; *Kearns v Evenson* [2020] IEHC 257; *AIB Mortgage Bank and AIB Banks plc v O'Brien* [2020] IECA 191; *Allied Irish Banks plc v Cuddy* [2020] IECA 211; *AIB plc v Griffin* [2020] IECA 221; *KBC Bank Ireland plc v Corrigan* [2012] IECA 9..

2 See *Allied Irish Banks Plc v O'Donoghue*, [2019] IEHC 526; *Allied Irish Banks Plc v McCarthy* [2019] IEHC 743.

3 See Rules of the Superior Courts, Ord 37, r7.

instance desires to have an account taken".[4] However, Ord 37, r 1 of the RSC, which deals with applications for summary judgment, is not applicable to proceedings for account taken. Order 37, r 14 of the RSC deals with such applications, and provides that:

> Where a summary summons has been indorsed with a claim for an account under Order 2, or where the indorsement on a summons involves taking an account, and the defendant does not after appearance, by affidavit or otherwise, satisfy the court that there is some preliminary question to be tried, the court shall forthwith make an order for the proper accounts, with all necessary inquiries and directions.

Particulars of a Debt in a Summary Summons

10–03 Order 4, r 4 of the RSC provides that the special indorsement of claim in a summary summons "shall state specifically and with all necessary particulars the relief claimed and grounds thereof". A defendant to a summary summons is in fact entitled by virtue of Ord 4, r 4 of the RSC to have necessary particulars to enable him "to satisfy his mind whether he ought to pay or resist".[5] As stated by Clarke CJ in *Bank of Ireland Mortgage Bank v O'Malley*[6]: what particulars are "necessary" is the real question. In that case, Clarke CJ went on to formulate the principles governing the level of "necessary particulars" that are required to be given in the special indorsement of claim of a summary summons. He stated:

> (i) There must be a level of particularity sufficient to allow a defendant to know whether he or she should concede or resist the claim.
> (ii) The indorsement on the summary summons may specify that the liquidated sum is due and calculated in accordance with some identified document or documents already sent to the defendant, then he or she has sufficient information, provided that those documents, in turn, themselves provide the necessary detail.
> (iii) There is an obligation on the plaintiff to produce *prima facie* evidence of his or her debt if he or she wishes the court to grant summary judgment.
> (iv) What a defendant wishes do to resist summary judgment the primarily/ focus will then turn on whether the *prima facie* claim to a debt is established, and whether the defendant wishes to put forward a positive defence.
> (v) It is necessary for the court to assess whether the defence amounts to mere assertion or meets the threshold for entitling the defendant to a full or plenary hearing.

[4] See *Aforge Finance SAS v HSBC Institutional Trust Services (Ireland) Ltd* [2009] IEHC 565; *AIB plc v Pierce* [2015] IECA 87; *ACC Loan Management Ltd v Connolly* [2017] IECA 119; *Best v Ghose* [2018] IEHC 376.

[5] *Bank of Ireland Mortgage Bank v O'Malley* [2019] IESC 84; see *The Governor and Company of the Bank of Ireland v Ward* [2020] IEHC 257; *Allied Irish Bank Plc v O'Driscoll* [2020] IEHC 253; *Kearns v Evenson* [2020] IEHC 257.

[6] [2019] IESC 84; see *The Governor and Company of the Bank of Ireland v Ward* [2020] IEHC 257; *Allied Irish Bank Plc v O'Driscoll* [2020] IEHC 253; *Kearns v Evenson* [2020] IEHC 257.

(vi) The obligation on a defendant is to establish an arguable defence is one which only arises if the plaintiff has first placed sufficient evidence before the court to establish *prima facie* the debt alleged is due.
(vii) Where the plaintiff seeking summary judgment puts sufficient evidence before the court to establish a prima facie debt the court then may consider whether the defendant has put forward a credible defence.
(viii) Where the plaintiff seeking summary judgment does not put sufficient evidence before the court to establish a prima facie debt then the plaintiff cannot be entitled to summary judgment in any event.
(ix) The court may take into account, "in assessing the adequacy of the manner in which a debt claim is particularised, any documentation which had been sent to the defendant in advance of the commencement of the proceedings."
(x) Summary proceedings "are not intended to involve an overly detailed account of every twist and turn of a banking relationship which might go back many years and involve, in at least some cases, thousands of transactions or measures potentially affecting the liability of the borrower."
(xi) It is necessary for a plaintiff who wishes to rely on previously supplied details to at least make some reference to those details in the special indorsement of claim.

In *Bank of Ireland Mortgage Bank v O'Malley*[7] Clarke CJ concluded that: **10–04**

> However, in my view, the special indorsement of claim in this case was not sufficient. There are absolutely no details of how the sum said to be due is arrived at. There are more than adequate particulars as to how it is said that monies generally are due having regard to the asserted loan, drawdown, failure to pay and calling in of the balance. But why the particular amount due should be the sum claimed is not at all clear. I cannot see that a person receiving such a summons could have the "necessary" details to decide whether they should concede or resist.

He went on to state: **10–05**

> If the special indorsement of claim had gone on to make specific reference to the relevant sum being calculated by reference to the details set out in the Statement of Account, then I would be happy that the document concerned would be incorporated by reference into the special indorsement of claim and regard could be had to it in deciding whether adequate particulars had been given. But even that simple step was not taken in this case. I would, therefore, conclude that the special indorsement of claim was not adequate.

Applications for Summary Judgment

An application for summary judgment may be commenced by the plaintiff issuing a notice of motion on the defendant together with a grounding affidavit setting out the facts of the case. The defendant may set out his or her case by replying affidavit. There may in fact be a multiplicity of **10–06**

[7] [2019] IESC 84; see *The Governor and Company of the Bank of Ireland v Ward* [2020] IEHC 257; *Allied Irish Bank Plc v O'Driscoll* [2020] IEHC 253; *Kearns v Evenson* [2020] IEHC 257.

affidavits involved in an application for summary judgment by motion on notice following upon the grounding affidavit by the plaintiff and replying affidavit by the defendant.[8] All such affidavits must be filed in the Central Office. The court may also on the application of either party to the motion order the attendance for cross-examination of the deponent of any such affidavit. In *McGrath v O'Driscoll*[9] Clarke J (as he then was), when referring to issues that may be litigated within the limited framework of a motion for summary judgment, stated:

> So far as questions of law or construction are concerned the court can, on a motion for summary judgment, resolve such questions, including, where appropriate, questions of the construction of documents, but should only do so where the issues which arise are relatively straightforward and where there is no real risk of an injustice being done by determining those questions within the somewhat limited framework of a motion for summary judgment.

10–07 Order 37 of the RSC sets out the procedural rules concerning applications for summary judgment. Under Ord 37, r 6 of the RSC:

> In contested cases, the Master shall transfer the case, when in order for hearing by the Court, to the Court list for hearing on the first opportunity; and, for this purpose, the Master may extend the time for filing affidavits and give such directions and adjourn the case before himself as he shall think fit. The Master may also, on consent, adjourn the case for plenary hearing as if the proceedings had been originated by plenary summons, with such directions as to pleadings, discovery, settlement of issues or otherwise as may be appropriate.

10–08 Order 37, r 7 of the RSC provides that:

> Upon the hearing of any such motion by the Court, the Court may give judgement for the relief to which the plaintiff may appear to be entitled or may dismiss the action or may adjourn the case for plenary hearing as if the proceedings had been originated by plenary summons, with such directions as to pleadings or discovery or settlement of issues or otherwise as may be appropriate, and generally may make such order for determination of the questions in issue in the action as may seem just.

10–09 In *Ulster Bank Ireland Ltd v Beades*[10] McKechnie J, when commenting on the summary judgment process, stated that "the general power given to the court when hearing a motion for liberty to enter final judgment is both widespread and extensive", and that this can be seen from Ord 37, r 7 of the RSC. He went on to state that:

> As can immediately be observed, the court on hearing such an application has a

---

[8] See *Allied Irish Banks Plc v O'Donoghue* [2019] IEHC 526; *Allied Irish Banks Plc v McCarthy* [2019] IEHC 743.

[9] [2006] IEHC 195.

[10] [2019] IESC 83, paras 23–24.

> variety of options available to it, including remitting the action for plenary hearing. As explained above, the summary process is different from that which follows if the proceedings have been commenced by plenary summons and if the normal route should be followed. To that extent it can be described as a truncated process. Nonetheless, it is an entirely valid and regular procedure and its utilisation may be critical in achieving justice between parties and in facilitating effective and efficient administration.

An application for summary judgment for a liquidated amount of money may be commenced by the plaintiff serving a notice of motion with a grounding affidavit on the defendant. Where an application for summary judgment is uncontested by the defendant, Ord 37, r 4 of the RSC provides that: **10–10**

> Upon the hearing of any such motion, the Master, in all uncontested cases, may deal with the matter summarily, and give liberty to enter judgment for the relief to which the plaintiff may appear to be entitled …

Where, however, an application for summary judgment is contested by the defendant, Ord 37, r 6 of the RSC provides that: **10–11**

> In contested cases, the Master shall transfer the case, when in order for hearing by the Court, to the Court list for hearing on the first opportunity; and, for this purpose, the Master may extend the time for filing affidavits and give such directions and adjourn the case before himself as he shall think fit. The Master may also, on consent, adjourn the case for plenary hearing as if the proceedings had been originated by plenary summons, with such directions as to pleadings, discovery, settlement of issues or otherwise as may be appropriate.

Under Ord 37, r 7 of the RSC, the court, upon hearing a motion for summary judgment, **10–12**

> may give judgement for the relief to which the plaintiff may appear to be entitled or may dismiss the action or may adjourn the case for plenary hearing as if the proceedings had been originated by plenary summons, with such directions as to pleadings or discovery or settlement of issues or otherwise as may be appropriate, and generally may make such order for determination of the questions in issue in the action as may seem just.

Where a defence relates to only part of the plaintiff's claim, under Ord 37, r 8 of the RSC, **10–13**

> the plaintiff shall have judgement forthwith for such part of his claim as the defence does not apply to or as is admitted, subject to such terms, if any, as to suspending execution, or the payment of the amount levied or any part thereof into Court by the sheriff, the taxation of costs, or otherwise, as the Court may think fit; and the defendant may be allowed to defend as to the residue of the plaintiff's claim.[11]

[11] Rules of the Superior Courts, Ord 37, r 8.

10–14 Under Ord 37, r 9 of the RSC, where it appears to the court at the hearing for summary judgment that

> any defendant has a good defence to or ought to be permitted to defend the action, and that any other defendant has not such defence and ought not to be permitted to defend, the former may be permitted to defend, and the plaintiff shall be entitled to enter final judgment against the latter, and may issue execution upon such judgment without prejudice to his right to proceed with his action against the former.

10–15 Further, under Ord 37, r 10:

> Leave to defend may be given unconditionally or subject to such terms as to give security, or time and mode of trial, or otherwise as the Court may think fit.

Grounding and Replying Affidavits

10–16 Grounding and replying affidavits are extremely important and fundamental to the litigation process involving applications for summary judgment. A grounding affidavit by the plaintiff sets out the facts of his or her case. In a replying affidavit the defendant may set out his or her account of the facts, and may counter or refute any of the facts set out in the plaintiff's grounding affidavit. A plaintiff may find it necessary to dispute the facts in a defendant's replying affidavit in a subsequent replying affidavit by him or her, and indeed, further replying affidavits may be exchanged between the parties before the hearing of the application. Legal submissions may also be made by the either of the parties based on established case law on the matter in dispute during the hearing of an application.

10–17 A good working example of an application for summary judgment by notice of motion and grounding affidavit by the plaintiff, and subsequent replying affidavits exchanged between plaintiff and defendant, may be found in *Allied Irish Banks Plc v O'Donoghue*.[12] In that case, the plaintiff by notice of motion for summary judgment and grounding affidavit claimed the sum of €1,541,000 stated to be owing and due on foot of guarantee executed by the defendant on 10 February 2009. It was alleged that the defendant guaranteed payment to the plaintiffs of all and every sum, or sums, of money due, or thereafter to become due, to the plaintiff by a company named Lodge Gaven Limited of which Mr O'Donoghue was a director. The application by the plaintiff was grounded on the affidavit of Ms June MacCabe sworn on 3 September 2015. She was an officer of the plaintiff's financial solutions group, Cork. She averred that the plaintiff provided banking facilities to Lodge Gaven Services Limited over a number of years, and that borrowings were habitually supported by a personal guarantee provided by the defendant,

[12] [2019] IEHC 526.

limited to a sum approximating to the aggregate liabilities of the sanctioned facilities.

In a replying affidavit by the defendant sworn on 12 February 2016, the defendant averred that he had always been advised by various solicitors never to sign a guarantee and that he had no recollection of ever doing so on this occasion. He averred that he did not believe that it was his signature on the guarantee and if the matter went to trial, he would retain the services of a handwriting expert. He also stated that he never received independent legal advice in relation to the execution of any guarantee, and as far as he was concerned, he was never a guarantor for a sum well in excess of €1,300,000. He further denied that he should be made responsible for the debts of the company, and was unaware of the origin of the amount in the guarantee. **10–18**

In a replying affidavit, dated 1 June 2016, Ms MacCabe averred that the defendant's contention that he had always been advised never to sign a guarantee and had no recollection of ever doing so lacked credibility because as a matter of fact he had executed such guarantees in the past in the presence of, and witnessed by, a solicitor. She referred to a guarantee which was executed by the defendant and his spouse in support of the company's borrowings on 14 December 2004. Guarantees were executed by him on 22 December 2003 and 3 May 2007, in the amount of €1,501,000, a copy of the latter being exhibited to her affidavit. It was witnessed by his then solicitor. The former two guarantees were not exhibited. She also averred that the letters of loan sanction were executed by the defendant and each was accompanied by a company resolution. Communications in respect of the said loans and facilities and in particular statements of the four company accounts were sent to the defendant's address. She also averred that the defendant was advised to obtain legal advice and referred to a document, exhibited to the affidavit of Mr Griffin sworn on 1 June 2016, evidencing that he waived his right to independent legal advice. A loan report prepared in February 2011 referred to the guarantee, but this had been redacted when documentation was given to Mr O'Donoghue pursuant to his data protection request. Ms MacCabe also exhibited to her affidavit what is described as "criticised loan report" dated February 2011, which referred to the defendant's guarantee in the sum of €1,541,000. **10–19**

In another replying affidavit on behalf of the plaintiff, Mr Griffin in his affidavit averred that he was acquainted with the defendant, who had been a significant business customer of the branch office where Mr Griffin worked. He confirmed that his signature was on the guarantee as witness. While he did not profess to have any specific recollection of the circumstances or occasion of the defendant's execution of the document, he had worked in the bank for 36 years, and throughout that time he had "not at any time or in any circumstances executed a document in my capacity as witness without **10–20** the individual concerned not being present in front of me". Also exhibited in Mr Griffin's affidavit was a "letter of waiver of independent legal advice", which was allegedly signed by the defendant on 10 February 2009.

10–21 In a replying affidavit, the defendant reiterated that he had no recollection of signing the guarantee, and argued that it was clear that Mr Griffin had no recollection of signing it either. Further, he had no recollection of executing a deed of waiver as suggested by Mr Griffin. He stated that he had spoken to all the solicitors involved and they had their own notes to prove that they did so advise him. No affidavit had been sworn in support of this averment by any solicitor nor had any notes been exhibited. In particular, in relation to the guarantee of 3 May 2007, no evidence had been adduced from the solicitor stated to have witnessed the document that it was not his signature, and no explanation had been given as to why such an affidavit had not been forthcoming. He reiterated that the letter of sanction allowed for a maximum amount of €1,340,000 and that "somehow the 'guarantee' which was allegedly signed on the same day as the letter of sanction is for €1,541,000". At para 9 of that affidavit Mr O'Donoghue averred that, as he did not accept that such a valid guarantee existed, "there is no need for me to address it here as it is simply not part of these proceedings".

10–22 The main arguments of defence were:

> (i) A dispute in relation to whether the guarantee was signed by the plaintiff.
> (ii) The absence of consideration.
> (iii) That the advance intended under the facility letter was never drawn down, and that property was not acquired by the company after the execution of the guarantee.

10–23 In his judgment MacGrath J, having identified the principles of summary judgment as found in *Aer Rianta cpt v Ryanair Ltd*[13] and *Harrisrange Ltd v Duncan*,[14] concluded that:

> an arguable defence has been raised concerning the absence of consideration. This defence is likely to involve a consideration of matters of fact and law. Counsel for the plaintiff does not expressly rely on a defence of forbearance to sue, rather it is submitted that consideration was provided in the form of the new guarantee as security for the borrowings and in the context of the extension and restructuring of facilities. The defendant, on the other hand, points to the stated purpose of the facility and the absence of evidence of drawdown of monies after the execution of the guarantee and contends that the guarantee is unsupported by consideration. Taking into account the constitutional rights of both parties and the threshold which has to be met on this application, in my view it cannot be concluded that it is clear that the defendant has no defence on this point, and in those circumstances I find

[13] [2001] 4 IR 607, 623.
[14] [2003] 4 IR 1, 7.

that this is an appropriate case in which to grant the defendant liberty to defend on this ground and to transfer the case to plenary hearing.

In an application for summary judgment the facts set out in the grounding affidavit by the plaintiff may be uncontested by the defendant, and in such case, the application may then turn on the legal submissions by the parties by reference to the principles of summary judgment.[15] Such was the case in *Danske Bank a/s t/a Danske Bank v Daniels*.[16] The plaintiff in that case, by notice of motion for summary judgment, claimed that the fourth-named defendant was liable on foot of a guarantee executed by him in favour of the plaintiff on 1 August 2006. There was no dispute regarding the sum now claimed by the plaintiff on foot of his guarantee signed in favour of the bank on 1 August 2006. **10–24**

The defendant put forward the following defences: **10–25**

(i) He received no benefit from the loan facilities, and any guarantee was not supported by any true consideration.
(ii) Any consideration was past consideration.
(iii) He did not receive any independent legal advice.
(iv) He was not allowed an opportunity to obtain independent legal advice.
(v) Untrue representations were made to him as to the effect of the guarantee.
(vi) Pressure was put upon him to sign the guarantee, amounting to duress, whether economic or otherwise.
(vii) In all the circumstances, the guarantee represented an unconscionable bargain which is unenforceable in equity.
(viii)The provisions of the Statute of Limitations applied so as to bar the claim. (This was asserted in argument, but not in the written submissions.)

In his judgment Hunt J stated that: **10–26**

4. The principles applicable to an application of this type have been set out many times and I do not propose to repeat them in detail in this case. It is sufficient to refer to the formulation adopted by the late Hardiman J. in *Aer Rianta CPT v Ryanair Limited* (No. 1) [2001] 4 I.R. 607 where he held, at page 623, that the test to be applied on an application for summary judgment involved the court asking itself the answer to one simple question, which he framed in the following terms: "Is it very clear that the defendant has no case? Is there either no issue to be tried or only issues which are simple and easily determined? Do the defendant's affidavits fail to disclose even an arguable defence?"

5. The observations of the Court of Appeal in *Close Invoice Finance Limited v Matthews* [2015] IECA 132 are also relevant. The Court of Appeal emphasised that the mere assertion in an affidavit of a given situation which is to form the basis of an intended defence does not of itself constitute a ground for granting leave to defend. Whether or not there is a fair and reasonable probability of the defendant having a real or *bona fide* defence has to be ascertained by looking at the situation

---

[15] See *Danske Bank a/s t/a Danske Bank v Daniels* [2018] IEHC 825.
[16] [2018] IEHC 825.

> as a whole, and assertions must be supported by some meaningful evidence such that a court could conclude that there is a fair or reasonable probability that the defendant has a *bona fide* defence based upon such assertions.

10–27 Having considered the various foregoing defences raised by the defendant, Hunt J found that the main area of concern was the assertion that the plaintiff was assured by the defendant prior to signature that execution of the guarantee was a formality required by the bank which would never be subsequently enforced, and as a result, the defendant had "a stateable defence to the effect that the guarantee was procured by such misrepresentations". He stated that the defendant had a defence "based on the assertion that the guarantee was procured by misrepresentation, and he was satisfied that the evidence of an absence of express reliance upon his guarantee in connection with subsequent advances is capable of supporting his assertions in this respect".

10–28 He concluded:

> 17. Having regard to the low threshold to be established by the defendant in meeting the test for remittal of the dispute for plenary hearing, I am satisfied that on the facts so far disclosed in relation to this case, and having regard to the issues which have been canvassed, that this is not an appropriate case in which to give summary judgment.

Applications for Account Taken

10–29 Applications to have account taken may be commenced by summary summons issued in compliance with the RSC. Under Ord 2, r1 of the RSC, procedure by summary summons may be adopted in claims in which "the plaintiff in the first instance desires to have an account taken". Order 37 of the RSC, r14, which deals with the hearing of proceeding commenced by summary summons for account taken, provides that:

> Where a summary summons has been indorsed with a claim for an account under Order 2, or where the indorsement on a summons involves taking an account, and the defendant does not after appearance, by affidavit or otherwise, satisfy the Court that there is some preliminary question to be tried, the Court shall forthwith make an order for the proper accounts, with all necessary inquiries and directions.

10–30 Order 37, r15 of the RSC provides that an application for such order as is mentioned in r14, "shall be made by motion on notice, and be supported by an affidavit, when necessary, filed on behalf of the plaintiff, stating concisely the grounds of his claim to an account. The application may be made at any time after the time for entering an appearance has expired." The claim to have an account taken must be the main issue for determination by the court, and not ancillary to other issues specified in the summary summons.

In *Aforge Finance SAS v HSBC Institutional Trust Services (Ireland) Ltd*,[17] Clarke J (as he then was) stated that:

> The order for the taking of an account as an ancillary order is "part of the process of determining the legal rights and obligations of parties to litigation rather than an entitlement in itself.

An application to have account taken is a separate, distinct and independent form and cause of action, and must be the substantive issue for decision in an action, and not merely ancillary to other issues. It is, therefore, an exclusive form and cause of action. In such action the plaintiff must show that he or she is entitled to have an account taken based on a fiduciary relationship existing between him or her and the defendant. Order 2, r1 (3) of the RSC allows "claims in which the plaintiff in the first instance desires to have an account taken" to be brought by summary summons.[18] As summary proceedings under Ord 2, r.3 "arise only in circumstances where the plaintiff can establish an entitlement as of right to the account concerned," Clarke J stated: **10–31**

> it seems to me that the term "preliminary question" as used in O. 37, r.14 of the RSC must logically refer to a question which (1) might be relevant to the entitlement of the plaintiff concerned to an account as of right or, (2) concern whether there might be any circumstances in which it would be appropriate for the court not to direct an account at that stage or, (3) relate to issues concerning the extent of the matters for which it might be appropriate for the defendant concerned to account. Those are the only sort of issues that are likely to arise before the court determines whether an account in the first instance should be directed.[19]

In *Aforge Finance SAS v HSBC Institutional Trust Services (Ireland) Ltd*[20] Clarke J also outlined the procedures involving a summary summons and claims to have account taken as follows: **10–32**

> Order 2 of the Rules of the Superior Courts deals with procedure by way of summary summons. Sub-rule 1 deals with liquidated claims. Sub-rule 2 deals with actions for the recovery of possession of land. The rule with which I am concerned in this case is sub-rule 3 which allows "claims in which the plaintiff in the first instance desires to have an account taken" to be brought by summary summons. There is no dispute but that, therefore, these proceedings are properly brought by summary summons in that what Aforge seeks is to have an account in the first instance taken.

---

17 [2009] IEHC 565, para 14.

18 See *Aforge Finance SAS v HSBC Institutional Trust Services (Ireland) Ltd* [2009] IEHC 565; *AIB plc v Pierce* [2015] IECA 87; *ACC Loan Management Ltd v Connolly* [2017] IECA 119; *Best v Ghose* [2018] IEHC 376.

19 [2009] IEHC 565, paras 4.2–4.3; see *Best v Ghose* [2018] IEHC 376.

20 [2009] IEHC 565; see *AIB plc v Pierce* [2015] IECA 87; *ACC Loan Management Ltd v Connolly* [2017] IECA 119.

> Order 37 deals with the hearing of proceedings commenced by summary summons. It is clear from the first sentence of r. 1 of O. 37, that the initial provisions of O. 37 (which deal with the fact that, where an appearance has been entered, the matter is to proceed by motion for liberty to enter final judgment before the Master) relate to each of the types of proceeding that can be brought by summary summons, other than those for an account. It is clear, therefore, that the general provisions of O. 37 have no application to proceedings in which an account in the first instance is what is sought. It is rules 13 to 15 of O. 37 that deal separately with the procedure to be followed in the case of a summary summons endorsed with a claim for an account. Rule 13, which is not material here, simply provides that the Master can make an order for accounts "with all necessary inquires and directions" where the defendant fails to appear. Rule 14 requires that, in the event that the defendant does not, having appeared, "by affidavit or otherwise, satisfy the court that there is some preliminary question to be tried", the court should make the relevant order for proper accounts with all necessary inquiries and directions. Rule 15 simply provides that the proper procedure to be followed in bringing the matter before the court is by motion supported by an affidavit.
>
> Its seems clear, therefore, that the stipulated procedure in summary summons cases where a plaintiff seeks an account in the first instance, and where the defendant enters an appearance, is that the matter should be brought before the court (and not the Master) by motion grounded on affidavit. The defendant is then required to satisfy the court that there is some preliminary question to be tried. The rule is silent as to the precise procedure to be followed in the event that the defendant does so satisfy the court that there is a preliminary question to be tried. In those circumstances, it seems to me to be clear that the court is at large as to the manner in which any preliminary question validly raised by a defendant is to be determined.[21]

10–33 He went on to state:

> It is a matter for the court to determine whether any particular matter is more conveniently dealt with by directing that an account be taken, rather than that the relevant issues be tried before the court. Such an account is, therefore, part of the process of determining the legal rights and obligations of parties to litigation rather than an entitlement in itself.[22]

[21] [2009] IEHC 565, paras 3.1–3.3; see *AIB plc v Pierce* [2015] IECA 87; *ACC Loan Management Ltd v Connolly* [2017] IECA 119.

[22] [2009] IEHC 565, para 4.1; see *AIB plc v Pierce* [2015] IECA 87; *ACC Loan Management Ltd v Connolly* [2017] IECA 119.

CHAPTER 11

PRINCIPLES OF SUMMARY JUDGMENT AND ACCOUNT TAKEN

INTRODUCTION

In *Allied Irish Banks Plc v Likely*[1] McDermott J, when considering the principles of summary judgment, stated that: **11–01**

> The legal principles applicable to an application for summary judgment are well established. They are summarised as follows by Ryan J. (as he then was) in Allied *Irish Banks plc v Farrell* [2014] IEHC 395 (at paras. 32 to 34) applying the decision of the Supreme Court in *Aer Rianta v Ryanair* [2001] 4 I.R. 607.

In *Harrisrange v Duncan*[2] McKechnie J summarised the legal principles which the court may apply when determining whether or not to grant summary judgment of a debt, and stated that the power of the court to grant summary judgment should be exercised with "discernible caution". In *Allied Irish Banks Plc v Likely*[3] McDermott J also stated: **11–02**

> These principles were also summarised by McKechnie J. in *Harrisrange Ltd. v Duncan* [2003] 4 I.R. 1. The learned judge emphasised that leave should not be granted where the only relevant averment in evidence is a mere assertion of a given situation which is to form the basis of the defence. The court should assess not only the defendant's response, but also in the context of that response, the cogency of the evidence adduced on behalf of the plaintiff, being mindful at all times of the unavoidable limitations which are inherent on any conflicting affidavit evidence and the overriding determinative consideration of the constitutional right of access to justice and the achievement of a just result.

In *Harrisrange v Duncan*[4] McKechnie J warned that the power of the court to grant summary judgment should be exercised with "discernible caution". **11–03**

---

1 [2016] IEHC 579, para 6; see *Emberton Finance Ltd v Cronin* [2018] IEHC 572.

2 [2003] 4 IR 1; see *Promontoria (Arrow) Limited v Burke* [2018] IEHC 773, paras 14–20.

3 [2016] IEHC 579, para 6; see *Emberton Finance Ltd v Cronin* [2018] IEHC 572.

4 [2003] 4 IR 1; see *Promontoria (Arrow) Limited v Burke* [2018] IEHC 773, paras 14–20.

11–04 In *Best v Ghose*[5] Baker J, when referring a claim to have an account taken, stated that:

> The account sought is more than what in everyday language would generally be called "an account" or "a statement" such as one furnished by a banker in the normal course of a banking transaction. What is sought is an account as long understood by the courts of equity, the giving of a narrative or an explanation in respect of transactions or events in the operation of the Fund.

11–05 An application to have an account taken must be the sole and exclusive issue for determination by the court. The entitlement of the plaintiff to make such application is based on an existing fiduciary relationship between the parties to the action.

Principles of Summary Judgment

11–06 When hearing a motion for summary judgment the court may apply the "low threshold" test set down by Hardiman J in *Aer Rianta cpt v Ryanair Limited*,[6] and the legal principles formulated by McKechnie J *Harrisrange Ltd v Duncan.*[7] In *Harrisrange Ltd v Duncan* McKechnie J stated that:

> (i) the power to grant summary judgment should be exercised with discernible caution;
> (ii) in deciding upon this issue the court should look at the entirety of the situation and consider the particular facts of each individual case ...
> (iii) in so doing the court should assess not only the defendant's response, but also in the context of that response, the cogency of the evidence adduced on behalf of the plaintiff ...
> (iv) where truly there are no issues or issues of simplicity only or issues easily determinable, then this procedure is suitable for use;
> (v) where, however, there are issues of fact which, in themselves, are material to success or failure, then their resolution is unsuitable for this procedure;
> (vi) where there are issues of law, this summary process may be appropriate but only so if it is clear that fuller argument and greater thought is evidently not required for a better determination of such issues ...

11–07 The court, by applying the principles of summary judgment, may decide to grant judgment to the plaintiff. In *ACC Loan Management Ltd v Connolly*[8]

---

5 [2018] IEHC 376, para 36; see *Aforge Finance SAS v HSBC Institutional Trust Services (Ireland) Ltd* [2009] IEHC 565; *AIB plc v Pierce* [2015] IECA 87; *ACC Loan Management Ltd v Connolly* [2017] IECA 119.

6 [2001] 4 IR 607, 623; see *First National Commercial Bank Plc v Anglin* [1996] 1 IR 75; *Allied Irish Banks Plc v Doran* [2018] IEHC 2; *McGrath v O'Driscoll* [2006] IEHC 195; *Bank of Scotland PLC v Mansfield* [2011] IEHC 463; *Bank of Ireland v Walsh* [2009] IEHC 220; *Allied Irish Banks Plc v Mullane* [2019] IEHC 636.

7 [2003] 4 IR 1, 7; see *Allied Irish Banks Plc v Doran* [2018] IEHC 2.

8 [2017] IECA 119; see *Allied Irish Banks Plc v Doran* [2018] IEHC 2.

certain loans to the first defendant, John Connolly, were guaranteed by way of two guarantees, one of 2005 and one of 2008, given by Maurice Connolly, co-defendant, appellant, and father of the first defendant. Maurice Connolly contended on appeal that account should have been taken of the fact that he had not been provided with independent legal advice before giving the guarantee and that the transaction was an improvident one for a man who was a vulnerable and not especially well person in his late 60s. No evidence of the son's supposed undue influence was given. Even so, it was argued that the low standard identified in *Aer Rianta v Ryanair*[9] was met where the lender knew of a close relationship (including father and son) and had not taken steps to ensure that independent legal advice had been obtained by the guarantor. However, in the Court of Appeal, Finlay Geoghegan J stated that:

> There was no evidence before the High Court upon which it could be concluded that an arguable defence of undue influence or other wrong by the son was made out … I am not satisfied that, in the absence of the father making out an arguable defence that he gave the guarantee under the undue influence of his son (or because of any other alleged wrong such as misrepresentation), there is any arguable defence available in Irish law to him that the bank was under an obligation by reason of the known fact that he, the proposed guarantor, was the father of the principal debtor to take steps to ensure that he received independent legal advice or otherwise ensure that the guarantee was freely entered into such that the failure of the bank to take such steps is an arguable defence to the enforcement of the guarantee against him.[10]

Finlay Geoghegan J also referred at para 29, to the decisions of the House of Lords in *Royal Bank of Scotland v Etridge (No 2)*[11] and Clarke J in *Ulster Bank v Roche and Buttimer*[12] and stated that those decisions provided **11–08**

> authority for an independent or distinct defence for a guarantor, albeit related to the principal debtor, seeking to vitiate a guarantee executed in favour of a bank by reason of a breach of an alleged duty owed by the bank to him to ensure that he has obtained independent legal advice or has taken some further steps to ensure that he fully understood the nature of the guarantee being given.

However, Finlay Geoghegan J concluded at para 49 that: **11–09**

> The appellant's unfortunate position is that as a person of full age he has signed a guarantee in favour of the bank. Whilst he was referred to in submission as a "vulnerable" person there was no evidence of any particular vulnerability. He has not put any evidence before the court upon which it could be argued that he did not freely enter into the commitments under the guarantee he signed and permitted to be delivered to the bank in connection with the loans being given to his son. In

---

9 [2001] 4 IR 607, 623; see *ACC Loan Management Ltd v Connolly* [2017] IECA 119; *Allied Irish Banks Plc v Doran* [2018] IEHC 2.

10 [2017] IECA 119, para 28; see *Allied Irish Banks Plc v Doran* [2018] IEHC 2.

11 [2002] 2 AC 773.

12 [2012] IEHC 166.

> the absence of evidence which would support an arguable duty imposed on the bank and arguable breach thereof there is no arguable defence.

11–10 In *Allied Irish Banks Plc v Doran*[13] the court also granted summary judgment to the plaintiff in relation to guarantees signed by the defendant. In that case, Mr Doran, an elderly father, signed guarantees in favour of his son, and the plaintiffs in the action sought to enforce the guarantees against him. During the course of his judgment, Barrett J, having referred to the judgment of Finlay Geoghegan J in *ACC Loan Management Ltd v Connolly*,[14] stated that:

> The case at hand, as will be seen, does not contend for such a free-standing duty. Here, submission is made that "historically the bank believed it necessary to ensure [that Mr Doran] … had independent legal advice but in 2010 … for some reason, the bank chose to deal with … Mr Doran where he had no independent advice … [I]nstead he relied exclusively on the bank". However, this submission is not borne out by Mr Doran's evidence. He avers, as will be seen below, that "Prior to my entering into the guarantee arrangement in 2006 I had the opportunity to receive and to consider independent legal advice … The plaintiff was aware that I had received independent legal advice". There is no mention in his evidence that the bank acted differently in 2006 and 2010; it is Mr Doran who acted differently as regards whether or not to obtain legal advice in respect of the respective guarantees. Moreover, Mr Doran's complaint in his affidavit evidence, as will be seen, is not that he relied exclusively on the bank but rather that through the concatenation of circumstances presenting, "I had no understanding of the nature and effect of the guarantee that I signed".

11–11 Barrett J concluded that on the facts:

> Notwithstanding the low threshold set in *Aer Rianta*, and mindful, *inter alia*, of that "discernible caution" which, to borrow from the judgment of McKechnie J. in *Harrisrange*, falls to be exercised by the court when it comes to the power to grant summary judgment, the court does not consider that Mr Doran has advanced any argument that would justify the within matter being sent to plenary hearing.

11–12 In *ADM v Arman*[15] Clarke J, when considering the defence of *non est factum* in relation to guarantees, stated that:

> On the facts of this case it is manifestly clear that the Defendants signed a document which is clearly, on its face, a guarantee. In those circumstances, even a cursory reading of the document would have brought to the Defendants' attention the fact that they were signing a guarantee. In those circumstances, it seems to me that the Defendants could not be said to have established any Defence under the non est factum doctrine. On that basis, it does not seem to me that that ground gives rise to any possible Defence or should lead to liberty to defend.

13 [2018] IEHC 2.
14 [2017] IECA 119.
15 [2006] IEHC 309.

In *ADM Londis Plc v Gibson*[16] the defendants sought leave to defend in relation to guarantees signed by them, and argued that: **11–13**

> They did not know they were signing a guarantee. It was not explained to them that it was a guarantee and they did not have any independent legal advice on same. Although they do not rely entirely on being "innocents abroad" as it was put, this was their first business venture. They thought they were signing an account opening form.

In his judgment, Hedigan J, when referring to the principles set out by Clarke J in *ADM v Arman Retail Ltd*,[17] stated that: **11–14**

> I gratefully adopt this statement of principle. Assertion, no matter how strongly made, is no defence. It is to the facts which are brought before it that the Court must look. If evidence of those facts could arguably give rise to a defence then leave to defend should be given. Questions of law or construction of documents may be resolved by the Court where relatively straightforward provided the limited framework of a motion for summary judgment does not involve a real risk of an injustice.

When considering the facts of the case, he went on to state that: **11–15**

> The same applies here. There is no conceivable way that a person could sign the guarantee document relied on herein without knowing it was a guarantee. It says so repeatedly throughout and is headed "Guarantee". To sign such a document without discovering it was a guarantee, fails utterly the third test set out above even were the first two met by the defendants.

He added: **11–16**

> The defendants in entering this contract of guarantee were acting as business people capable of contracting on their own without independent legal advice or any cooling off period. The guarantee was signed by both as directors of the company and they were free to contract or not as they wished. The fact that Mrs. Gibson's name did not appear in block letters opposite her admitted signature is of no substance.

Principles of Account Taken

The first principle is that a claim to have an account taken must be the main issue for determination by the court, and not ancillary to other issues specified in the summary summons. In *Aforge Finance SAS v HSBC Institutional Trust Services (Ireland) Ltd*,[18] Clarke J (as he then was) stated that: "The order for the taking of an account as an ancillary order is part **11–17**

16 [2010] IEHC 432.
17 [2006] IEHC 195, para 3.
18 [2009] IEHC 565, para 14.

of the process of determining the legal rights and obligations of parties to litigation rather than an entitlement in itself."

11–18 In *Best v Ghose*[19] Baker J added that:

> Because the claim is one brought for the taking of an account and not as part of another substantive cause of action, the plaintiffs must establish an entitlement to an account as of right and not by way of ancillary relief or in support of an already claimed allegation of wrongdoing.

11–19 The second principle is that the plaintiff must also show that he or she is entitled to have an account taken. The question of entitlement to have an account taken is dependent on the existence of a fiduciary relationship between the parties. There are various types of fiduciary relationship and the list of such relationships is not exhaustive. In *Clements v Meagher*[20] Feeney J, when referring to fiduciary relationships and the equitable remedy of account taken, stated that:

> It is not possible to provide a complete definition of the categories of persons who occupy fiduciary positions. The categories of fiduciary relationships are not closed and it is well recognised that fiduciary duties may be owed notwithstanding the fact that the relationship in question does not fall within one of the settled categories of fiduciary relationships. That is so, provided the circumstances justify the imposition of fiduciary duties. A fiduciary is not subject to fiduciary obligations because he is a fiduciary; it is because he is subject to them that he is a fiduciary. It follows that a fiduciary is a person who owes fiduciary duties. A fiduciary relationship, therefore, is a relationship between two or more persons in which at least one of them is a fiduciary who owes fiduciary duties to the other or others.

11–20 In *Aforge Finance SAS v HSBC Institutional Trust Services (Ireland) Ltd*[21] Clarke J, when considering the question of entitlement to have an account taken, stated:

> Where the only relief claimed is for an account in circumstances where no allegation of wrongdoing is made, then it follows that the account can only be ordered where the plaintiff bringing the claim is legally entitled to an account of the matter sought. The most obvious example of such circumstances will arise where, as here, it is said that the defendant owes a fiduciary duty to the plaintiff and is, thus, obliged to account.

11–21 In *Bristol and West Building Society v Mothew*[22] the characteristics of the fiduciary relationship were described by Millet LJ as follows:

---

19 [2018] IEHC 376, para 39.

20 [2008] IEHC 258; see *Best v Ghose* [2018] IEHC 376, para 45; *Fermoy Fish Ltd. v Canestar Ltd* [2015] IESC 93; *Moore v McGlynn* [1894] 1 IR 76.

21 [2009] IEHC 565; see *Best v Ghose* [2018] IEHC 376.

22 [1998] Ch 1, 18; see *McMullen v Clancy (No 2)* [2005] IESC 10, [2005] 2 IR 445, 470; *Clements v Meagher* [2008] IEHC 258; *Best v Ghose* [2018] IEHC 376.

> A fiduciary is someone who has undertaken to act for or on behalf of another in a particular matter in circumstances which give rise to a relationship of trust and confidence. The distinguishing obligation of a fiduciary is the obligation of loyalty. The principal is entitled to the single-minded loyalty of his fiduciary. This core liability has several facets. A fiduciary must act in good faith; he must not make a profit out of his trust; he must not place himself in a position where his duty and his interest may conflict; he may not act for his own benefit or the benefit of a third person without the informed consent of his principal. This is not intended to be an exhaustive list, but it is sufficient to indicate the nature of fiduciary obligations. They are the defining characteristics of the fiduciary.

In *Best v Ghose*[23] Baker J, adopting the foregoing *dicta* of Millet LJ as a statement of principle, and went on to state that: **11–22**

> In his first judgment in *Aforge Finance v HSBC Institutional Trust*, at para. 15, Clarke J. considered that the "most obvious example" of the circumstances giving rise to an entitlement to an account as of right is where a defendant owes a fiduciary duty to the plaintiff and is obliged to account by virtue of the fiduciary relationship. He quoted from the judgment of Chatterton V.C. in *Moore v McGlynn* [1894] 1 IR 74, also quoted with approval by Kenny J. in *Chaine-Nickson v Bank of Ireland* [1976] IR 393, that the relationship of trustee and beneficiary imports such a right. *Moore v McGlynn* is an authority for the general and established principle that a cestui que trust is entitled to have an account of the trust property as of right, the right deriving from the nature of the relationship between trustee and beneficiary and not being dependent upon any allegation of wrongdoing on the part of the trustee.

Baker J went on to state: **11–23**

> I find of particular benefit the statement of principle contained in McGhee, *Snell's Equity* (33rd ed., Sweet & Maxwell, 2015), where the obligation to account is explained as one which arises out of the receipt by a person of property "in an accountable capacity", at para. 20-015, and although that description might appear to be tautological, it is useful as it identifies the key component. The accountable capacity is one that arises in any circumstance where it can be shown that a person has control of property which belongs to another. As Snell says, the central case is that of an express trustee but the principles apply to various categories of relationships, including "agents who control property belonging to the principals", at para. 20-012.
>
> Snell also suggests that "[t]he claimant bears the onus of proving that the defendant has received property into their control in circumstances sufficient to import an equitable obligation to handle the property for the benefit of another", at para. 20-015.[24]

---

23 [2018] IEHC 376, para 49.

24 [2018] IEHC 376, paras 40–44.

11–24 In *Fermoy Fish Ltd v Canestar Ltd*[25] Dunne J, when considering the duties of a fiduciary, stated that:

> By virtue of the agreements entered into between the parties, Canestar [...] undertook to manage the customer accounts of Fermoy Fish for a period of twenty-four months in consideration of a sum of money. Fermoy Fish was entitled to payments made by customers to Canestar on behalf of Fermoy Fish. Clearly, in circumstances where Canestar received a sum of €484,895 on behalf of Fermoy Fish it was under an obligation to pay that sum to Fermoy Fish. It could hardly be thought otherwise than that Canestar had a relationship of trust and good faith towards Fermoy Fish. Despite that, Canestar received money belonging to Fermoy Fish from its customers and, instead of paying it over to Fermoy Fish as it was obliged to do, used the money to discharge its creditors.

11–25 In *In Re Belfast Theatre of Varieties Ltd*[26] Kenny J held that a liquidator does not have an obligation to account and is, at best, an agent who might have special duties imposed by statute or otherwise.[27] In *In Re DR Developments (Youghal) Ltd (In Liquidation)*[28] Finlay Geoghegan J held that the relationship between the clients of the company in liquidation and the company was contractual, and not one of trustee and beneficiary. In *Best v Ghose*[29] Baker J found that the liquidator could not be described as having any fiduciary duty or any direct contractual obligation to the plaintiffs. In relation to stockbrokers in *In Re Money Markets International Ltd*[30] Laffoy J found that the effect of s 52(5)(a) of the Stock Exchange Act 1995, as substituted by s 78 of the Investor Compensation Act 1998, was to ring-fence the funds deposited with a stockbroker in the client bank account and preserve them for the client creditors who had provided the funds. The funds so held in the client account were clients' funds and were held by the firm in a fiduciary capacity as trustee.

11–26 In *Aforge Finance SAS v HSBC Institutional Trust Services (Ireland) Ltd*[31] Clarke J, when considering the question of entitlement to have an account taken, stated:

> It logically follows that a plaintiff invoking the summary summons procedure and seeking an account in the first instance (and that, by definition, means that the account sought is not as an ancillary relief to a substantive claim) must establish an entitlement as of right to the account sought.

---

25 [2015] IESC 93; see *Best v Ghose* [2018] IEHC 376, para 46; *Moore v McGlynn* [1894] 1 IR 76.

26 [1963] 1 IR 41; *Knowles v Scott* (1891) 1 Ch 717, 723; see *In re Uniacke (No 2)* [1944] 78 ILTR 154.

27 See *Best v Ghose* [2018] IEHC 376.

28 [2011] IEHC 307; see *In re Custom House Capital Ltd (In Liquidation)* [2012] IEHC 382; *Best v Ghose* [2018] IEHC 376.

29 [2018] IEHC 376.

30 [2000] 3 IR 437, 447–48; see *Best v Ghose* [2018] IEHC 376.

31 [2009] IEHC 565; see *Best v Ghose* [2018] IEHC 376.

Chapter 12

ARGUABLE DEFENCES

Introduction

The court, when deciding on whether or not to grant summary judgment of a debt owing on a contract of loan or a guarantee relating to a debt, may be guided by the "low threshold" test formulated by Hardiman J *Aer Rianta cpt v Ryanair*,[1] and by addressing the following four questions posed by him in the same case: **12–01**

> First, is it very clear that a defendant has no case? Second, are the issues simple and easily determined? Third, has a defendant disclosed even an arguable defence? Fourth, where there is no notice to cross-examine, can a court be confident, on the affidavit evidence alone, where the justice of the case lies?

In *Harrisrange Ltd v Duncan*[2] McKechnie J formulated the legal tests that may be applied by the court when determining whether or not the defendant had an arguable defence. The court will also consider whether there is a fair and reasonable probability of a defendant having a real or *bona fide* defence, either in law, or on the facts.[3] In *Ulster Bank Ireland Ltd v Beades*[4] McKechnie J stated that "leave to defend should be granted where there is a fair and reasonable probability that a real or bona fide defence exists, or that what is averred to in the defendant's affidavit is credible". He also stated: "This approach, admittedly with some modification of emphasis if not more, has to a substantial degree, continued to be the law to this day." He went to state that the court "may give leave to defend unconditionally or subject to such terms, as the court thinks fit. In brief but subject to what is later stated, such leave will be granted where an arguable defence has been plausibly asserted." **12–02**

---

1 [2001] 4 IR 607, 623; see *Promontoria (Arrow) Limited v Burke* [2018] IEHC 773, paras 21–23; *AIB Mortgage Bank and AIB Banks plc v O'Brien* [2020] IECA 191; *Allied Irish Banks plc v Cuddy* [2020] IECA 211; *AIB plc v Griffin* [2020] IECA 221.

2 [2003] 4 IR 1, 7; *Aer Rianta cpt v Ryanair Ltd* [2001] 4 IR 607, 623; see *Allied Irish Banks plc v Farrell* [2014] IEHC 395, paras 32–34.

3 See *Allied Irish Banks plc v Farrell* [2014] IEHC 395, paras 32 to 34; *Promontoria (Arrow) Limited v Burke* [2018] IEHC 773, paras 21–23.

4 [2019] IESC 83, para 16; see *Banque de Paris v De Naray* [1984] 1 Lloyds Reports 21.

12–03 In *Allied Irish Banks plc v Farrell*[5] Ryan J (as he then was), when addressing the standard and onus of proof in such matters, set out:

> Is what the defendant says credible? If it is not credible, then there is no fair or reasonable probability of the defendant having a defence.
> (i) The standard of proof for a defendant at this stage must as a matter of principles be a low one.
> (ii) The onus of proving lack of credibility is on the plaintiff.

12–04 In *IBRC Ltd v McCaughey*[6] Clarke J (as he then was), when considering the meaning of the credibility of a defence, stated:

> It is important, therefore, to re-emphasise what is meant by the credibility of a defence. A defence is not incredible simply because the judge is not inclined to believe the defendant. It must, as Hardiman J. pointed out in *Aer Rianta v Ryanair Ltd.* … be clear that the defendant has no defence. If issues of law or construction are put forward as providing an arguable defence, then the court can assess those issues to determine whether the propositions advanced are stateable as a matter of law and that it is arguable that, if determined in favour of the defendant, they would provide for a defence. In that context, and subject to the inherent limitations on the summary judgment jurisdiction … the court may come to a final resolution of such issues. That the court is not obliged to resolve such issues is also clear from *Danske Bank v Durkan New Homes* [2010] IESC 22, …

12–05 Where a defendant establishes that he or she has an arguable defence, the court may then, pursuant to Ord 37, r7 of the Rules of the Superior Court (RSC), remit the issue to plenary hearing. In *Promontoria (Arrow) Limited v Burke*[7] Barniville J stated that:

> It is well established that the court has a jurisdiction pursuant to O.37, rr.7 and 10 RSC where the defendant seeks to raise a number of defences, to adjourn to plenary hearing only that defence or those defences which meet the threshold of a *bona fide* or arguable defence in accordance with the test referred to earlier.

12–06 The issue for plenary hearing may involve the application of an equitable or legal principle, such as equitable mistake, *non est factum*, undue influence or misrepresentation and rescission, and will have to be substantiated at plenary hearing.[8] Where the issue remitted for plenary hearing involves promissory estoppel or estoppel by convention, the prerequisites for applying the relevant estoppel must be substantiated by the erstwhile defendant at plenary hearing.[9] The court may also remit a particular issue to plenary

---

5 [2014] IEHC 395, paras 32–34; see *Promontoria (Arrow) Limited v Burke* [2018] IEHC 773, paras 21–23.

6 [2014] 1 IR 749, para 22; see *Allied Irish Banks PLC v Likely* [2016] IEHC 579; *Danske Bank v Shortt* [2020] IECA 137.

7 [2018] IEHC 773, paras 21–23.

8 See Chapters 6, 7, 8 and 9.

9 See Chapter 5.

hearing, such as an issue involving the amount of interest accruing on a sum of money lent.[10] However, where a defendant is unable to establish an arguable defence, judgment will be entered for the amount of money claimed by the plaintiff.[11] Furthermore, a defence based on an issue not recognised by Irish law will not be entertained by the court.[12]

In *Allied Irish Banks plc v Likely*[13] McDermott J, when considering the principles applicable to cross-claims or set-offs in applications for summary judgment, stated that: **12–07**

> The relevant principles applicable to a claim of set-off in an application for summary judgment were considered by Clarke J. in *Moohan v S & R Motors (Donegal) Ltd.* [2008] 3 I.R. 650 in which he held that when a cross-claim is advanced the court has a somewhat wider discretion than that available under the test formulated in *Aer Rianta* for the granting of leave to defend.

Arguable Defences

For a defence to be deemed arguable, a defendant must show "that a real or bona fide defence exists, or that what is averred to in the defendant's affidavit is credible".[14] In *Ulster Bank Ireland Ltd v Beades*[15] McKechnie J, when referring to the competing rights of the plaintiff and defendant in applications for summary judgment, stated: **12–08**

> Whatever the initiating process may be, it is however necessary to remain mindful that justice is, at least, a two-way process involving the party who institutes the proceedings and the party against whom a cause of action is asserted, and some relief or remedy is sought: the public interest in the general administration of justice should be added. In assessing how any action should be conducted, irrespective of its origin, the court is frequently called upon to have regard to a number of potentially competing rights. On the plaintiff's side there is principally a right to litigate a judiciable grievance to a merit based conclusion and, depending on the circumstances including the subject matter of the action, a defendant may assert some right or entitlement which may impact on the course of that litigation.[16]

He concluded that: **12–09**

> In general, where in issue, these rights are assessed by the application of many

[10] See *Bank of Ireland Mortgage Bank v Mavroudis* [2020] IEHC 136.
[11] *Ulster Bank Ireland Ltd v Beades* [2019] IESC 83.
[12] See *ICS Building Society v Grant* [2010] IEHC 17; *Healy v Stepstone Mortgages* [2014] IEHC 134; *Allied Irish Banks Plc v McCarthy* [2019] IEHC 743.
[13] [2016] IEHC 579, para 32.
[14] See *Ulster Bank Ireland Ltd v Beades* [2019] IESC 83, para 16; *First Commercial Bank Plc v Anglin* [1996] 1 IR 75.
[15] [2019] IESC 83, para 16; see *Banque de Paris v De Naray* [1984] 1 Lloyds Reports 21.
[16] [2019] IESC 83, para 19.

different rules either created by statute, rules of court, or by case law: whichever, all have been developed so as to ensure that the litigation process is conducted fairly and proportionately and that the outcome is just.[17]

12–10 In *Harrisrange Ltd v Duncan*[18] McKechnie J stated that the following legal tests (vii) to (xii) may be applied by the court when determining whether or not the defendant had an arguable defence:

> (vii) the test to be applied, as now formulated is whether the defendant has satisfied the court that he has a fair or reasonable probability of having a real or bona fide defence; or as it is sometimes put, "is what the defendant says credible?"
> (viii) this test is not the same as and should not be elevated into a threshold of a defendant having to prove that his defence will probably succeed or that success is not improbable, it being sufficient if there is an arguable defence;
> (ix) leave to defend should be granted unless it is very clear that there is no defence;
> (x) leave to defend should not be refused only because the court has reason to doubt the bona fides of the defendant or has reason to doubt whether he has a genuine cause of action;
> (xi) leave should not be granted where the only relevant averment is the totality of the evidence, is a mere assertion of a given situation which is to form the basis of a defence and finally;
> (xii) the overriding determinative factor, bearing in mind the constitutional basis of a person's right of access to justice either to assert or respond to litigation, is the achievement of a just result whether that be liberty to enter judgment or leave to defend, as the case may be.

12–11 In *McGrath v O'Driscoll*[19] Clarke J (as he then was), when considering arguable defences within the limited framework of a motion for summary judgment, stated:

> So far as factual issues are concerned it is clear, therefore, that a mere assertion of a defence is insufficient. But any evidence of fact which would, if true, arguably give rise to a defence will, in the ordinary way, be sufficient to require that leave to defend be given so that that issue of fact can be resolved.
>
> So far as questions of law or construction are concerned the court can, on a motion for summary judgment, resolve such questions, including, where appropriate, questions of the construction of documents, but should only do so where the issues which arise are relatively straightforward and where there is no real risk of an injustice being done by determining those questions within the somewhat limited framework of a motion for summary judgment.
>
> It seems to me that that is the appropriate test that I need to apply to the issues of defence raised. Can it be shown, insofar as the defences raised are based on facts, that the defendant has put forward facts which, if true, might arguably give

---

[17] [2019] IESC 83, para 20.

[18] [2003] 4 IR 1, 7; *Aer Rianta cpt v Ryanair Ltd* [2001] 4 IR 607, 623; see *Allied Irish Banks plc v Farrell* [2014] IEHC 395, paras 32–34.

[19] [2006] IEHC 195.

rise to a defence? And insofar as issues of law or construction are concerned, are those issues straightforward and capable of resolution on *a motion such as this or are they complex and should await a full plenary hearing?*

In *Allied Irish Banks plc v Farrell*[20] Ryan J (as he then was) when commenting on the principles of summary judgment and arguable defences, stated that: **12–12**

1. Is there a fair or reasonable probability of the defendant having a real or *bona fide* defence? If so, judgment must be refused and the matter determined at plenary hearing. If not, the plaintiff is entitled to judgment.
2. The mere assertion in an affidavit of a given situation as the basis of a defence does not of itself provide leave to defend.
3. To grant summary judgment to a plaintiff and to refuse leave to defend it is not sufficient that the court should have reason to doubt the *bona fides* of the defendant or to doubt whether the defendant has a genuine cause of action.
4. The court looks at the case as a whole to see whether the defendant has established that there is a fair or reasonable probability of having a real or *bona fide* defence.
5. Is what the defendant says credible? If it is not credible, then there is no fair or reasonable probability of the defendant having a defence.
   (i) The standard of proof for a defendant at this stage must as a matter of principles be a low one.
   (ii) The onus of proving lack of credibility is on the plaintiff.
6. In *Aer Rianta*, McGuinness J. identified the issue whether the proposed defence is so far-fetched, so self-contradictory as not to be credible.
7. Hardiman J. asked: Is it "very clear" that the defendant has no case?
   (i) Is there either no issue to be tried or only issues which are simple and easily determined?
   (ii) Do the defendant's affidavits fail to disclose even an arguable defence?
8. The court takes the nature and context of the dispute into account. Hardiman J. referred to the facts of the cases in the authority cited and observed that in *First National Commercial Bank v Anglin* [1996] 1 I.R. 75, "the indisputable documentation of a commercial transaction rendered the alternatively chronology proposed by the defendant quite untenable"."

The court will also focus on the issue of the credibility of the defence in ascertaining whether there was a "fair or reasonable probability" of the defendants having a real or bona fide or arguable defence.[21] In the Supreme Court in *IBRC Limited v McCaughey*[22] Clarke J (as he then was), when considering the question of credibility of a defence, stated that: **12–13**

A defence is not incredible simply because the judge is not inclined to believe the defendant. It must, as Hardiman J. pointed out in *Aer Rianta* ..., be clear that the defendant has no defence. If issues of law or construction are put forward as providing an arguable defence, then the court can assess those issues to determine whether the propositions advanced are stateable as a matter of law and that it is arguable that, if determined in favour of the defendant, they would provide for a

[20] [2014] IEHC 395, paras 32–34.
[21] See *First National Commercial Bank plc v Anglin* [1996] 1 IR 75.
[22] [2014] 1 IR 749, 759.

> defence. In that context, and subject to the inherent limitations on the summary judgment jurisdiction identified in *McGrath v O'Driscoll* [2006] IEHC 195, [2007] 1 I.L.R.M. 203, the court may come to a final resolution of such issues. That the court is not obliged to resolve such issues is also clear from *Danske Bank a/s (t/a National Irish Bank) v Durkan New Homes* [2010] IESC 22.

12–14 However, he also stated that:

> It needs to be emphasised again that it is no function of the court on a summary judgment motion to form any general view as to the credibility of the evidence put forward by the defendant.

12–15 The court will also consider the quality of evidence adduced by a defendant when deciding whether or not he or she has an arguable defence. Mere assertions made by a defendant will not be accepted by the court as sufficient evidence of an arguable defence. In *IBRC Limited v McCaughey*[23] Clarke J (as he then was) stated that:

> The sort of factual assertions, which may not provide an arguable defence, are facts which amount to a mere assertion unsupported either by evidence or by any realistic suggestion that evidence might be available, or, facts which are in themselves contradictory and inconsistent with uncontested documentation or other similar circumstances such as those analysed by Hardiman J. in *Aer Rianta* ...

12–16 In *Ulster Bank Ireland Limited v O'Brien*[24] MacMenamin J stated that where there is "real conflict on the facts or law, the matter must be remitted for plenary hearing", and went on to state:

> I would point out that a simple, bald denial of indebtedness, whether in correspondence or on affidavit, will not be sufficient to discharge the burden, so far as a defendant is concerned. A defendant's evidence must set out in a clear way why the sum claimed is said not to be due and owing to a plaintiff.

Issues Raised in Arguable Defences

12–17 The following issues were raised in arguable defences put forward by defendants:

(i) Misrepresentation

12–18 An arguable defence may be based on an issue of misrepresentation.[25] In *Danske Bank a/s t/a Danske Bank v Daniels*,[26] the plaintiff by notice of

[23] [2014] 1 IR 749, 759.
[24] [2015] 2 IR 656, 659; *Allied Irish Banks plc v O'Callaghan* [2020] IECA 318.
[25] See Chapter 7.
[26] [2018] IEHC 825.

motion for summary judgment claimed that the fourth-named defendant on foot of a guarantee executed by him in favour of the plaintiff on 1 August 2006, which was limited to the sum of €700,000, and given in respect of banking facilities and advanced in favour of Adelphi Distributors Limited (the company). Mr Gerry McGovern provided the grounding affidavit and a replying affidavit on behalf of the plaintiff. Mr Michael Crowley also provided a replying affidavit. Mr Cantwell provided two replying affidavits. However, the essential facts of the matter were not in issue. Mr Cantwell did not deny that the company entered into the four facilities set out in the summary summons, or that the company drew down the various amounts set out in respect of these facilities, or that it subsequently failed to repay the loan monies in question. Therefore, there was no dispute about the company's debt which was the sum claimed by the plaintiff from Mr Cantwell on foot of his guarantee, which he did not dispute signing in favour of the bank on 1 August 2006 as security for the debts of the company.

Hunt J stated that: **12–19**

> The main area of concern in this case is the assertion that, in effect, Mr. Crowley assured Mr. Cantwell prior to signature that execution of the guarantee was a formality required by the bank which would never be subsequently enforced. In the ordinary course of events, I would treat such assertions with a considerable degree of scepticism. However, in this case, there are two evidential reasons to believe that the bare assertions are backed by a fair or reasonable probability that Mr. Cantwell has a stateable defence to the effect that the guarantee was procured by such misrepresentations.[27]

He concluded: **12–20**

> In these circumstances, I am satisfied that there is sufficient evidence to support a fair and reasonable probability that Mr. Cantwell has a defence based on the assertion that the guarantee was procured by misrepresentation. I am satisfied that the evidence of an absence of express reliance upon his guarantee in connection with subsequent advances is capable of supporting his assertions in this respect.
>
> Having regard to the low threshold to be established by the defendant in meeting the test for remittal of the dispute for plenary hearing, I am satisfied that on the facts so far disclosed in relation to this case, and having regard to the issues which have been canvassed, that this is not an appropriate case in which to give summary judgment.[28]

(ii) *Non Est Factum*

An arguable defence may be based on an issue of *non est factum*.[29] In **12–21**

---

[27] [2018] IEHC 825, para 13.
[28] [2018] IEHC 825, paras 16–17.
[29] See Chapter 9.

Emberton Finance Ltd v Cronin[30] the plaintiff sought summary judgment against the defendant in the sum of €259,966.45. The claim was brought on foot of a loan agreement made on 9 October 2007 whereby Friends First Finance Ltd agreed to lend the sum of €250,000 to the defendant that was repayable over a period of 60 months by way of 60 monthly interest payments amounting to €1,498.39 per month, followed by a "balloon" payment of €250,000. The sum of €250,000 was advanced to the defendant on 11 October 2007. The annual percentage rate of interest charged was 7.39 per cent. The purpose of the loan was to facilitate the acquisition by the defendant of a share in a new office building then under construction in New York City. The loan facility was to repaid on or before 1 December 2012. It was not repaid. The benefit of the loan was transferred by Friends First Finance Ltd to Emberton Finance Ltd by deed of transfer dated 3 March 2014. The defendant relied on the defence of *non est factum*. The defendant contended that in signing the loan facility, he did so believing its terms to be otherwise than stated. He believed himself to be signing a "non-recourse" loan agreement.

12–22 In his judgment, McDermott J stated:

> The principles applicable to the court's consideration of an application to grant summary judgment are well established and summarised by McKechnie J. in *Harrisrange Ltd. v Duncan* [2003] 4 I.R. 1, Hardiman J. in *Aer Rianta c.p.t. v Ryanair Ltd.* [2001] 4 I.R. 607 and the Supreme Court in *IBRC Ltd. v McCaughey* [2014] 1 I.R. 749.[31]

12–23 In relation to the defence of *non est factum*, he stated that:

> It would appear that the defendant in this case chose not to read the document or obtain legal advice in respect of the document. He chose not to respond to the invitation to withdraw from the agreement if he had any difficulty with it when a copy was furnished to him on 29th October. There is no evidence that the creditor contributed in any way to any alleged lack of understanding on his part as to the nature and legal character or consequences of the loan facility. It may be thought odd that a business man whose main concern in the transaction he was about to enter was that he was obtaining a non-recourse loan and considered this to be the main "selling point" of the entire enterprise would not take steps to read the relatively short loan facility letter and/or the copy with which he was later furnished to ensure that it was not the standard type loan facility to which he did not wish to commit himself. However, I also note that the plaintiff has not set out on affidavit any evidence which challenges Mr. Cronin's account of how the loan was negotiated or describing its dealings through Mr. Loughnane with the defendant.
>
> This is a case that goes beyond mere assertion. It is not the court's function to form an overall view of the defendant's veracity on this issue at this stage. I am

[30] [2018] IEHC 572; see *Allied Irish Banks plc v Higgins* [2010] IEHC 219.
[31] [2018] IEHC 572, para 6.

> satisfied that the facts as presented by the defendant are capable of giving rise to a defence if accepted and amount to an arguable defence as defined in the case-law cited above.[32]

McDermott J concluded at para 33: "For all of the above reasons I am satisfied that the defendant has established an arguable or *bona fide* case within the principles set out above in respect of the *non est factum* defence." **12–24**

(iii) Promissory Estoppel or Estoppel by Convention

An arguable defence may be based on an issue of promissory estoppel or estoppel by convention.[33] The equitable principle of promissory estoppel is based on the notion of unconscionable behaviour or unconscionability, ie it would be unconscionable for a contractual party to renege on representations made by him or her which were relied on and acted upon by the party to whom they were made, and who suffered a detriment by doing so. An arguable defence may involve the equitable principle of estoppel by convention where contractual parties tacitly recognise and accept changed circumstances surrounding their contract as a result of a mistake, and yet they continue with the performance of their contract knowing of the mistake, it will be assumed that they have accepted the changed contractual circumstances following upon the mistake. **12–25**

(iv) A Statute-Barred Claim by a Bank

An arguable defence may be based on an issue involving a statute-barred claim. In *Danske Bank v Kelly*[34] the appellant's submission was that the bank's claim was statute-barred. In her judgment, Power J stated that: **12–26**

> 26. The appellant, in my view, should not be deprived of raising an arguable defence in circumstances where the bank's own records raise a question as to whether the claim was brought within six years of the demand having been made. Whether the period of 6 years or 12 years is the relevant statutory limitation period in this case is not a matter which this Court has to decide. As noted earlier, I confine myself strictly to the matters which were before the High Court.
>
> 27. Given the significance of what is involved when summary judgment is granted I approach this appeal in the light of what McKechnie J. said in *Harrisgrange Limited v Duncan* [2003] 4 I.R. 1, namely, "the power to grant summary judgment should be granted with discernible caution". Since issues concerning the Statute are, inevitably, associated with issues of fact, I am not satisfied that the issue of fact as to whether or not a letter of demand did issue in April 2009 is something that can be determined without having recourse to a plenary hearing. A document is before the Court which states that "demand letters issued in April 09" and this

---

[32] [2018] IEHC 572, paras 28–30.
[33] See Chapter 5.
[34] [2020] IECA 12.

> is a matter which, when finally determined, may go to the defence of this claim. Discovery may shed further light on this.
>
> 28. Applying the test for summary judgment (per Hardiman J.) I cannot say that it is "very clear" that the defendant has no case. I cannot say that the issue of whether a letter issued in April 09 is one which is "easily determined". I cannot say that the appellant has failed to disclose even an "arguable defence".
>
> 29. I consider that the appellant is entitled to have the matter proceed to plenary hearing, which may involve the trial of a preliminary issue on the Statute.
>
> 30. In view of the reasons set out herein I would allow the appeal.

12–27 However, a defence based on an issue not recognised by Irish law will not be entertained by the court, such as the tort of reckless lending.[35] There is no such tort as reckless lending in Irish law, and therefore, a defence based on such by a defendant in a motion for summary judgment by a plaintiff will not be entertained by the court. The following case law decided between 2010 to 2019 all emphasise that there is no such tort of reckless lending in Irish law. In *ICS Building Society v Grant*[36] Charleton J stated "the tort of reckless lending does not exist in law as a civil wrong", and that:

> It is difficult to imagine the parameters of such a law since those who seek a loan will have a view as to what should be borrowed, and if a loan is badly made by a bank, how can the issue of contribution be escaped from by the borrower who sought the money in the first place.

12–28 The decision in *ICS Building Society* was followed by Kelly J (as he then was) in *McConnan v President of Ireland*,[37] who was satisfied that the alleged tort of "reckless lending" did not exist as a civil wrong in Irish law. In *Healy v Stepstone Mortgages*[38] Hogan J, referring to *ICS Building Society v Grant* and *McConnan v President of Ireland*, also stated, "There is simply no tort of reckless lending which is known to the law."

12–29 In *Allied Irish Banks Plc v McCarthy*[39] the court again considered whether a defence of reckless lending by banks existed in Irish law. In that case, the plaintiff applied for summary judgment in the sum of €119,402.09 against the defendant in respect of a loan advanced to the defendant in 2007. The defendant raised a number of issues in his affidavits which amounted to

---

[35] See *ICS Building Society v Grant* [2010] IEHC 17; *Healy v Stepstone Mortgages* [2014] IEHC 134; *Allied Irish Banks Plc v McCarthy* [2019] IEHC 743.

[36] [2010] IEHC 17; see *Healy v Stepstone Mortgages* [2014] IEHC 134; *Allied Irish Banks Plc v McCarthy* [2019] IEHC 743.

[37] [2012] IEHC 184.

[38] [2014] IEHC 134; see *The Governor and Company of the Bank of Ireland v McMahon* [2017] IEHC 600.

[39] [2019] IEHC 743.

the allegation that the plaintiff bank was reckless in advancing the loan to him. However, Barr J, having referred to *ICS Building Society v Grant*,[40] *McConnan v President of Ireland*[41] and *The Governor and Company of the Bank of Ireland v McMahon*,[42] stated:

> Having regard to the submissions of both parties and the above mentioned case law, I am satisfied that there is no tort of "reckless lending" in Irish law, accordingly there is no substance to this ground of defence raised by the defendant.

He concluded: **12–30**

> 44. Having regard to the findings made by me herein, I am not satisfied that the defendant has persuaded the Court that he has a real or bona fide defence sufficient to cross the threshold provided for in the *Aer Rianta* and *Harrisrange* cases. Accordingly, I refuse to remit the matter to plenary hearing.
>
> 45. I am satisfied that the defendant is indebted to the plaintiff on foot of the loan in the sum set out in Ms. Clancy's affidavit. Accordingly, the plaintiff is entitled to summary judgment herein. I award the plaintiff judgment against the defendant in the sum of €119,402.09.

Cross-Claims

In *Moohan v S & R Motors (Donegal) Ltd*[43] Clarke J, when considering cross-claims in applications for summary judgment, stated that when a cross-claim is advanced the court has a somewhat wider discretion than that available under the test formulated in *Aer Rianta* for the granting of leave to defend. He stated at para 4.2: **12–31**

> (a) It is firstly necessary to determine whether the defendant has established a defence as such to the plaintiff's claim. In order for the asserted cross claim to amount to a defence as such, it must arguably give rise to a set off in equity, and must, thus, stem from the same set of circumstances as give rise to the claim but also arise in circumstances as give rise to the claim but also arise in circumstances where, on the basis of the defendant's case, it would not be inequitable to allow the asserted set off.
> (b) If, and to the extent that, a prima facie case for such a set off arises the defendant will be taken to have established a defence to the proceedings and should be given liberty to defend the entire (or an appropriate portion of) the claim (…)
> (c) If the cross claim amounts to an independent claim, then judgment should be entered on the claim but the question of whether execution of such judgment should be stayed must be determined in the discretion of the court

---

40 [2010] IEHC 17.
41 [2012] IEHC 184.
42 [2017] IEHC 600.
43 [2008] 3 IR 650; see *Allied Irish Banks Plc v Likely* [2016] IEHC 579.

by reference to the principles set out by Kingsmill Moore J. in *Prendergast v Biddle* (Unreported, Supreme Court, 21st July, 1957).

Substantiating Issues at Plenary Hearing

12–32 Under Ord 37, r 7 of the RSC, the court upon the hearing of a motion for summary judgment, and finding that a defendant has an arguable defence, may give "such directions as to pleadings or discovery or settlement of issues or otherwise as may be appropriate, and generally may make such order for determination of the questions in issue in the action as may seem just".

12–33 In *Allied Irish Bank Plc v Griffin* [44] Murray J when allowing the defendant's appeal gave the following directions:

> Therefore, I would allow this appeal and substitute for the Order of the High Court Judge an Order refusing the application for summary judgment and making in its stead an Order remitting this case to plenary hearing. The Order made by the High Court Judge granting the plaintiff its costs of the summary judgment application should be vacated, and it is my provisional view that an Order should be made that the costs of that application in the High Court and of this appeal should be costs in the cause. I would also propose directing the delivery of pleadings – the Statement of Claim by 5 pm on Monday September 7, any particulars on that to be raised within three weeks and replied to within three weeks, and the Defence to be delivered three weeks thereafter.

12–34 At plenary hearing of the remitted issue involving an equitable principle or contractual concept, the issue will have to be substantiated and developed by the erstwhile defendant by showing that the prerequisites for applying the principle or concept are present. An issue remitted by the court for plenary hearing may involve an equitable principle, such as *non est factum* or undue influence; the issue will have to be substantiated by showing that the prerequisites for application of the principle *vis-à-vis* the issue are present.[45] Where the issue remitted by the court for plenary hearing involves a contractual concept such as misrepresentation, mistake or rectification, the erstwhile defendant will have to show that the prerequisites required for the application of the concept have been satisfied in relation to the remitted issue.[46] Where the issue remitted by the court for plenary hearing involves promissory estoppel or estoppel by convention it must be shown at plenary hearing of the issue that the prerequisites for applying the relevant estoppel are present at the time of plenary hearing of the issue.[47]

12–35 Thus, the "truncated" process of summary judgment begins with an

---

[44] [2020] IECA 221, para 34.
[45] See Chapters 8 and 9.
[46] See Chapters 6 and 7.
[47] See Chapter 5.

application by the plaintiff for an order of summary judgment for a debt of a liquidated sum of money against the defendant that may be granted by the court, or may not be granted where the defendant shows that he or she has an arguable defence. Where an arguable defence is established by the defendant, the court may remit the issue for plenary hearing where it has to be substantiated and established by the defendant.[48] The issue whether it involves an equitable principle or contractual concept may be substantiated and established by showing that the prerequisites for its application at the time of the plenary hearing of the issue.

In *Ulster Bank Ireland Ltd v Beades*[49] McKechnie J commented on summary judgment proceedings: **12–36**

> Overall therefore, one can see that the procedure is quite different to that of a plenary hearing. It is envisaged as being a speedier process and a more efficient manner of dealing with cases to which it applies: in addition, there is less cost and expense involved. However, whatever its virtues may be, it must be acknowledged that where judgment results at this point in the proceedings, the overall process falls short of the more complete hearing inherent in the plenary process. Where appropriately utilised however, there is nothing fundamentally wrong with this procedure, a point I will come back to in a moment.[50]

48 See *Ulster Bank Ireland Ltd v Beades* [2019] IESC 83.
49 [2019] IESC 83.
50 [2019] IESC 83, para 18.

Chapter 13

CONTRACTS WITH BANKS

Introduction

At common law a contract between bank and customer traditionally establishes a debtor and creditor relationship between the parties.[1] Under the contract a bank is answerable for monies lodged by a customer together with a duty to repay, when demanded, a sum equivalent to that paid into the bank.[2] A bank is also obliged to act on foot of a customer's instructions, unless it has received notice of a customer's incapacity or death, and such notices terminate the mandate of a bank to act in relation to the customer's account.[3] It appears that a bank owes no further duty, either express or implied, to its customers.[4] In *Best v Ghose*,[5] Baker J stated that: **13–01**

> The ordinary relationship of banker/customer involves the bank agreeing to hold money on behalf of a customer, to act on instructions with regard to payments into and from the account, and a bank in general does not actively take decisions which can result in a gain or loss of monies so held.

She added: **13–02**

> The normal relationship of banker/customer is not a relationship which imports fiduciary obligations, and this is established in a number of recent judgments, including that of Finlay Geoghegan J. in *IBRC Ltd. v Morrissey* [2013] IEHC 208.

However, in *Bourke v O'Donnell*[6] Hedigan J stated that: **13–03**

> where there are circumstances attendant upon a transaction that clearly raise substantial grounds to doubt the capacity of its customer to give instructions, the bank has a duty to make enquiry. It is obvious that such a situation would be rare. Certainly, the mere fact that a customer is elderly could not give rise to such a duty. Something more would have to be present in the mix of circumstances.[7]

---

1 See *Best v Ghose* [2018] IEHC 376.
2 *Foley v Hill* [1848] 2 HL Cas 28.
3 See *Bank of Ireland v Hussey* [1965] IR 46, 55; *Bourke v O'Donnell* [2010] IEHC 348.
4 See *Lipkin Gorman v Karpnale Ltd* [1989] 1 WLR 1340, 1352; *Bourke v O'Donnell* [2010] IEHC 348.
5 [2018] IEHC 376, para 58.
6 [2010] IEHC 348.
7 [2010] IEHC 348, para 8.6.

13–04 Under Ord 37 of the Rules of the Superior Courts (RSC), a bank may seek summary judgment enforcing payment of a debt owing to it by a customer or guarantee relating to the debt. However, the court, upon the hearing of a motion for summary judgment, may find that the customer has an arguable defence, and may remit the matter to plenary hearing, and may give "such directions as to pleadings or discovery or settlement of issues or otherwise as may be appropriate, and generally may make such order for determination of the questions in issue in the action as may seem just".[8]

13–05 An arguable defence may involve the consideration given in support of a contract of loan or guarantee between bank and customer, or may involve a conflict in the wording of a guarantee and facility letter, or may concern actual evidence of the contract between bank and customer, or a dispute concerning the amount of interest due on a loan, and where an arguable defence is established the matter may be remitted by the court for plenary hearing. It may also be argued that the bank's duty to make enquiries in the circumstances envisaged by Hedigan J in *Bourke v O'Donnell*, especially, where there are substantial grounds to doubt a customer's incapacity to give instructions apropos an improvident transaction, and that such circumstances may also have the effect of superimposing a constructive trust on a bank's duty to make enquiries, and as such form the basis of an arguable defence. Such circumstances may also have the effect of establishing a fiduciary relationship between bank and customer arising out of the superimposed constructive trust.

Bank and Customer Relationships

13–06 The nature of the relationship between bank and customer is that of debtor and creditor.[9] A bank "is of course answerable for the amount, because he has contracted, having received that money, to repay to the principle, when demanded, a sum equivalent to that paid into his hands".[10] A bank's failure to honour its customers' instructions "may redound to the discredit of its customer".[11] In *IBRC Ltd v Morrissey*[12] Finlay Geoghegan J affirmed that the relationship between bank and customer did not go beyond the traditional contractual relationship. In *Bank of Ireland v Hussey*[13] McLoughlin J, when considering the question of notice to a bank of a customer's death or unsoundness of mind, stated, "It is also the position that it is not the death or insanity of the customer that amounts to a withdrawal of authority but

[8] Rules of the Superior Courts, Ord 37, r7; see Chapter 12.
[9] See *Foley v Hill* [1848] 2 HL Cas 28; *Best v Ghose* [2018] IEHC 376.
[10] *Foley v Hill* [1848] 2 HL Cas 28.
[11] *Bourke v O'Donnell* [2010] IEHC 348.
[12] [2013] IEHC 208; see *Best v Ghose* [2018] IEHC 376.
[13] [1965] IR 46, 55.

the notice of the customer's death or insanity." Where a bank has no notice of a customer's incapacity it is still obliged to act on instructions until such notice is received.

In *Bourke v O'Donnell*[14] Hedigan J, when considering the question of knowledge of a customer's incapacity, stated that: **13–07**

> The requirement for knowledge of the alleged mental incapacity on the part of the bank is crucial. Clearly, the bank cannot treat every elderly customer as being unable to give instructions in relation to their accounts merely because of their age. Further, although the bank had no knowledge of the fact that the plaintiff had been ill and was now living in fulltime residential care, even if it had, that fact alone would not have been sufficient for the bank to assume that she lacked mental capacity as opposed to being physically infirm.

He continued: **13–08**

> I accept that the bank has no duty to advise on the wisdom of carrying through what the customer wishes and instructs. I accept that, in the circumstances of this case, any fiduciary duty the bank might have does not arise. I accept further that the bank must follow the instructions of its customer until it has knowledge of the customer's incapacity. When it has such knowledge, the mandate is revoked. Until it has such knowledge, the mandate is operative.

However: **13–09**

> It seems to me to follow from this that where there are circumstances attendant upon a transaction that clearly raise substantial grounds to doubt the capacity of its customer to give instructions, the bank has a duty to make enquiry. It is obvious that such a situation would be rare. Certainly, the mere fact that a customer is elderly could not give rise to such a duty. Something more would have to be present in the mix of circumstances.[15]

A Bank's Duty to Make Enquiries

Where "substantial doubts" arise regarding a customer's capacity to give instructions to his or her bank and who is about to enter into what might be termed improvident transactions, the bank has a duty to make enquiry. In *Bourke v O'Donnell*[16] Hedigan J stated that "where there are circumstances attendant upon a transaction that clearly raise substantial grounds to doubt the capacity of its customer to give instructions, the bank has a duty to make enquiry".[17] **13–10**

[14] [2010] IEHC 348.
[15] [2010] IEHC 348, para 8.6.
[16] [2010] IEHC 348.
[17] [2010] IEHC 348, para 8.6.

13–11 In *Bourke v O'Donnell*[18] Hedigan J, when referring to a customer's incapacity and a bank's lack of inquiry concerning her incapacity, stated that:

> In this case, I consider that the evidence given by the plaintiff was telling. She presented as an elderly lady, a little infirm and very hard of hearing. She answered clearly and firmly, albeit at times a little confused. She was emphatic that she never intended to give her money to the first and second defendants. This, above all else, was clear in her mind and I have no doubt there was no confusion in this regard. I accept her evidence. She had been, during six months before the transaction, in very frail health. In particular, until relatively shortly before, she had been in various stages of confusion and disorientation. It appears to me, on the evidence, that on the balance of probabilities, the plaintiff, at the time of this transaction, was so mentally disordered as to have lost her contractual capacity. The fact she may have been under no such incapacity before or after the transaction does not render such a finding inconsistent with the evidence. The medical evidence clearly shows that, as her General Practitioner stated – "*she was coming and going from time to time*". As late as 23rd November, 2007, she was reported, and her GP agreed, as "*sometimes confused*". This was only two weeks before the transaction.

13–12 He added:

> The bank had, I accept, no direct notice of this incapacity. The only thing, in my view, that could engage the bank's duty would be that the circumstances of the transaction itself were such as should have raised substantial doubt as to the plaintiff's capacity to give instructions. I have considerable sympathy with the bank manager. He gave frank and direct answers to all questions asked. He agreed it was an unusual transaction. He had not before or since come across another like it. There were no written protocols in existence to guide him. He clearly had reservations at the time and did his best as he saw it. I can only look to the facts that presented themselves to him at that time. He had before him an elderly, but apparently capable lady. She was a customer. He owed her the respect due to her status, both as a customer and a senior citizen. I find that he did not know she was in a nursing home nor did he know she had been ill. Yet the requested transaction was a bizarre one. He himself agreed with that. As far as his knowledge of her assets went, she was proposing to divest herself almost entirely and for no consideration whatever. It seems to me that these circumstances alone raise substantial doubts that ought to have been investigated further and resolved. There was no suggestion made of any need for urgency. The manager might have temporised. He might have asked for a medical certificate. He might have insisted on only dealing with her in the company of her solicitor unless she produced such a medical certificate. There may have been other ways in which the process could have been delayed to allow some further investigation or cooling off period. I would consider there should be written protocols to assist managers in such a situation.

13–13 He concluded:

> It seems to me that there were substantial grounds arising from the circumstances herein to doubt the capacity of the plaintiff to give instructions. The manager, in the absence of any protocols to guide him in this most unusual transaction, did not make any real enquiry as to her capacity. His questions to her were only to

[18] [2010] IEHC 348, paras 8.7–8.8.

> elicit her intentions and to advise she give less and also that she see a solicitor. Any further enquiry would have elicited the information that she was living in a nursing home, that she had a nephew who looked out for her and that she had been ill in a way that gave rise to very serious questions about her mental capacity. In my view, the bank breached a duty to enquire as to their customer's capacity where substantial grounds to doubt existed.[19]

Arguable Defences by Bank Customers

13–14 During a hearing for summary judgment a customer may raise an arguable defence, and where successful in doing so, the issue may be remitted to plenary hearing.[20] An arguable defence may be raised relating to the absence of consideration in the contract between bank and customer. In *Allied Irish Banks Plc v O'Donoghue*,[21] the plaintiff by notice of motion for summary judgment claimed that the sum of €1,541,000 was owing and due on foot of a guarantee executed by the defendant on 10 February 2009. It was alleged that the defendant guaranteed payment to the plaintiffs of all and every sum, or sums, of money due, or thereafter to become due, to the plaintiff by a company named Lodge Gaven Limited of which Mr O'Donoghue was a director. The application was grounded upon the affidavit of Ms June MacCabe sworn on 3 September 2015. She was an officer of the plaintiff's financial solutions group, Cork. She averred that the plaintiff provided banking facilities to Lodge Gaven Services Limited over a number of years and that borrowings were habitually supported by a personal guarantee provided by the defendant, limited to a sum approximating to the aggregate liabilities of the sanctioned facilities.

13–15 In his judgment MacGrath J, having identified the principles of summary judgment as found in *Aer Rianta cpt v Ryanair Ltd*[22] and *Harrisrange Ltd v Duncan*,[23] concluded that:

> an arguable defence has been raised concerning the absence of consideration. This defence is likely to involve a consideration of matters of fact and law. Counsel for the plaintiff does not expressly rely on a defence of forbearance to sue, rather it is submitted that consideration was provided in the form of the new guarantee as security for the borrowings and in the context of the extension and restructuring of facilities. The defendant, on the other hand, points to the stated purpose of the facility and the absence of evidence of drawdown of monies after the execution of the guarantee and contends that the guarantee is unsupported by consideration. Taking into account the constitutional rights of both parties and the threshold which has to be met on this application, in my view it cannot be concluded that it is clear that the defendant has no defence on this point, and in those circumstances I find

19 [2010] IEHC 348, paras 8.7–8.8.
20 See Chapter 12.
21 [2019] IEHC 526.
22 [2001] 4 IR 607, 623.
23 [2003] 4 IR 1, 7.

> that this is an appropriate case in which to grant the defendant liberty to defend on this ground and to transfer the case to plenary hearing.

13–16 The court upon hearing a motion for summary judgment may decide that a defendant has an arguable defence on grounds that there was a potential for a conflict between the wording of a guarantee and a facility letter, and remit the issue for plenary hearing. In *Stapleford Finance DAC v Tuthill*,[24] proceedings were instituted by way of summary summons issued on 16 March 2017. The plaintiff claimed, in total, the sum of €143,364.86 against the defendants on foot of guarantees provided by them on 22 March 2001, in respect of the debts of Adson Salons Limited to whom monies were advanced by way of facility letter dated 22 March 2001 by Anglo Irish Bank Corporation. The sum advanced to the company was €250,000 to be repaid by instalments over 84 months. Letters of demand were issued to the company on 7 December 2015 seeking immediate repayment of the sum which was then due of €134,760.44. On 16 December 2016 the plaintiff served a demand on the defendants in respect of their alleged liability for sums due on foot of the guarantees. Letters of demand were issued to the company on 7 December 2015 seeking immediate repayment of the sum which was then due of €134,760.44. On 16 December 2016 the plaintiff served a demand on the defendants in respect of their alleged liability for sums due on foot of the guarantees. By application pursuant to the notice of motion dated 5 April 2018 the plaintiff sought an order pursuant to Ord 37 of the RSC for judgment against the defendants in the sum of €143,364.89.

13–17 In his judgment at paras 20 and 21, MacGrath J stated:

> There is no disagreement between the parties as to the principles applicable in an application such as this. As described by Irvine J. in *AIB v Stack* [2018] IECA128, the court must be satisfied that it is very clear that the defendant has no defence of the proceedings, otherwise the case ought to be adjourned for plenary hearing. She also stated that the threshold which the defendant must achieve in order to satisfy the court to transfer the case to plenary hearing is a low one. Nevertheless, the suggested defence must amount to more than a mere assertion. There must be substance to the proposed defence and it must be based on facts which, if true and established, would amount to a defence. It also must be credible.
>
> Applying these principles, the defendants contend that the defence which they wish to advance is demonstrably stateable as a matter of law.

13–18 He went on to state at para 27:

> Having considered the submissions of the parties, and the authorities upon which reliance has been placed, it is clear that the terms of the guarantee, as a matter of law, that any ambiguity or lack of clarity surrounding the guarantee ought to be resolved in favour of the guarantor. In this case, the guarantee upon which the

[24] [2020] IEHC 44.

> plaintiff seeks to rely is that which is contained in a document which, in sequence, appears and arises immediately after the main facility letter, prior to that part of the document which contains the resolution executed by the company and also prior to where the general conditions are contained. The facility letter states that if there is any conflict between the terms of the facility letter and the general conditions, the terms of the facility letter shall prevail. The general conditions do not appear to make any specific reference to the terms of the guarantee and it seems to me, on the face of it, it is arguable that given the reference to the facility letter under the heading "borrowers acceptance", that they must be read together. That being the case, there is a potential for a conflict between the wording of the guarantee as relied upon by the plaintiff, and clause 3 of the facility letter. The court does not have to be satisfied that this is a case which will ultimately be made out at trial, merely that it is arguable. Bearing in mind the constitutional rights of the first named defendant to defend proceedings brought against her, I am not satisfied that it is clear that the defendant has no arguable defence either as a matter of law or as a matter of fact. The position of the second named defendant is somewhat less clear. She has not sworn any affidavit but it seems to me that in the interests of justice the entire matter should be referred to plenary hearing where all issues concerning the liability of the defendants and the validity of the guarantees can be agitated.

He concluded: "In all the circumstances, I must refuse the relief sought and transfer the matter to plenary hearing." **13–19**

Where the arguable defence shows that there is incomplete evidence of the contract between the bank and a customer the court may refer the matter to plenary hearing. In *Allied Irish Banks Plc v Purcell*[25] Barrett J stated that: **13–20**

> Given AIB's failure, for no good reason, to put the complete loan agreement before the court – thereby rendering it impossible for the court to identify the nature of the liability arising on the part of the third-named defendant – the clear respective answers to questions [1], [2] and [3] in the just-quoted text is, for the reasons outlined previously above, [1] "No", [2] "No", and [3] "No". What the position would be if the court had the complete loan agreement before it cannot be known; it may be, for example, that the complete contract makes provision concerning waivers of security requirements. However, for the avoidance of doubt, on the basis of such (incomplete) evidence as is now before the court, and confronted, as it is, with a situation where (a) a lending institution has elected not to insist on compliance with a particular security obligation, (b) in circumstances where compliance with such obligation (I) would have conferred a benefit on a borrower and (II) that security obligation had been agreed to be a pre-condition to drawdown, the court arrives at the same conclusion in respect of questions [1], [2] and [3] above.
>
> Having regard to all of the foregoing, and mindful, *inter alia*, of that "*discernible caution*" which McKechnie J. indicates in *Harrisrange Ltd v Duncan* [2003] 4 IR 1, 7, should be brought to the exercise of the power to grant summary judgment, there is no question but that this is a case which requires to be sent to plenary hearing.[26]

[25] [2018] IEHC 534, para 33.

[26] [2018] IEHC 534, paras 7–9.

13–21 Where a partial issue concerning the amount of interest owing and due on a loan is raised and accepted as an arguable defence the court may remit that issue only to plenary hearing, though otherwise granting summary judgment to the plaintiff. In *Bank of Ireland Mortgage Bank v Mavroudis*[27] the court remitted a single issue regarding the amount of interest accruing on a loan to plenary hearing. In that case, the plaintiff sought summary judgment in the sum of €300,401.66, plus interest accruing from 3 October 2015. These were monies lent by the plaintiff to the defendant and were not repaid. The defendant did not dispute the fact that he borrowed these monies, and that he had not repaid them. However, the defendant sought to have the plaintiff's claim remitted to plenary hearing. The defendant also alleged that he was overcharged on interest in the sum of €16,201.08 in respect of a facility letter between the plaintiff and defendant. Meenan J stated that the principles which the court had to apply on an application for summary judgment were well established, and referred to the decision of Hardiman J in *Aer Rianta cpt v Ryanair Ltd*,[28] and that of Clarke J (as he then was) in *McGrath v O'Driscoll*,[29] and found:

> I am satisfied that, save for the issue of interest, the defendant has failed to establish any defence as would permit this court to direct a plenary hearing in the action. I therefore will grant the plaintiff judgment in the sum of €284,101 (plus interest that may have accrued), and remit the sum of €16,300 to plenary hearing.

An Arguable Defence Based on the Superimposition of a Constructive Trust on a Bank's Duty to Enquire

13–22 It may be argued that a bank's duty to enquire in cases where a customer is incapable of giving instructions may create a constructive trust superimposed on the bank's duty to enquire, and indeed, as a result, may also establish a fiduciary relationship between the bank and such customer, and further, as such, may be recognised by the court as forming the basis of an arguable defence in an application for summary judgment.

13–23 Equity has traditionally protected vulnerable persons by providing a variety of remedies such as undue influence or improvident transactions to address circumstances where vulnerable persons were exploited or taken advantage of when entering into transactions. In furtherance of the traditional role, equity may also intervene to assist a vulnerable person who is customer of a bank and who is incapable of giving instructions when negotiating the terms of a loan with his or her bank due to illness and old age or a "mix of

---

[27] [2020] IEHC 136.
[28] [2001] 4 IR 607.
[29] [2007] 1 ILRM 203, 210.

circumstances", and who intends to engage in an improvident transaction to the knowledge of the bank. In *Bourke v O'Donnell*,[30] Hedigan J, when referring to a bank's duty to enquire in such circumstances, stated that:

> where there are circumstances attendant upon a transaction that clearly raise substantial grounds to doubt the capacity of its customer to give instructions, the bank has a duty to make enquiry. It is obvious that such a situation would be rare. Certainly, the mere fact that a customer is elderly could not give rise to such a duty. Something more would have to be present in the mix of circumstances.

It may be argued that equity may intervene and superimpose a constructive trust to protect a vulnerable customer in circumstances that give rise to a bank's duty to enquire, and indeed, equity may further render a bank a fiduciary arising out of the creation of the superimposed constructive trust.[31] The superimposition of a constructive trust on a bank's duty to enquire may also be raised as an arguable defence in such circumstances where a bank seeks to enforce payment of a debt by summary judgment. **13–24**

The argument for the superimposition of a constructive trust on a bank's duty to enquire, and also for the purposes of rendering a bank a fiduciary of a vulnerable or incapacitated customer and owing duties accordingly, may be advanced and based on the following propositions: **13–25**

(i) A bank has duty to enquire where there are substantial doubts surrounding a customer's capacity to give instructions, and who is about to enter an improvident transaction.[32]
(ii) The protection of vulnerable persons has always been a major concern to equity, and that this concern may also be extended to vulnerable and incapacitated customers of banks.[33]
(iii) The circumstances which give rise to a duty to enquire by a bank may also give rise to the creation of a constructive trust superimposed on that duty.[34]
(iv) The imposition of a constructive trust superimposed on a bank's duty to enquire may also have the effect of elevating the relationship of bank and vulnerable customer to that of a fiduciary relationship.
(v) The relationship of bank and vulnerable customer does not fall within the settled categories of fiduciary relationships.
(vi) However, in *Clements v Meagher*[35] Feeney J, when speaking of persons who occupy fiduciary positions, stated that:
"It is not possible to provide a complete definition of the categories of persons who occupy fiduciary positions. The categories of fiduciary

---

30 [2010] IEHC 348, para 8.6.
31 See *Clements v Meagher* [2008] IEHC 258.
32 See *Bourke v O'Donnell* [2010] IEHC 348, paras 8.7–8.8).
33 See *Grealish v Murphy* [1946] IR 35, 49–50; *McGuirk v Branigan*, unreported, High Court, Morris J, 9 November 1992; *Carroll v Carroll* [1998] 2 ILRM 218; *Prendergast v Joyce* [2009] IEHC 199; *Secured Property Loans Ltd v Floyd* [2011] IEHC 189.
34 See *Bourke v O'Donnell* [2010] IEHC 348, paras 8.7–8.8.
35 [2008] IEHC 258, para 3.1.

relationships are not closed and it is well recognised that fiduciary duties may be owed notwithstanding the fact that the relationship in question does not fall within one of the settled categories of fiduciary relationships."

(vii) There is nothing to prevent the extension of the categories of persons who occupy fiduciary positions to include a bank and vulnerable customer arising out of the imposition of a constructive trust, and also rendering a bank a trustee and fiduciary of the vulnerable customer.

(viii) The foregoing propositions may also give rise to the superimposition of a constructive trust on a bank's duty to enquire may form the basis of an arguable defence in applications for summary judgment of debts.

Part IV

DISCOVERY OF DOCUMENTS, DELIVERY OF INTERROGATORIES, INJUNCTIONS AND COSTS

Chapter 14

DISCOVERY OF DOCUMENTS

Introduction

Where a litigant party withholds relevant, necessary and material documents the other party to the action may apply to the court for discovery of those documents. Order 31, r 12(1) of the Rules of the Superior Courts (RSC) as amended by SI No 93 of 2009 provides the rules relating to applications to the court by notice of motion for discovery of documents. Order 31, r 12(1) of the RSC provides that: **14–01**

> (1) Any party may apply to the court by way of notice of motion for an order directing any other party to any cause or matter to make discovery on oath of the documents which are or have been in his possession, power or procurement relating to any matter in question therein. Every such notice of motion shall specify the precise categories of documents in respect of which discovery is sought and shall be grounded upon the affidavit of the party seeking such an order of discovery which shall:
>
> (a) verify that the discovery of documents sought is necessary for disposing fairly of the cause or matter or for saving costs;
>
> (b) furnish the reasons why each category of documents is required to be discovered, and
>
> (c) where the discovery sought includes electronically stored information, specify whether such party seeks the production of any documents in searchable form and if so, whether for that purpose the party seeking discovery seeks the provision of inspection and searching facilities using any information and communications technology system owned or operated by the party requested.

The court may order discovery of documents where the documents sought "are both relevant and necessary for the fair disposal of the case or to save costs".[1] In *Ryanair plc v Aer Rianta cpt*[2] Fennelly J stated that, in order to discover particular categories of documents it must be shown that they are "necessary for disposing fairly of the cause or matter", but the applicant for discovery does not have to prove that they are in any sense "absolutely necessary" to the cause or matter. However, instead of applying for discovery of documents "more efficient methods of disclosure should first be pursued", **14–02**

---

1 See Rules of the Superior Courts, Ord 31, r12, as amended by 2009 by SI No 93 of 2009; *Tobin v Minister for Defence* [2019] IESC 57; *Promontoria (Aran) Ltd v Sheehy* [2020] IECA 104.

2 [2003] IESC 62, [2003] 4 IR 264, 277; see *Compagnie Financiere et Commerciale du Pacifique v Peruvian Guano* (1882) 11 QBD 55.

to seek the same information, such as by the delivery of interrogatories.[3] In *Dunnes Stores v McCann*[4] Barniville J stated that:

> If it can be shown that there are alternative means of establishing the issues in respect of which the discovery is sought other than by discovery, then the party seeking discovery may have a difficulty in discharging the onus of showing that the discovery sought is necessary in that sense.

14–03 The principles applied by the courts when considering whether or not to make an order for discovery of documents were summarised by Clarke CJ in *Tobin v Minister for Defence*.[5]

Rules of Discovery of Documents

14–04 The rules for discovery of documents are found in Ord 31 of the RSC as amended by the RSC (Discovery) 2009, SI No 93 of 2009. The RSC (Discovery) 2009, SI No 93 of 2009, amended Ord 31, r12(2) of the RSC primarily to include the discovery of electronically stored information. In relation to the hearing of applications by the court for discovery of documents Ord 31, r12(2) of the RSC provides that:

> On the hearing of application for discovery of documents the court may:
> (a) either refuse or adjourn the same, if satisfied that such discovery is not necessary, or not necessary at that stage of the cause or matter, or by virtue of non-compliance with the provisions of sub-rule (6), or
> (b) make an order for discovery either in terms of some or all of the categories of documents sought or limited to certain documents or classes of documents within any or all of those categories, or otherwise as may be thought fit, and on terms as to security for the costs of discovery or otherwise, and for this purpose may adjourn the application in part;
> (c) where the discovery ordered includes electronically stored information and the Court is satisfied that such electronically stored information is held in searchable form and can be provided in the manner hereinafter referred to without significant cost to the party from whom discovery is requested:
> (i) further order that the documents or classes of documents specified in such order be provided electronically in the searchable form in which they are held by the party ordered to make discovery, or
> (ii) where the Court is satisfied that such documents or classes of documents, or any information within such documents, could not, if provided electronically, be subjected to a search by the party

[3] See *Anglo Irish Bank Corporation Ltd. v Browne* [2011] IEHC 140; *McCabe v Irish Life Assurance Plc* [2015] IECA 239, [2015] 1 IR 346; *Dunnes Stores & Anor v McCann* [2018] IEHC 123; *Allied Irish Bank Plc v Doran* [2020] IEHC 210.

[4] [2018] IEHC 123, para 36; see *McCabe v Irish Life Assurance Plc* [2015] IECA 239.

[5] See *Tobin v Minister for Defence* [2019] IESC 57, paras 6–7.

seeking discovery without incurring unreasonable expense, further order that the party ordered to make discovery make available inspection and searching facilities using its own information and communications technology system, so as to allow the party seeking discovery to avail of any search functionality available to the party ordered to make discovery.

(3) (a) Any order made under sub-rule (2)(c) may include such provision or restriction and be subject to such undertakings from any party or person as the Court may consider necessary to ensure that documents discovery of which has not been ordered are not accessed or accessible, and otherwise to secure the information and communications technology system concerned.

(b) Such order may in particular include a provision that the inspection and searching of documents shall be undertaken by an independent expert or person agreed between the parties, or appointed by the Court in default of agreement (instead of being undertaken by the party seeking discovery), who may conduct such inspections and searches as may be required and report the results to the party seeking discovery.

(c) Where such order makes provision for inspection and searching of documents in the manner referred to in paragraph (b), the party seeking the order shall indemnify such independent expert or person in respect of all fees and expenses reasonably incurred by him, and the fees and expenses so indemnified shall form part of the costs of that party for the purposes of Order 99.

(4) (a) Documents of the same or a similar nature and not in electronic form, when numerous, shall so far as possible be grouped together and numbered or otherwise sufficiently marked so as to be identifiable.

(b) Parties providing discovery shall list documents or categories of information, and shall provide documents and information for inspection, in a manner corresponding with the categories in the agreement or order for discovery and, subject to any such agreement or order, in a sequence corresponding with the manner in which the documents or information have been stored or kept in the usual course of business by the party making discovery.

(5) An order shall not be made under this rule if and so far as the Court shall be of opinion that it is not necessary either for disposing fairly of the cause or matter or for saving costs.

(6) An order under sub-rule (2) directing any party or under rule 29 directing any other person to make discovery shall not be made unless:

(*a*) the applicant for same shall have previously applied by letter in writing requesting that discovery be made voluntarily—

(i) specifying the precise categories of documents in respect of which discovery is sought,

(ii) furnishing the reasons why each category of documents is required to be discovered,

(iii) where the discovery sought includes electronically stored information, specifying whether the applicant seeks the production of any documents in searchable form and if so, whether for that purpose the applicant seeks the provision of inspection and searching facilities using any information and communications technology system owned or operated by the party requested, and

(*b*) a reasonable period of time for such discovery has been allowed, and

(*c*) the party or person requested has failed, refused or neglected to make such discovery or has ignored such request.

Provided that in any case where by reason of the urgency of the matter or the consent of the parties, the nature of the case or any other circumstances which to the Court seem appropriate, the Court may make such order as appears proper, without the necessity for such prior application in writing.

(7) Any such discovery sought and agreed between parties or between parties and any other person shall, subject to sub-rule (9), be made in like manner and form and have such effect as if directed by order of the Court.

(8) In any case in which discovery has been sought and agreed and has not been made within the time agreed, the party who has sought same may make application pursuant to rule 21 provided that when seeking discovery the party requested was informed that:

(*a*) such voluntary discovery was being sought pursuant to Order 31, rule 12;

(*b*) agreement to make discovery would require it to be made in like manner and form and would have such effect as if directed by order;

(*c*) failure to make the discovery may result in an application pursuant to rule 21;

and the Court may if satisfied that it is proper so to do, make such order under this rule, rule 19 or rule 21 as is appropriate or such other order as appears just in the circumstances.

(9) An application for discovery whether under sub-rule (1) or (6) shall be made not later than twenty-eight days after the action has been set down or in matters which are not set down, twenty-eight days after it has been listed for trial provided that the Court may order or the party requested may agree, to extend the time for the application for discovery in any case in which it appears just and reasonable to do so.

(10) The costs of an application to Court for discovery in any case in which prior written application has not been made or in which application has not been made within the time provided, shall be in the discretion of the Court.

(11) Any party concerned by the effect of an order or agreement for discovery may at any time, by motion on notice to each other party concerned, apply to the Court for an order varying the terms of the discovery order or agreement. The Court may vary the terms of such order or agreement where it is satisfied that—

(i) further discovery is necessary for disposing fairly of the case or for saving costs, or

(ii) the discovery originally ordered or agreed is unreasonable having regard to the cost or other burden of providing discovery.

(12) An order under sub-rule (11) shall not be made unless:

(*a*) the applicant for same shall have previously applied by letter in writing to the other party specifying the variations sought to the order, furnishing the reasons why each variation is sought and requesting that party's agreement to the variations sought, and

(*b*) a reasonable period of time for agreement has been allowed, and
(*c*) the party or person requested has failed, refused or neglected to agree to such variation or has ignored such request.

(13) "documents", for the purposes of this rule and rule 29, includes all electronically stored information, and the reference to "business documents" in rule 20 shall be construed accordingly.

The precedent affidavit of discovery of documents pursuant to Ord 31, r13 is as follows: **14–05**

AFFIDAVIT AS TO DOCUMENTS
[Title of action]

I .... make oath and say as follows:—

1. I have in my possession, power or procurement the documents [*and electronically stored information*]* relating to the matters in question in this suit and falling within the relevant categories of documents specified

*in the letter requesting voluntary discovery dated ……. 20....

*in the order of the Master of this Honourable Court made on ……….. 20…..

set forth in the first and second parts of the first schedule hereto.

2. I object to produce the said documents [and electronically stored information]* set forth in the second part of the said first schedule hereto.

3. That [*here state upon what grounds the objection is made, and verify the facts as far as may be*].

4. I have had, but have not now, in my possession, power or procurement the documents [*and electronically stored information*]* relating to the matters in question in this suit set forth in the second schedule hereto.

5. The last mentioned documents [*and electronically stored information*]* were last in my possession, power or procurement on [*state when*].

6. That [*here state what has become of the last-mentioned documents or information, and in whose possession they now are*].

7. According to the best of my knowledge, information, and belief, I have not now, and never had in my possession, power or procurement or in the possession, custody or power of my solicitors or agents, solicitor or agent,

or in the possession, custody or power of any other persons, or person on my behalf, any document of any kind or any electronically stored information, or any copy of or extract from any such document or information, relating to the matters in question in this suit, or any of them, or wherein any entry has been made relative to such matters, or any of them, and falling within the relevant categories of documents specified

*in the letter requesting voluntary discovery dated ……... 20....

*in the order of the Master of this Honourable Court made on ……….. 20…..

other than and except the documents [*and information*]* set forth in the said first and second schedules hereto.

8. I understand that the obligation on a party giving discovery is to discover all documents and electronically stored information within his/her/its possession, power or procurement within the categories agreed or ordered to be delivered that contain information which may enable the party receiving the discovery to advance its own case or to damage the case of the party giving discovery or which may fairly lead to a train of inquiry which may have either of those consequences.

Sworn, &c.

Note—

(i) Documents of the same or a similar nature, when numerous, must so far as possible, be grouped together and numbered or otherwise sufficiently marked so as to be identifiable.

(ii) Parties providing discovery shall list documents or categories of information, and shall provide documents and information for inspection, in a manner corresponding with the categories in the agreement or order for discovery, or in a sequence corresponding with the manner in which the documents or information have been stored or kept in the usual course of business by the party making discovery.

The Clarke Principles of Discovery

14–06 The principles relating to the discovery of documents were summarised by Clarke CJ in *Tobin v Minister for Defence*[6] as follows:

[6] See *Tobin v Minister for Defence* [2019] IESC 57, paras 6–7.

(i) The primary principles are relevance and of necessity.[7]
(ii) The proportionality test may be viewed as a refinement of the concept of "necessity".[8]
(iii) "Necessity" means that the disclosure of the documents concerned may be necessary for the fair and just resolution of the proceedings and potentially for saving costs.
(iv) If it cannot be demonstrated that documents are relevant, then there could be no basis for requiring that they be discovered.
(v) The default position should be that a document whose relevance has been established should be considered to be one whose production is necessary.
(vi) A default position is capable of being displaced for a range of other reasons.
(vii) Access to justice has been impaired even where it cannot be demonstrated that a relevant party could not afford the burden of making full discovery.[9]
(viii) A party required to expend a great deal of money on making full discovery may be inhibited in its ability to properly conduct litigation even if could not be heard to say that it did not have the money to do so.[10]
(ix) It is incumbent on a party who may wish to argue that the discovery sought is excessively burdensome, to set forward in its response, and in some reasonable detail, just why that is said to be so.
(x) A requested party should, in its response, indicate why it does not consider that what might otherwise be regarded as "full" discovery should be ordered, set out any facts relevant to an assessment of that question and go on, if it is thought appropriate, to suggest any alternative means by which, short of full discovery, the legitimate requirements of the proper administration of justice, in all the circumstances of the case in question, could be met.
(xi) The initial burden of establishing both relevance and necessity rests on the requesting party.
(xii) In the event of a court being required to adjudicate on such matters, then, to the extent that the reasons for suggesting that discovery of any particular category of document is not "necessary" is dependent on facts, it is for the requested party to place evidence before the courts to establish the relevant facts. To the extent that the opposition to discovery may be based on legal argument, then it is for the requested party to put forward its reasons as to why production is not necessary.
(xiii) It is for the requesting party to establish the relevance of the documents whose discovery is sought but it is for the requested party to establish, whether by facts or argument, that discovery is not necessary even though the documents sought have been shown to be relevant.
(xiv) It is for the requesting party to establish the relevance of the documents whose discovery is sought but it is for the requested party to establish, whether by

---

7 See *Ryanair plc v Aer Rianta cpt* [2003] IESC 62, [2003] 4 IR 264, 277; see *Compagnie Financiere et Commerciale du Pacifique v Peruvian Guano* (1882) 11 QBD 55; *Framus Ltd v CRH plc* [2004] IESC 25, [2004] 2 IR 20, 36.

8 See *Tobin v Minister for Defence* [2019] IESC 57; *Dome Telecom Ltd. v Eircom Ltd* [2007] IESC 59, [2008] 2 IR 726; *Astrazeneca AB and Ors v Pinewood Laboratories Ltd & Ors* [2011] IEHC 159; *Persona Digital Telephony Limited & Anor v Minister for Public Enterprise & Ors* [2017] IESC 27 and *SPV Osus Ltd v HSBC Institutional Trust Services (Ireland) Limited & Ors* [2018] IESC 44.

9 See *Tobin v Minister for Defence* [2019] IESC 57; See *Tobin v Minister for Defence* [2019] IESC 57, paras 6.3–6.5; *Persona Digital Telephony Limited & Anor v Minister for Public Enterprise & Ors* [2017] IESC 27; and *SPV Osus Ltd v HSBC Institutional Trust Services (Ireland) Limited & Ors* [2018] IESC 44.

10 See *Tobin v Minister for Defence* [2019] IESC 57, paras 7.7–7.9.

facts or argument, that discovery is not necessary even though the documents sought have been shown to be relevant.

(xv) A requesting party must establish that they have exhausted all other procedures available to establish relevant facts before discovery can be sought. In many straightforward cases, there would be no conceivable basis for declining discovery of all relevant documents, for the imposition of an obligation to make such discovery may not be burdensome at all and questions of proportionality or alternative methods of obtaining relevant information and evidence may not truly arise.

(xvi) A requesting party needs to deal with those issues of necessity after a case has been made to the effect that it is not necessary, for any of the reasons explored in this judgment, that all potentially relevant documents be discovered.

(xvii) The question of relevance is determined by reference to the pleadings.

(xviii) It is appropriate for a court to take into account the manner in which the case is pleaded, not only for the purposes of determining relevance, but also to assess the extent to which a party who objects to making discovery, on the grounds that it is excessively burdensome, has contributed to that situation by the manner in which they have pleaded their case.

(xix) As the application of the above principles is one for judges dealing with the preparation of cases and since issues as to relevance, necessity and proportionality involve an adjudication based on a detailed understanding of the case, in general decisions as to discovery should involve a significant measure of appreciation by any appellate court reviewing a decision at first instance.

(xx) Where litigation is under case management by a judge with an intimate knowledge of the issues involved, those considerations heighten. In any event, where an order made on a consideration of affidavit evidence and pleadings is appealed, the burden of demonstrating as a probability that the decision made is wrong rests on the appellant from the original High Court order.

(xxi) It would be disproportionate to order an immediate discovery of confidential documents in circumstances where it was unclear whether they would be relevant to the issues which will arise at the trial. Instead, an order was made requiring that the relevant documents were recorded and preserved in order to ensure that they would be available, if required, for production at trial, if it was established that they were necessary to the proper resolution of the case.[11]

(xxii) The fact that confidentiality (as opposed to privilege) does not provide a legitimate basis for refusing to require disclosure of documents should they prove necessary to the proper administration of justice. But they do provide a warrant for the court adopting appropriate measures to respect the importance of confidentiality by ensuring that it is only displaced when the production of confidential documentation proves truly necessary to the just resolution of proceedings.[12]

14–07 In *Tobin v Minister for Defence*[13] Clarke CJ also pointed out that the "default

---

[11] See *Tobin v Minister for Defence* [2019] IESC 57, para 7.11; *Yap v Children's University Hospital* (Unreported, High Court, Clarke J, 1 June 2006); *Hartside Ltd v Heineken Ireland Ltd* [2010] IEHC 3; *Flogas Ireland Ltd v Tru Gas Ltd & Ors* [2012] IEHC 259.

[12] See *Tobin v Minister for Defence* [2019] IESC 57, para 7.12.

[13] [2019] IESC 57, para 7.16; see *Clydaville Investments Ltd v Setanta Centre* [2020]

position" is that "a document whose relevance has been established should be considered to be one whose production is necessary". He went on to state:

> However, that remains only a default position and one which is capable of being displaced for a range of other reasons. If it can be demonstrated that compliance with the obligation to make the discovery sought would be particularly burdensome, then a court will have to weigh in the balance, in deciding whether discovery is truly "necessary", a range of factors, including the extent of the burden which compliance will be likely to place on the party concerned, the extent to which it might reasonably be expected that any of the contested documentation whose discovery is sought will play a reasonably important role in the proper resolution of proceedings and, importantly, the extent to which there may be other means of achieving the same end as that which is sought to be achieved by discovery but at a much reduced cost.

In *Promontoria (Aran) Ltd v Sheehy*[14] the primary claim in the proceedings was to recover monies claimed on foot of loan facilities with Ulster Bank, which loans together with associated security had been acquired by the appellant. The respondent sought and obtained discovery in Category 4 of all documents relating to the amount paid by the appellant for the transfer of the loans. Discovery was resisted by the appellant on grounds that the documents were confidential and commercially sensitive. Haughton J, having referred to *Tobin v Minister for Defence*[15] and *Yap v Children's University Hospital*,[16] *Independent Newspapers (Ireland) Ltd v Murphy*,[17] *Hartside Ltd v Heineken Ireland Ltd* [2010] IEHC 3, *Flogas Ireland Ltd v Tru Gas Ltd*,[18] concluded that: **14–08**

> The Appellant has failed to demonstrate that the trial judge erred in principle in his decision to grant Category 4 discovery to the limitations and undertakings set out in his Order, or that the trial judge was probably wrong. The discovery so ordered is relevant to advance the defence of the case pleaded in the alternative by the Appellant, and is necessary for fairly disposing of issues that arise. In that the documents may be confidential and commercially sensitive the trial judge carried out an appropriate balancing exercise in reaching his decision, and the order made is proportionate having regard to the restrictions and undertakings which adequately protect the Appellant and all of borrowers from any wider disclosure than is necessary for the purpose of defending the proceedings. I would dismiss the appeal and affirm the judgment and order of the High Court.

The time, cost and effort involved in making discovery must also be proportionate to the objective to be attained. The onus of proof rests upon the party seeking discovery to prove that the documents sought are relevant to the issues in the case and necessary for its fair disposal or for saving costs. **14–09**

IEHC 287.

14 [2020] IECA 104.

15 [2019] IESC 57.

16 Unreported, High Court, Clarke J, 1 June 2006.

17 [2006] IEHC 276, [2006] 3 IR 566.

18 [2012] IEHC 259.

14–10 A party is only obliged to produce on discovery documents either in his possession or in respect of which he has a legal right to demand their production.[19] In *Dwyer v Dowling*[20] Noonan J stated that:

> ... while a party making discovery is required to discover relevant documents within his or her possession or procurement, there is no onus on a deponent to carry out an extensive investigation to establish if other parties might potentially have in their possession documents which could possibly have some relevance to the issues in the case.

14–11 He also commented that:

> Many judges in recent times have expressed serious misgivings about the discovery process as it currently stands and of the fact that frequently, grossly disproportionate costs are incurred in the pursuit of discovery which often bears little or no fruit. It is widely recognised as an area of the law in need of urgent reform.

[19] See *Thema International v HSBC* [2013] 1 IR 274; *Dwyer v Dowling* [2019] IEHC 271.

[20] [2019] IEHC 271.

Chapter 15

DELIVERY OF INTERROGATORIES AND PRIVILEGED COMMUNICATIONS

Introduction

The rules relating to the delivery of interrogatories are found in Ord 31, rr1–11 of the Rules of the Superior Courts (RSC). Order 31, r1 of the RSC provides as follows: **15–01**

> 1. In any cause or matter where relief by way of damages or otherwise is sought on the ground of fraud or breach of trust, the plaintiff may at any time after delivering his statement of claim, and a defendant may at or after the time of delivering his defence, without any order for that purpose, and in every other cause or matter any party may by leave of the Court, upon such terms as to security for costs or otherwise as the Court may direct, deliver interrogatories in writing for the examination of the opposite parties, or any one or more of such parties, and such interrogatories when delivered shall have a note at the foot thereof, stating which of such interrogatories each of such persons is required to answer: provided that no party shall deliver more than one set of interrogatories to the same party without an order for that purpose; provided also that interrogatories which do not relate to any matters in question in the cause or matter shall be deemed irrelevant, notwithstanding that they might be admissible on the oral cross-examination of a witness.

The delivery of interrogatories, besides providing an alternative method of seeking relevant and necessary information, is also a less expensive and less time-consuming method. In *McCabe v Irish Life Assurance plc*[1] the Court of Appeal stated that: **15–02**

> Often the delivery of interrogatories can obviate the necessity for expensive and time consuming discovery, can dispose of issues prior to trial, can lessen the number of witnesses and result in an overall shortening of trials. In many cases which lend themselves to the delivery of interrogatories the procedure is simply ignored.

In *Allied Irish Bank plc v Doran*[2] Simons J summarised the general principles that govern the delivery of interrogatories garnered from former case law on the matter. **15–03**

---

1 [2015] IECA 239.
2 [2020] IEHC 210.

15–04 Where a party claims that communications in his or her possession are privileged, a distinction may be made between communications seeking legal advice that are privileged, and communications seeking legal assistance that are not privileged. In *Smurfit Paribas Limited v AAB Export Finance Limited*[3] Finlay CJ stated that privilege should:

> therefore, in my view, only be granted by the courts in instances which have been identified as securing an objective which in the public interest in the proper conduct of the administration of justice can be said to outweigh the disadvantage arising from the restriction of disclosure of all facts.

15–05 In *Prendergast v McLoughlin*[4] Clarke J (as he then was), when considering what kind of documents may be classified as privileged, referred to *Ochre Ridge Limited v Cork Bonded Warehouses Limited and Port of Cork Company Limited*[5] where Lavan J set out twelve criteria which can assist in determining whether a relevant communication can be said to be made in the context of legal advice on the one hand or legal assistance on the other. When accepting and applying the criteria formulated by Lavan J in *Ochre Ridge Limited v Cork Bonded Warehouses Limited and Port of Cork Company Limited*,[6] Clarke J stated that they were of considerable assistance in attempting to define the boundary between legal advice and legal assistance.

Delivery of Interrogatories

15–06 The rules relating to the delivery of interrogatories are found in Ord. 31, rr1–11 of the RSC. Order 31, rr2–11 provide as follows:

> 2. A copy of the interrogatories proposed to be delivered shall be delivered with the notice of application for leave to deliver them, unless the Court shall otherwise order, and the particular interrogatories sought to be delivered shall be submitted to and considered by the Court. In deciding upon such application, the Court shall take into account any offer which may be made by the party sought to be interrogated, to deliver particulars, or to make admissions, or to produce documents, relating to any matter in question. Leave shall be given as to such only of the interrogatories as shall be considered necessary either for disposing fairly of the cause or matter or for saving costs.
>
> 3.[4] In adjudicating the costs of the cause or matter, inquiry shall at the instance of any party be made into the reasonableness of exhibiting such interrogatories. If it is the opinion of the Legal Costs Adjudicator or of the Court, with or without an application for inquiry, that such interrogatories have been exhibited unreasonably,

[3] [1990] 1 IR 469; *Prendergast v McLoughlin* [2008] IEHC 296.
[4] [2008] IEHC 296.
[5] Unreported, High Court, Lavan J, 13 July 2004.
[6] Unreported, High Court, Lavan J, 13 July 2004.

the costs occasioned by those interrogatories and the answers thereto shall be paid in any event by the party found to have behaved unreasonably.

4. Interrogatories shall be in the Form No 8 in Appendix C.

5. If any party to a cause or matter be a body corporate or a joint stock company, whether incorporated or not, or any other body of persons, empowered by law to sue or be sued, whether in its own name or in the name of any officer or other person, any opposite party may apply for an order allowing him to deliver interrogatories to any member or officer of such corporation, company, or body, and an order may be made accordingly.

6. Any objection to answering any one or more of several interrogatories on the ground that it is or they are scandalous or irrelevant, or not bona fide for the purpose of the cause or matter, or that the matters inquired into are not sufficiently material at that stage, or on any other ground, may be taken in the affidavit in answer.

7. Any interrogatories may be set aside on the ground that they have been exhibited unreasonably or vexatiously, or struck out on the ground that they are prolix, oppressive, unnecessary, or scandalous: and any application for this purpose may be made within seven days after service of the interrogatories.

8. Interrogatories shall be answered by affidavit to be filed within ten days, or within such other time as the Court may allow.

9. An affidavit in answers to interrogatories shall be in the Form No 9 in Appendix C.

10. No exception shall be taken to any affidavit in answer but the sufficiency or otherwise of any such affidavit objected to as insufficient shall be determined by the Court on motion.

11. If any person interrogated omits to answer, or answers insufficiently, the party interrogating may apply to the Court for an order requiring him to answer, or to answer further, as the case may be; and an order may be made requiring him to answer or answer further, either by affidavit or by viva voce examination, as the Court may direct.

The following precedent may be used when issuing interrogatories: **15–07**

INTERRROGATORIES

[*Title of action*]

Interrogatories on behalf of the (*plaintiff or defendant*) for the examination of the *[defendant or plaintiff]*.

1. Did not, &c.,?

2. Has not, &c.,?

&c., &c.,

ANSWER TO INTERROGATORIES.

[*Title of action*].

The answer of the to the interrogatories for his or her examination by the (*plaintiff or defendant*)

In answer to the said interrogatories, I, the above-named (*plaintiff or defendant*) make oath and say as follows:—

15–08 In *Anglo Irish Bank Corporation Ltd v Browne*[7] Kelly J, when considering the issuing of interrogatories as an alternative to discovery of documents, stated that:

> Discovery ought not to be ordered where the information sought to be gleaned by it is capable of being obtained by an alternative less expensive and less time consuming method. In this regard, I have in mind the use of interrogatories.

15–09 And went on to state:

> When seeking to obtain information from their opponents, the first port of call ought not to be requests for discovery if it is probable that the information which is being sought is capable of being elicited by an adroit use of interrogatories.

15–10 In *Allied Irish Bank plc v Doran*[8] Simons J, when commenting on the delivery and objectives of interrogatories, observed:

> One of the procedural tools available to a litigant is the ability, in certain circumstances, to compel the other party to the proceedings to answer questions on oath prior to the trial. This is done by the delivery of interrogatories. These take the form of written questions (usually admitting of a "yes or no" answer) which the other party is required to answer on affidavit. Employed properly, the delivery of interrogatories can have the benefit of saving costs and reducing the amount of court time required for the hearing of an action. These are laudable objectives.

15–11 He referred to *McCabe v Irish Life Assurance plc*,[9] where the Court of Appeal encouraged the delivery of interrogatories by stating:

> Often the delivery of interrogatories can obviate the necessity for expensive

---

7 [2011] IEHC 140.
8 [2020] IEHC 210.
9 [2015] IECA 239.

> and time consuming discovery, can dispose of issues prior to trial, can lessen the number of witnesses and result in an overall shortening of trials. In many cases which lend themselves to the delivery of interrogatories the procedure is simply ignored.

Simons J went on to identify the general principles which govern the delivery of interrogatories, as follows: **15–12**

> First, interrogatories may be served not only in relation to facts directly in issue, but also in respect of facts the existence or non-existence of which is relevant to the existence or non-existence of facts directly in issue. (*Goodbody Ltd v Clyde Shipping Company Ltd*, unreported, Supreme Court, 9 May 1967).
>
> Secondly, the right to serve interrogatories is not confined to facts which are in the peculiar knowledge of the other party. Rather, they may also be used for the purpose of obtaining an admission from the other side. (*Goodbody Ltd v Clyde Shipping Company Ltd*, unreported, Supreme Court, 9 May 1967).
>
> Thirdly, interrogatories will only be allowed where they are necessary either for disposing fairly of the cause or matter or for saving costs. (Order 31, rule 2). See also *McCabe v Irish Life Assurance plc* [2015] IECA 239; [2015] 1 I.R. 346.
>
> Fourthly, interrogatories will not be allowed where what is being sought is not an answer in respect of a factual matter, but rather relates to the interpretation of the contents of a document. (*Bula Ltd. v Tara Mines* [1995] 1 I.L.R.M. 401 (at 406); *Woodfab Ltd v Coillte Teoranta* [2000] 1 I.R. 20 (at 26)).

Privileged Communications

In *Smurfit Paribas Limited v AAB Export Finance Limited*[10] Finlay CJ, when debating the question of privilege, stated that privilege should "only be granted by the courts in instances which have been identified as securing an objective which in the public interest in the proper conduct of the administration of justice can be said to outweigh the disadvantage arising from the restriction of disclosure of all facts". He went on to state that legal privilege should only be extended to communications that "were closely and proximately linked to the conduct of litigation and the function of administering justice in the courts". In *Prendergast v McLoughlin*[11] Clarke J (as he then was), when discussing what kind of documents may be classified as privileged, stated that: **15–13**

> There may, however, be documents which pass between a client and the client's solicitor, in the context of making a will, which may be privileged, where the dominant purpose of the document concerned is designed for the purposes of obtaining or giving legal advice connected with the making of a will, as opposed

[10] [1990] 1 IR 469.
[11] [2008] IEHC 296.

to legal assistance in the drawing of the will concerned. This will be the case where the client concerned expressly seeks legal advice as to matters such as those which I have noted earlier, or where it is implicit in the nature of the instructions tendered that the relevant solicitor was under a duty to give legal advice, arising out of the circumstances concerned, rather than simply perform the task of converting the client's instructions into a properly drafted will. Likewise, where the dominant purpose of a document which arises in the context of the giving or receiving of instructions for the making of a will is not, either expressly or by implication, for the purposes of obtaining or giving legal advice, then it may nonetheless be possible that a portion of such a document can properly be redacted, if it contains instructions necessary for obtaining legal advice, or the tendering of the advice concerned. Like considerations seem to me to apply where a document, such as an attendance, records oral versions of the above.

15–14 In his judgment, Clarke J also referred to *Ochre Ridge Limited v Cork Bonded Warehouses Limited and Port of Cork Company Limited*[12] where Lavan J set out twelve criteria which can assist in determining whether a relevant communication can be said to be made in the context of legal advice on the one hand or legal assistance on the other. In *Prendergast v McLoughlin*[13] Clarke J summarised the Lavan criteria relating to privilege as follows:

i. The communication must be made between a person and a lawyer acting on behalf of such person as a lawyer for the purpose of obtaining from such lawyer legal advice;
ii. The dominant purpose of the communication must be the seeking or giving of legal advice;[14]
iii. Advice does not extend to business matters or to conveyancing documents but does cover correspondence associated with a conveyance for the purpose of seeking or giving legal advice;[15]
iv. The necessity to obtain legal advice envisages the possibility of a legal challenge or query as to the correctness or effectiveness of some step which a person is contemplating;[16]
v. The provision of legal assistance may, in certain circumstances, also entail the provision of legal advice because of the fact that a solicitor's duty of care extends beyond the scope of instructions and requires the solicitor concerned to consider the legal implications of the facts;
vi. There may be circumstances where surrounding documents consulted for the purpose of drafting and for the purpose of obtaining legal advice which included elements of assistance, are privileged;[17]
vii. Communications between solicitor and client giving advice in respect of conveyancing transactions may be privileged if they contain legal advice;[18]
viii. A solicitor will not be required to disclose information as to the details of

[12] Unreported, High Court, Lavan J, 13 July 2004.
[13] [2008] IEHC 296.
[14] *Three Rivers Council v Governor and Company of the Bank of England (No 5)* [2003] QB 1156.
[15] *Balabel v Air India* [1988] Ch 317.
[16] *Smurfit Paribas Bank Ltd v AAB Export Finance Ltd* [1990] 1 IR 469, 478.
[17] *Hustridge Finance Ltd v Lismore Homes*, unreported, High Court, Costello J, 15 February 1991.
[18] See *R v Crown Court exp. Baines* [1988] 1 QB 579, 587.

a client where it is so intertwined with the legal advice that the effect of revealing it would be to disclose the advice;[19]

ix. Privilege does not attach to copies of pre-existing documents which are made for the purpose of obtaining legal advice;[20]

x. The details of when a client met with their lawyer are usually not the subject of legal advice privilege unless in the exceptional instance of where such details are required by a solicitor to give legal advice;[21]

xi. Communications from an opponent's solicitor to a client do not benefit from legal advice privilege as such communication is hardly likely to convey legal advice, unless it contemplates settlement; and

xii. Finally, the objective, as stated by Finlay CJ in *Smurfit Paribas* that, "the public interest in the proper conduct of the administration of justice" arising from the restriction of a disclosure should be kept in mind in any discussion on legal privilege.[22]

When accepting and applying the foregoing criteria formulated by Lavan J in *Ochre Ridge Limited v Cork Bonded Warehouses Limited and Port of Cork Company Limited*,[23] Clarke J stated that they were of considerable assistance in attempting to define the boundary between legal advice and legal assistance. He went on to say that "the criteria that are relevant in any particular circumstances will vary significantly depending on the facts of the case and on the nature of the contact between the client and the solicitor concerned". For the purpose of the issue before him he identified *ii*, *iii*, *v* and *vii* of the foregoing criteria as being of particular relevance. He concluded by saying that he was satisfied that the balance of all of the documents are properly described as arising in the context of legal assistance, rather than legal advice, and cannot be said to be privileged. In the circumstances he disallowed the privilege claimed by the defendant and directed that the plaintiff be entitled to inspection of all of the relevant documents with the exception of the redactions to which he referred. **15–15**

[19] *Miley v Flood* [2001] 2 IR 50.
[20] *TromsoSparebank v Beirne* [1989] ILRM 257.
[21] *R v Manchester Crown Court, exp Rogers* [1991] 4 All ER 35.
[22] *Smurfit Paribas Bank Ltd v AAB Export Finance Ltd* [1990] 1 IR 469, 473.
[23] Unreported, High Court, Lavan J, 13 July 2004.

Chapter 16

INJUNCTIONS

Introduction

Before the hearing of an action for the enforcement of a contract by specific performance an issue may arise between the contractual parties that may require an injunction to deal with it. An application may be made for an interlocutory or mandatory interlocutory injunction. An interlocutory or mandatory interlocutory injunction may be granted for the primary reason of retaining the status quo between the parties before the hearing of the action. The main distinction between an interlocutory injunction and mandatory interlocutory injunction is that in the case of the former there must be a fair bona fide or serious question to be tried, and in the case of the latter the applicant must show that he or she has a strong case that he or she is likely to succeed in the hearing of the action. The court when entertaining an application for an interlocutory injunction may apply the following principles when deciding on whether or not to grant it, that: **16–01**

(i) there is a fair *bona fide* or serious question to be tried;
(ii) damages would not be an adequate remedy for the plaintiff; and
(iii) the balance of convenience favours the granting of the injunction.[1]

The court when entertaining an application for a mandatory interlocutory injunction may apply the following principles when deciding on whether or not to grant it, that: **16–02**

(i) the applicant has a strong case and likely to succeed in the hearing of the action;
(ii) damages would not be an adequate remedy; and
(iii) the balance of convenience favours the granting of the injunction at the interlocutory stage.[2]

The court may also apply the foregoing injunctive principles in applications for springboard injunctions.[3] **16–03**

---

1 *Campus Oil v Minister for Industry (No 2)* [1983] IR 88; see *American Cyanamid Co v Ethicon Limited* [1975] AC 396; *Okanade v The Minister for Justice* [2012] IESC 49, para 9.42; [2012] 3 IR 152; *Osmond Ireland on Farm Business Ltd v McFarland* [2010] IEHC 295; *Curust Financial Services Ltd v Loewe-Lack-Werk*1994] 1 IR 450.

2 *Maha Lingham v Health Service Executive* [2006] ELR 137; see *Shelbourne Hotel Holdings Ltd v Torriam Hotel Operating Company* Ltd [2008] IEHC 376; *Boyhan v Tribunal of Enquiry into the Beef Industry* [1993] 1 IR 210.

3 See *AIB v Diamond* [2011] IEHC 505.

16–04 The court, by exercising its discretionary powers, may award damages *in lieu* of equitable relief for injunctions and, indeed, may also award damages in addition to such equitable relief under s 2 of the Chancery Amendment Act 1858 (known as Lord Cairns' Act). Where the court decides to grant an injunction to the plaintiff it may also require him or her to give an undertaking as to damages for any loss incurred by the defendant before the hearing of the action.

16–05 A plaintiff may make an *ex parte* application to the court seeking a mareva injunction for the purpose of restraining the defendant from disposing of his or her funds before the hearing of an action on a contract between them.[4] The plaintiff is obliged to make full disclosure of all matters relevant and material in his or her application for a mareva injunction.[5]

Interlocutory and Mandatory Interlocutory Injunctions

16–06 An interlocutory or mandatory interlocutory injunction or, indeed, springboard injunction, may be sought by a contractual party to retain the status quo between him or her and the other party to the contract before the hearing of the action on the contract.

(i) Interlocutory Injunctions

16–07 When entertaining an application for an interlocutory injunction by notice of motion the court will also be mindful of the purpose for which such injunctions are sought. In *O'Sullivan's Pharmacies and Beauticians (Sarsfield Street) Limited v Health Service Executive*[6] Laffoy J stated:

> I suppose, to get down to basics, the purpose of seeking an interlocutory injunction is to preserve the status quo between the parties pending the trial of the action. What the Court has to consider at this juncture is whether there is a fair issue to be tried between the parties, whether damages would be an adequate remedy for the party seeking the injunction, and where the balance of convenience lies.

16–08 Applications for interlocutory injunctions may be evaluated by the court on the basis of whether (a) had the plaintiff made out a fair case to be tried, (b) if so, would damages be an adequate remedy in the event that such a case was ultimately successful and (c) in the event that damages would not be an adequate remedy, where does the balance of convenience lie.[7] In

---

4 *O'Mahony v Horgan* [1995] 2 IR 411; *Bambrick v Cobley* [2011] IEHC 505.

5 *Bambrick v Cobley* [2011] IEHC 505; *Third Chandris Shipping Corporation v Unimarine SA* [1979] 2 All ER 972, 984.

6 [2008] IEHC 106; *Claystone v Larkin* [2007] IEHC 89.

7 *Evans v IRFB Services (Ireland) Ltd* [2005] 2 ILRM 358, 361.

Osmond Ireland on Farm Business Ltd v McFarland[8] Laffoy J stated that the plaintiff's application for an interlocutory injunction was determinable by reference to the principles set out by the Supreme Court in *Campus Oil Ltd v Minister for Industry and Energy (No 2)*.[9] According to the principles in *Campus Oil* to establish an entitlement to an interlocutory injunction the plaintiff must show that:

(a) there is a fair *bona fide* or serious question to be tried;
(b) damages would not be an adequate remedy for the plaintiff if it was refused interlocutory relief but was successful at the trial of the action; and
(c) the balance of convenience favours the granting of the injunction.

In *Okanade v The Minister for Justice*[10] Clarke J (as he then was), when referring to the "overall" test for granting interlocutory injunctions, stated that: **16–09**

> As to the overall test I am of the view, therefore, that in considering whether to grant a stay or an interlocutory injunction in the context of judicial review proceedings the court should apply the following considerations:–
> (a) The court should first determine whether the applicant has established an arguable case; if not the application must be refused, but if so then;
> (b) The court should consider where the greatest risk of injustice would lie. But in doing so the court should:
> (i) Give all appropriate weight to the orderly implementation of measures which are prima facie valid;
> (ii) Give such weight as may be appropriate (if any) to any public interest in the orderly operation of the particular scheme in which the measure under challenge was made; and
> (iii) Give appropriate weight (if any) to any additional factors arising on the facts of the individual case which would heighten the risk to the public interest of the specific measure under challenge not being implemented pending resolution of the proceedings;
> but also,
> (iv) Give all due weight to the consequences for the applicant of being required to comply with the measure under challenge in circumstances where that measure may be found to be unlawful.
> (c) In addition the court should, in those limited cases where it may be relevant, have regard to whether damages are available and would be an adequate remedy and also whether damages could be an adequate remedy arising from an undertaking as to damages.
> (d) In addition, and subject to the issues arising on the judicial review not involving detailed investigation of fact or complex questions of law, the court can place all due weight on the strength or weakness of the applicant's case.

As a springboard injunction is an interlocutory application, the court may apply the well-established principles when deciding whether or not to grant **16–10**

8 [2010] IEHC 295.
9 [1983] IR 88.
10 [2012] IESC 49, para 9.42; [2012] 3 IR 152.

an interlocutory injunction. In *AIB v Diamond*[11] Clarke J, when describing the purpose of springboard injunctions, stated that:

> The only legitimate purpose of a springboard injunction is to put in place measures designed to redress an improper head start in competition obtained by unlawful activity. It follows that the only orders which can be made are those which are reasonably necessary to achieve that end. That overall consideration has potential to limit both the scope of orders that can be made and the length of time for which any such orders might be in place.

16–11 In *AIB v Diamond* Clarke J, when considering the granting of a springboard injunction and an undertaking as to damages, stated:

> While it may not strictly be the case that the interlocutory decision brings the case to an end the grant of a springboard injunction at the interlocutory stage has some similarities to such cases. It will, of course, be the case that a plaintiff will be required, if obtaining a springboard injunction, to give the usual undertaking as to damages.

(ii) Mandatory Interlocutory Injunctions

16–12 In applications for mandatory interlocutory injunctions Fennelly J in *Maha Lingham v Health Service Executive*[12] stated that:

> It is well established that the ordinary test of a fair case to be tried is not sufficient to meet the first leg of the test for the grant of interlocutory injunction where the injunction sought is in effect mandatory. In such a case it is necessary for the applicant to show at least that he has a strong case that he is likely to succeed in the hearing of the action. Secondly, the court must consider whether damages would be an adequate remedy for the party seeking the injunction, if he was successful at the trial of the action; and thirdly, whether the balance of convenience favours the grant or refusal of an injunction at the interlocutory stage.

16–13 In *Tola Capital Management LLC v Linders (No 1)*[13] Cregan J, when referring to the relevant principles applied in mandatory interlocutory injunctions, stated that:

> In my view, therefore, it is clear from this review of the authorities that, in the case of mandatory injunctions, there is what Clarke J. has described as "a refinement" or "a variation" of the "pure" *Campus Oil* test. This variation has been applied to mandatory injunctions in two recent Supreme Court decisions – *Maha Lingham* and *Okanade*. In my view, it appears from the decision of Fennelly J. in *Maha Lingham* and the decision of Clarke J. in *Okanade* that where the order sought is a mandatory order, then the appropriate test is that the plaintiff must establish, in

---

11 [2011] IEHC 505, para 10.

12 [2006] ELR 137; see *Shelbourne Hotel Holdings Ltd v Torriam Hotel Operating Company Ltd* [2008] IEHC 376; *Boyhan v Tribunal of Enquiry into the Beef Industry* [1993] 1 IR 210.

13 [2014] IEHC 316, paras 47–48.

> the words of Fennelly J. in *Maha Lingham*, that he has "a strong case that he is likely to succeed at the hearing of the action".
>
> It also appears to be the case that, where a mandatory injunction is being sought, the court should also particularly adopt "whatever course would carry the lower risk of injustice" as stated by Kelly J. in *Shelbourne Hotel* and Clarke J. in *Okanade*.

The plaintiff may also be required to furnish an undertaking as to damages. In *Irish Bank Resolution Corporation Ltd v Quinn*[14] Peart J, when considering the nature of the undertaking as to damages and its purpose, stated that: **16–14**

> As explained, the need for the plaintiff to give an undertaking as to damages is to strike a fair balance as far as possible between the plaintiff's right to be protected from damage and loss which could not be adequately compensated by an award of damages against the defendant, and the defendant's right to be compensated for loss and damage he may suffer as a result of the injunction, in the event that the plaintiff is unsuccessful at trial, and if it is shown that the injunction ought not to have been granted. It is part of the Court's consideration as to where lies the balance of convenience.

In *Sheehan v Breccia*[15] Haughton J, when considering the discretion of the court to vary or discharge interlocutory injunctions, stated, "In relation to the varying and discharge of injunctions, I accept that the court has a wide discretion." **16–15**

He continued: **16–16**

> The court has the power to vary or discharge interlocutory injunctions even if made on consent. This jurisdiction arises *inter alia* where there has been breach of agreement between the parties, change of circumstance or inordinate delay. The principles applicable to granting an interlocutory injunction guide the court, but the relief is discretionary and flexible, the court is guided by equitable principles, and ultimately the court must do what is "just and convenient" and best designed to minimise the risk of injustice in all the circumstances.

Adequacy of Damages

Where it is established that there is a fair or bona fide or serious question to be tried, the court may then consider the question of adequacy of damages. In *Okanade v The Minister for Justice*[16] the Supreme Court summarised the test for deciding the adequacy of damages as follows: **16–17**

---

14 [2013] IEHC 437; see *F Hoffmann-La Roche & Co ASG v Secretary of State for Trade and Industry* [1975] AC 295; *American Cyanamid Co v Ethicon Limited* [1975] AC 396.

15 [2017] IEHC 692, paras 44 and 47; see *Purcell v Trigell Ltd* [1971] 1 QB 358.

16 [2012] 3 IR 152; see *Stena Line Limited v Doyle Shipping Group; Doyle Shipping Group v Stena Line Limited* [2017] IEHC 727.

> First, the court must consider whether, if it does not grant an injunction at the interlocutory stage, a plaintiff who succeeds at the trial of the substantive action will be adequately compensated by an award of damages for any loss suffered between the hearing of the interlocutory injunction and the trial of the action. If the plaintiff would be adequately compensated by damages the interlocutory injunction should be refused subject to the proviso that it appears likely that the relevant defendant would be able to discharge any damages likely to arise.

16–18 However, if damages would not adequately compensate either party, then the court must consider where the balance of convenience lies. Where all other matters are equally balanced the court should attempt to preserve the status quo.[17]

16–19 In *American Cyanamid Co v Ethicon Limited*[18] Lord Diplock, when addressing the issue of adequacy of damages and interlocutory injunctions, stated that:

> It is where there is a doubt as to the adequacy of the respective remedies in damages available to either party or to both that the question of balance of convenience arises. It would be unwise to attempt even to list all of the various matters which may need to be taken into consideration in deciding where the balance lies, let alone to suggest the relative weight to be attached to them. These will vary from case to case.

Undertaking as to Damages

16–20 The undertaking as to damages is not viewed as a contract between the plaintiff and the defendant. It is an undertaking that the plaintiff gives to the court, and a breach of it may be considered to be a contempt of court. In *F Hoffmann-La Roche & Co ASG v Secretary of State for Trade and Industry*[19] Diplock LJ stated that:

> … the defendant may have suffered loss as a result of having been prevented from doing it while the interim injunction was in force; and any loss is likely to be damnum absque injuria for which he could not recover damages from the plaintiff at common law. So unless some other means is provided in this event for compensating the defendant for his loss there is a risk that injustice may be done.
>
> It is to mitigate this risk that the court refuses to grant an interim injunction unless the plaintiff is willing to furnish an undertaking by himself or by some other willing and responsible person …

---

17 See *Okanade v The Minister for Justice* [2012] IESC 49, para 9.42; [2012] 3 IR 152; *Osmond Ireland on Farm Business Ltd v McFarland* [2010] IEHC 295; *Curust Financial Services Ltd v Loewe-Lack-Werk* [1994] 1 IR 450.

18 [1975] AC 396; see *Okanade v The Minister for Justice* [2012] IESC 49, para 9.42; [2012] 3 IR 152; *Whelan Frozen Foods Ltd v Dunnes Stores* [2006] IEHC 171.

19 [1975] AC 295, 361.

In *Okanade v The Minister for Justice*[20] the Supreme Court, in relation to the question of an undertaking as to damages by the plaintiff, stated: **16–21**

> If damages would not be an adequate remedy for the plaintiff, then the court must consider whether, if it does grant an injunction at the interlocutory stage, a plaintiff's undertaking as to damages will adequately compensate the defendant, should the latter be successful at the trial of the action, in respect of any loss suffered by him due to the injunction being enforced pending the trial. If the defendant would be adequately compensated by damages, then the injunction will normally be granted. This last matter is also subject to the proviso that the plaintiff would be in a position to meet the undertaking as to damages in the event that it is called on.

The undertaking as to damages is never intended as a complete indemnity to the defendant. In *Irish Bank Resolution Corporation Ltd v Quinn*[21] Peart J, when referring to the nature and purpose of the undertaking as to damages, stated that: **16–22**

> It is necessary to consider the nature of the undertaking as to damages, and its purpose. What is said by Lord Diplock in *F Hoffmann-La Roche & Co ASG v Secretary of State for Trade and Industry* [1975] AC 295, and also by him in *American Cyanamid Co v Ethicon Limited* [1975] AC 396 is useful in that regard. As explained, the need for the plaintiff to give an undertaking as to damages is to strike a fair balance as far as possible between the plaintiff's right to be protected from damage and loss which could not be adequately compensated by an award of damages against the defendant, and the defendant's right to be compensated for loss and damage he may suffer as a result of the injunction, in the event that the plaintiff is unsuccessful at trial, and if it is shown that the injunction ought not to have been granted. It is part of the Court's consideration as to where lies the balance of convenience.

The court may refuse to grant an injunction which would otherwise be granted where it is satisfied that the undertaking as to damages offered by the plaintiff is of no real value.[22] In *Irish Bank Resolution Corporation Ltd v Quinn*[23] Peart J stated: **16–23**

> There is no doubt that the Court can refuse to grant an injunction which would otherwise be granted, where it is satisfied that the undertaking as to damages offered by the plaintiff is of no real value.

In *F Hoffmann-La Roche & C ASG v Secretary of State for Trade and Industry*[24] Diplock LJ, when considering the question of enforcement of **16–24**

---

[20] [2012] IESC 49, para 9.42; [2012] 3 IR 152; see *Stena Line Limited v Doyle Shipping Group; Doyle Shipping Group v Stena Line Limited* [2017] IEHC 727.
[21] [2013] IEHC 437, para 75.
[22] *Irish Bank Resolution Corporation Ltd v Quinn* [2013] IEHC 437, para 76.
[23] *Irish Bank Resolution Corporation Ltd v Quinn* [2013] IEHC 437, para 79.
[24] [1975] AC 295, 361.

an undertaking as to damages and the assessment of such damages, stated that the court

> retains a discretion not to enforce the undertaking if it considers that the conduct of the defendant in relation to the obtaining or continuing of the injunction or the enforcement of the undertaking makes it inequitable to do so, but if the undertaking is enforced the measure of damages is not discretionary. It is assessed on an inquiry into damages at which principles to be applied are fixed and clear. The assessment is made upon the same basis as that upon which damages for breach of contract would be assessed if the undertaking had been a contract between the plaintiff and the defendant that the plaintiff would not prevent the defendant from doing that which he was restrained from doing by the terms of the injunction.

16–25 The court will not enforce the undertaking if the defendant's own conduct would make it unjust or inequitable to do so. In *Irish Bank Resolution Corporation Ltd v Quinn*[25] Peart J stated:

> It will be noted that the Court enjoys a discretion not to enforce the undertaking as to damages if the defendant's own conduct would make it unjust/inequitable to do so, even though the normal practice will be to do so absent special circumstances. ... The circumstances include delay by the defendant in seeking to enforce the undertaking, the unmeritorious conduct of the defendant, and the "inequitable conduct" of a defendant.

16–26 He went on to state:

> The fact that upon the failure of the plaintiff's case at trial the judge retains a discretion not to enforce the undertaking as to damages so as to do justice between the parties, begs the question whether there can be circumstances where the Court upon an application for an interlocutory injunction may grant the injunction notwithstanding that there is no undertaking of substance or worth forthcoming from the plaintiff. In normal circumstances, the Court cannot insist on an undertaking, but in the absence of one being offered the injunction will normally be refused, because an undertaking is the price which a plaintiff pays for the granting of the injunction.

Mareva Injunctions

16–27 A mareva injunction may be sought by *ex parte* application to the court where there is an anticipated disposal of funds by the defendant with a view to evading his or her contractual obligations.[26] A plaintiff when seeking a mareva injunction must make full disclosure of all matters relevant and material to the application.[27] Where it is later shown that a plaintiff did not

[25] *Irish Bank Resolution Corporation Ltd v Quinn* [2013] IEHC 437, paras 77–78.

[26] *O'Mahony v Horgan* [1995] 2 IR 411; *Bambrick v Cobley* [2011] IEHC 505.

[27] *Bambrick v Cobley* [2011] IEHC 505; *Third Chandris Shipping Corporation v Unimarine SA* [1979] 2 All ER 972, 984.

make full disclosure of all material facts and information the injunction may be discharged.[28] The primary purpose for seeking an injunction is to retain the status quo between the plaintiff and defendant or as near as possible to it before the hearing of the action between the parties. The plaintiff when making an *ex parte* application to the court must make a full disclosure of all matters relevant and material to the application.[29] In *O'Mahony v Hogan*[30] Hamilton CJ stated that the applicant for a mareva injunction should:

> (a) make full and frank disclosure of all matters in his knowledge which are material for the court to know;
> (b) give particulars of his claim and the amount thereof, fairly stating the points made against it by the Defendant;
> (c) give some grounds for believing the Defendant has assets within the jurisdiction: the existence of a bank account is normally sufficient;
> (d) give some grounds for believing that there is a risk of the assets been removed or dissipated; and
> (e) give an undertaking in damages in the event that he should fail.

28 *Bambrick v Cobley* [2005] IEHC 43.
29 *Bambrick v Cobley* [2011] IEHC 505; *Third Chandris Shipping Corporation v Unimarine SA* [1979] 2 All ER 972, 984.
30 [1995] 2 IR 411, 416–18; see *Bambrick v Cobley* [2011] IEHC 505; *Third Chandris Shipping Corporation v Unimarine SA* [1979] 2 All ER 972, 984.

CHAPTER 17

THE COSTS OF ENTIRE PROCEEDINGS

INTRODUCTION

The Rules of the Superior Courts (RSC) (Costs) 2019[1] which came into operation on 3 December 2019 now governs the issue of costs of the entire proceedings, as opposed to costs of interlocutory applications.[2] Since the enactment of the Legal Services Regulation Act 2015 (the 2015 Act) the provisions contained s 196 deal with the powers of the court to award costs of proceedings. In *Chubb European Group SE v The Health Insurance Authority*[3] Murray J, having stated that Ord 99 of the RSC (Costs) 2019 and the relevant parts of ss 168 and 169 of the 2015 Act may be read in conjunction with each other, went on to summarise the general principles "now applicable to the costs of proceedings as a whole (as opposed to the costs of interlocutory applications)". The fundamental principles for awarding costs are that the award of costs is discretionary and that generally costs will "follow the event" are still applicable However, in *Crowley v Promontoria (Oyster) DAC*[4] Sanfey J stated that: **17–01**

> Section 169(1) of the Legal Services Regulation Act 2015 ("LSRA") sets out a non-exhaustive list of circumstances in which the court may depart from this rule "having regard to the particular nature and circumstances of the case, and the conduct of the proceedings by the parties …"

He also stated that the court is required by Ord 99 of the RSC (Costs) 2019 "to have regard to the matters set out in s.169(1) of the [LSRA] where applicable". In *Chubb European Group SE v The Health Insurance Authority*[5] Murray J summarised the general principles applicable to the costs of proceedings as a whole (as opposed to the costs of interlocutory applications). In *Harrison v Charleton*[6] Noonan J stated that the "new regime" applying post the RSC (Costs) 2019 is that as identified by Murray J in *Chubb European Group SE v The Health Insurance Authority*.[7] **17–02**

---

1 SI No 584 of 2019.
2 See Chapter 18.
3 See Chapter 18.
4 [2020] IEHC 365, para 4.
5 [2020] IECA 183.
6 [2020] IECA 197, para 4.
7 [2020] IECA 183.

Costs of the Entire Proceedings

17–03 In *Chubb European Group SE v The Health Insurance Authority*[8] Murray J stated that Ord 99 of the RSC (Costs) 2019 and the relevant parts of ss 168 and 169 of the Legal Services Regulation Act 2015 may be read in conjunction with each other when deciding on an issue of costs. The RSC (Costs) 2019,[9] which came into operation on the 3 December 2019, provides that:

> 2. Subject to the provisions of statute (including sections 168 and 169 of the 2015 Act) and except as otherwise provided by these Rules:
>
> (1) The costs of and incidental to every proceeding in the Superior Courts shall be in the discretion of those Courts respectively.
>
> (2) No party shall be entitled to recover any costs of or incidental to any proceeding from any other party to such proceeding except under an order or as provided by these Rules.

17–04 Sections 168 and 169 of the 2015 Act introduced new statutory provisions dealing with the *powers* of the courts to award costs. Section 168 provides that:

> Subject to the provisions of this Part, a court may, on application by a party to civil proceedings, at any stage in, and from time to time during, those proceedings—
>
> (a) order that a party to the proceedings pay the costs of or incidental to the proceedings of one or more other parties to the proceedings, or
>
> (b) where proceedings before the court concern the estate of a deceased individual, or the property of a trust, order that the costs of or incidental to the proceedings of one or more parties to the proceedings be paid out of the property of the estate or trust.
>
> (2) Without prejudice to *subsection (1)*, the order may include an order that a party shall pay—
>
> (a) a portion of another party's costs,
>
> (b) costs from or until a specified date, including a date before the proceedings were commenced,
>
> (c) costs relating to one or more particular steps in the proceedings,
>
> (d) where a party is partially successful in the proceedings, costs relating to the successful element or elements of the proceedings, and
>
> (e) interest on costs from or until a specified date, including a date before the judgment.
>
> (3) Nothing in this Part shall be construed as—
>
> (a) restricting any right of action for the tort of maintenance, or
>
> (b) restricting any right of a trustee, mortgagee or other person, existing on the day on which this section commences, to be paid costs out of a particular estate or fund to which he or she would be entitled under any rule of law or equity.

8 See Chapter 18.

9 SI No 584 of 2019.

Section 169(1) of the 2015 Act introduced new statutory powers which may be applied by the courts when awarding costs of proceedings. Section 169(1) provides that: **17–05**

> A party who is entirely successful in civil proceedings is entitled to an award of costs against a party who is not successful in those proceedings, unless the court orders otherwise, having regard to the particular nature and circumstances of the case, and the conduct of the proceedings by the parties, including—
> (a) conduct before and during the proceedings,
> (b) whether it was reasonable for a party to raise, pursue or contest one or more issues in the proceedings,
> (c) the manner in which the parties conducted all or any part of their cases,
> (d) whether a successful party exaggerated his or her claim,
> (e) whether a party made a payment into court and the date of that payment,
> (f) whether a party made an offer to settle the matter the subject of the proceedings, and if so, the date, terms and circumstances of that offer, and
> (g) where the parties were invited by the court to settle the claim (whether by mediation or otherwise) and the court considers that one or more than one of the parties was or were unreasonable in refusing to engage in the settlement discussions or in mediation.

Principles of Costs of the Entire Proceedings

In *Chubb European Group SE v The Health Insurance Authority*[10] Murray J summarised the general principles now applicable to the costs of proceedings as a whole (as opposed to the costs of interlocutory applications) as follows: **17–06**

> (a) The general discretion of the Court in connection with the ordering of costs is preserved (s.168(1)(a) and O.99, r.2(1)).
> (b) In considering the awarding of costs of any action, the Court should "have regard to" the provisions of s.169(1) (O.9, r.3(1)).
> (c) In a case where the party seeking costs has been "entirely successful in those proceedings", the party so succeeding "is entitled" to an award of costs against the unsuccessful party unless the court orders otherwise (s.169(1)).
> (d) In determining whether to "order otherwise" the court should have regard to the "nature and circumstances of the case" and "the conduct of the proceedings by the parties" (s.169(1)).
> (e) Further, the matters to which the court shall have regard in deciding whether to so order otherwise include the conduct of the parties before and during the proceedings, and whether it was reasonable for a party to raise, pursue or contest one or more issues (s. 169(1)(a) and (b)).
> (f) The Court, in the exercise of its discretion may also make an order that where a party is "partially successful" in the proceedings, it should recover costs relating to the successful element or elements of the proceedings (s.168(2)(d)).
> (g) Even where a party has not been "entirely successful" the court should still have regard to the matters referred to in s.169(1)(a)-(g) when deciding whether to award costs (O.99, r.3(1)).

[10] [2020] IECA 183.

(h) In the exercise of its discretion, the Court may order the payment of a portion of a party's costs, or costs from or until a specified date (s.168(2)(a)).

17–07 Murray J found:

> 37. Chubb, not having been "entirely successful" in its proceedings has no entitlement under s 169(1) of the 2015 Act to its costs. The Court has, however, the power under s 168(2)(a) to make an order in its favour to the extent that it was "partially successful" in the proceedings, just as it has the power to make an order on the same basis in favour of HIA. That power extends to awarding "costs relating to the successful element" of the proceedings. The difference between the two provisions is important: the party who prevails entirely has a right to costs unless there is a reason not to order them. A party who only succeeds partially may obtain an order for costs in respect of the successful aspect of its claim if, having regard inter alia to the criteria specified in s.169(2), it is appropriate to award them. Issues will arise in other cases as to what exactly "entirely successful" means. Depending on the precise construction placed on that phrase, the pre-existing position that a party who won "the event" but succeeds in respect of only some of the issues addressed in support of the relief it obtains is presumptively entitled to all its costs, may have been changed by the Act.
>
> 38. In this case, it is in my view appropriate that Chubb obtain the costs attributable to that part of the proceeding in which it succeeded, and the same applies to HIA. In determining the costs so attributable, I do not see that the Act limits the power of the Court to award only those costs directly attributable to those issues and in determining the level of such costs I believe – 19 – that the allowance to Chubb of the costs of the presentation of the background issues is appropriate.

17–08 He concluded:

> 43. (a) HIA will recover as against Chubb all of the costs of the judicial review proceedings except the costs of the hearing of the appeal in those proceedings.
> (b) For the purposes of determining the costs of the High Court hearing of the judicial review proceedings, those proceedings shall be treated as having lasted one and a half days. – 21 –
> (c) For the avoidance of doubt, I am making no order as to the costs of the hearing of the appeal of the judicial review proceedings because those proceedings were so enmeshed with the statutory application that they are properly and fairly treated for the purposes of the hearing as a single appeal. However, again for the avoidance of doubt, HIA is entitled to recover the costs of the appeal of the judicial review proceedings excluding the hearing costs (including solicitor's instruction fees and counsel's brief fees) and comprising the costs attending response to the notice of appeal and legal submissions.
> (d) HIA shall recover from Chubb one third of its costs of the High Court proceedings and of the appeal in the statutory application.

17–09 In *Harrison v Charleton*[11] Noonan J observed:

[11] [2020] IECA 197.

> 4. Neither of the parties has specifically addressed the provisions of the Legal Services Regulation Act, 2015 and in particular sections 168 and 169 thereof, together with the relevant provisions of Order 99 of the Rules of the Superior Courts as they stand since the 3rd December, 2019. The new regime applying post that date is considered in detail in the judgment of this court in *Chubb European Group SE v The Health Insurance Authority* [2020] IECA 183. In the course of delivering a judgment with which the other members of the court agreed, Murray J. helpfully set out at para. 19 the principles to be applied by the court in determining costs issues post-December 2019. Section 169(1) provides that where the party seeking costs has been "entirely successful" in the proceedings, such party "is entitled to an award of costs unless the court orders otherwise." In determining whether to order otherwise, the court should have regard to the "nature and circumstances of the case" and "the conduct of the proceedings by the parties". This includes conduct both before and during the proceedings and whether it was reasonable for a party to raise, pursue or contest one or more issues. The court's overriding general discretion is preserved by section 168(1)(a) and O. 99, r. 2(1).

He concluded: **17–10**

> 5. It is clear that the respondent has been entirely successful in these proceedings. All issues considered by this court to be material have been determined against the appellant. Therefore, whether one adopts the criterion of costs following the event, or of being entirely successful, under either rubric the respondent should be entitled to his costs unless the appellant can demonstrate that there are special reasons why the court should depart from the normal rule.

CHAPTER 18

THE COSTS OF INTERLOCUTORY APPLICATIONS

INTRODUCTION

The Rules of the Superior Courts (RSC) (Costs) 2008 amended Ord 99 of the RSC 1986, and provides that: **18–01**

> 1. Order 99 of the Rules of the Superior Courts is hereby amended by:
>   (i) the substitution for sub-rules (3) and (4) of rule 1 thereof of the following:
>   (3) Subject to sub-rule (4A), the costs of every action, question, and issue tried by a jury shall follow the event unless the Court, for special cause, to be mentioned in the order, shall otherwise direct.
>   (4) Subject to sub-rule (4A), the costs of every issue of fact or law raised upon a claim or counterclaim shall, unless otherwise ordered, follow the event.
>   (4A) The High Court or the Supreme Court, upon determining any interlocutory application, shall make an award of costs save where it is not possible justly to adjudicate upon liability for costs on the basis of the interlocutory application.

Under Ord 99, r1(4A) of the RSC (Costs) 2008, where interlocutory applications are involved, as opposed to costs of the whole proceedings, the court may make an award costs except where it is not "possible justly" to do so. In *Glaxo Group Limited v Rowex Limited*[1] Barrett J summarised the principles relating to the right to costs in interlocutory applications pursuant to Ord 99, r 1(4A) of the RSC (Costs) 2008.[2] **18–02**

The RSC (Costs) 2019,[3] which came into operation on 3 December 2019, provides that: **18–03**

> 2. Subject to the provisions of statute (including sections 168 and 169 of the 2015 Act) and except as otherwise provided by these Rules:
>   (1) The costs of and incidental to every proceeding in the Superior Courts shall be in the discretion of those Courts respectively.
>   (2) No party shall be entitled to recover any costs of or incidental to any

1 [2015] 1 IR 185, 208–15.
2 SI No 12 of 2008.
3 SI No 584 of 2019.

> proceeding from any other party to such proceeding except under an order or as provided by these Rules.
>
> (3) The High Court, the Court of Appeal or the Supreme Court, upon determining any interlocutory application, shall make an award of costs save where it is not possible justly to adjudicate upon liability for costs on the basis of the interlocutory application.

18–04 Under Ord 99, r 2(3) of the RSC (Costs) 2019, and where interlocutory applications are involved, as opposed to costs of the whole proceedings, the court may make an award of costs except where it is not "possible justly" to do so. It can be seen that the provisions relation to costs of interlocutory applications in Ord 99, r 2(3) of the RSC (Costs) 2019 are similar to those in Ord 99, r 1(4A) of the RSC (Costs) 2008, except that the provisions of Ord 99, r 2(3) of the RSC (Costs) 2019 are made subject to ss 168 and 169 of the Legal Services Regulation Act 2015 (the 2015 Act). In *Paddy Burke (Builders) Limited (in liquidation and in receivership) v Tullyvaraga Management Company Limited*[4] McDonald J, and in *Crowley v Promontoria (Oyster) DAC*[5] Sanfey J, applied principles summarised by Barrett J in *Glaxo Group Limited v Rowex Limited*[6] when deciding on the issue of costs pursuant to Ord 99 r 2(3) of the RSC (Costs) 2019. Sanfey J added that Ord 99, r 2(3) of the RSC (Costs) 2019 contain provisions similar to those in Ord 99, r 1(4A) of the RSC (Costs) 2008.

Costs of Interlocutory Applications

18–05 Order 99, r1(4A) of the RSC (Costs) 2008 provides that:

> The High Court or the Supreme Court, upon determining any interlocutory application, shall make an award of costs save where it is not possible justly to adjudicate upon liability for costs on the basis of the interlocutory application.

18–06 In *Haughey v Synnott*[7] Laffoy J, when considering the question of costs pursuant to Ord 99, r 1(4A) of the RSC (Costs) 2008 and interlocutory applications, referred to the judgment of Clarke J in *Veolia Water UK plc v Fingal County Council*[8]:

> The prospect of a court being in a position to make an award of costs in relation to an application for interlocutory injunctive relief after the determination of the application is less likely than in the case of other forms of interlocutory applications, for example, interlocutory applications dealing with procedural matters. That is because, in the case of an application for interlocutory injunctive

4 [2020] IEHC 199.
5 [2020] IEHC 365.
6 [2015] 1 IR 185, 208–15.
7 [2012] IEHC 403.
8 [2007] 2 IR 81.

> relief, it is frequently "not possible justly to adjudicate upon liability for costs" at that juncture, so that the case comes within the saver in rule 1(4A).

She also referred to the decision of Clarke J in *Allied Irish Banks Plc v Diamond*[9] and stated that Clarke J had gone on to: **18–07**

> draw a distinction between cases where the decision on an interlocutory injunction application turns on issues relating to the merits of the proceedings such that a different picture may emerge at the trial and cases where the application turns on matters such as adequacy of damages or balance of convenience which will not be addressed again at the trial. In the former category of cases, a risk of injustice may arise in determining costs at the stage of the interlocutory injunction application whereas the same risk may not arise where the application does not turn on the merits of the proceedings.

In *ACC Bank plc v Hanrahan and Sheeran*[10] Clarke J, when referring costs pursuant to Ord 99, r 1(4A) and interlocutory applications stated that: **18–08**

> 3.2 The reason for the introductions of [r 1(4A)] seems to me to be clear. While, historically, there had been a tendency to reserve the costs of most motions to the trial judge, a view has been taken that this can lead to injustice for, at least in very many cases, a judge who has heard a motion is in a better position than the trial judge to consider the justice of where the costs of that motion should lie. This will especially be so in cases where the trial court will not have to revisit the merits or otherwise of the precise issue that was raised by motion … [For example, a] judge hearing a discovery motion will … in almost all cases, be in a better position than the trial judge to decide where the costs of such a motion should lie. Like considerations apply to many other cases such as motions for further and better particulars.
>
> 3.3 It is, of course, the case that such motions are very much "events" in themselves. There are issues as to the appropriate scope of discovery or particulars. They are decided once and for all on the motion. The merits of the results of these motions are not, in the vast majority of cases, in any way revisited at trial.
>
> 3.4 Slightly different considerations seem to me to apply in cases where, at least to a material extent, some of the issues which are before the Court at an interlocutory stage arise or are likely to arise again at the trial in at least some form.
>
> 3.5 It follows that in such cases there may well be good grounds for not dealing with the costs at the interlocutory stage for the trial court may be in a better position to assess the justice of the costs of an interlocutory hearing when it has been able to decide where the true costs lie. It is not necessarily just that a plaintiff who secures an interlocutory injunction on the basis of putting up false facts should get the costs of that interlocutory injunction even if it was fairly clear that an injunction would be granted on the basis of the facts as asserted.

---

9 Unreported, High Court, Clarke J, 7 November 2011.
10 [2014] IESC 40 11.

Principles of Costs of Interlocutory Applications

18–09 In *Glaxo Group Limited v Rowex Limited*[11] Barrett J helpfully summarised the principles relating to costs of interlocutory applications pursuant to Ord 99, r 1 (4A) of the RSC (Costs) 2008 as follows:

> 12. It seems to the court that the following principles as to whether or not to make an order for costs in favour of the victor following an application for interlocutory injunctive relief can be derived from the cases considered above.
>
> A. Reason for introduction of r.1(4A).
> i. While, historically, there was a tendency to reserve the costs of most motions to the trial judge, a view has been taken that this can lead to injustice: a judge who has heard a motion is often better placed than the trial judge to consider the justice of where costs of that motion should lie. (Hanrahan).
>
> B. Effect of r.1(4A).
> ii. The effect of r.1(4A) is that a court is required to adjudicate upon and make a costs order in respect of an interlocutory application, rather than reserve the costs. (Haughey).
>
> C. Discretion and options of court.
> iii. The court retains a wide discretion in deciding what costs order to make. (Haughey).
>
> iv. Options include making (a) an order awarding all or part of the costs to one party, (b) no order as to costs, or (c) the costs of the application costs in the cause. (Haughey).
>
> v. Costs may only be reserved where it is not possible justly to adjudicate upon the costs of the interlocutory application. (Haughey).
>
> D. Factors influencing exercise of discretion.
> vi. Important factors in determining how to deal with the costs of an interlocutory application include (a) whether an application was required to be brought, (b) the success, or degree of success, of a party on the application, (c) whether the party bringing the application gave the opposing party an adequate opportunity to deal with the subject matter of the motion prior to its issue, and (d) whether the opposing party acted reasonably in refusing to deal with the particular matter on a consensual basis. (Haughey).
>
> vii. In the case of interlocutory injunction applications, the diversity of outcomes following which the court may be asked to determine where the burden of costs should lie will inevitably bear on the court's determination. (Tekenable, Hanrahan).
>
> viii. Another factor is the inherent nature of an interlocutory injunction which is to preserve the status quo. (Tekenable, Campus Oil).
>
> E. Interlocutory injunction vs. other interlocutory applications.

[11] [2015] 1 IR 185, 208–15.

ix. There is a wide range of interlocutory applications where there is not the remotest possibility of injustice if costs are awarded in a particular manner. An obvious example is the award of costs to a plaintiff on a motion for judgment in default of defence. (Tekenable).

x. The prospect of a court being in a position to make an award of costs in relation to an application for interlocutory injunctive relief is less likely than in the case of other forms of interlocutory applications. (Haughey, O'Dea, Tekenable, Hanrahan).

xi. A distinction falls to be drawn between (a) cases where the decision on an interlocutory injunction application turns on issues in respect of which a different picture may emerge at trial and (b) cases where the application turns on matters such as adequacy of damages or balance of convenience which will not be addressed again at the trial. In the former category of cases, a risk of injustice may arise in determining costs at the stage of the interlocutory injunction application; in the latter the same risk may not arise. (Haughey, Diamond, Hanrahan).

xii. Factors making an application for an interlocutory injunction less susceptible to a determination as to liability for costs include (a) that there may be matters which can only be resolved by the court of trial on oral evidence at plenary hearing of the action, and (b) matters may come to light by way of discovery or new evidence not available to the parties at the time of the interlocutory application which will bring about a result which seemed unlikely or improbable at the time that application was heard. (O'Dea, Dubcap).

xiii. It is not necessarily just that a plaintiff who secures an interlocutory injunction should get the costs of that interlocutory injunction even if it was fairly clear that an injunction would be granted on the basis of the facts as asserted. (Hanrahan).

Order 99, r 2(3) of the RSC (Costs) 2019,[12] which came into operation on the 3 December 2019, provides that: **18–10**

The High Court, the Court of Appeal or the Supreme Court, upon determining any interlocutory application, shall make an award of costs save where it is not possible justly to adjudicate upon liability for costs on the basis of the interlocutory application.

In *Paddy Burke (Builders) Limited (in liquidation and in receivership) v Tullyvaraga Management Company Limited*[13] McDonald J, when considering the question of costs pursuant to Ord 99 r 2(3) of the RSC (Costs) 2019 in relation to an interlocutory application, stated: **18–11**

3. In considering the question of costs, I am obliged to approach the matter in accordance with the provisions of O.99 r.2 (3) R.S.C. which replaces the former O.99 r.1 (4A). Order 99 r.2 (3) provides as follows:– "The High Court … upon determining any interlocutory application, shall make an award of costs save

---

12 SI No 584 of 2019.

13 [2020] IEHC 199; see *Crowley v Promontoria (Oyster) DAC* [2020] IEHC 365.

where it is not possible justly to adjudicate upon liability for costs on the basis of the interlocutory application."

4. Order 99 r.2 (3) is in identical terms to the former O.99 r.1 (4A). The latter rule has been addressed in a number of authorities including the decision of Laffoy J. in *Tekenable Ltd v Morrissey* [2012] IEHC 391 which was expressly approved by the Supreme Court in *ACC Bank Plc v Hanrahan* [2014] 1 I.R. 1. In turn, the decision of Laffoy J. in *Tekenable* was influenced by the earlier decisions of Clarke J. (as he then was) in *Allied Irish Banks v Diamond* (High Court, unreported, 7th November, 2011) referred to in Delaney & McGrath on "Civil Procedure in the Superior Courts", 4th ed., 2018, at para. 24-79 and the previous decision of Laffoy J. herself in *O'Dea v Dublin City Council* [2011] IEHC 100.

7. The relevant principles (and the authorities on which they are based) were also comprehensively considered by Barrett J. in his judgment in *Glaxo Group Ltd v Rowex Ltd* [2015] 1 I.R. 185 at p.p. 208-215.

18–12 He referred to principle xii in the judgment of Barrett J in *Glaxo Group Ltd v Rowex Ltd* where he stated:

xii. Factors making an application for an interlocutory injunction less susceptible to a determination as to liability for costs include (a) that there may be matters which can only be resolved by the court of trial on oral evidence at plenary hearing of the action, and (b) matters may come to light by way of discovery or new evidence not available to the parties at the time of the interlocutory application which will bring about a result which seemed unlikely or improbable at the time that application was heard. (*O'Dea v Dublin City Council…*); *Dubcap Ltd v Microcrop Ltd …*

18–13 In the light of principle xii in *Glaxo* McDonald J stated:

In my view, the observations of Barrett J. in that paragraph (which succinctly summarise the approach suggested by Laffoy J. in *O'Dea* and of Keane J. (as he then was) in *Dubcap*) are of particular relevance in the present case. As appears from the judgment which I delivered on 8th April, 2020, the issue of priority as between Promontoria, the secured creditor, on the one hand and the management company, on the other, was critical to my conclusion that, on the basis of the evidence and arguments currently before the court, the management company had failed to make out either a strong case or even a serious issue to be tried. On the basis of the evidence before the court at this point in the proceedings, it appeared to me to be clear that the mortgage in favour of Promontoria has priority over any of the management agreements with the management company.

18–14 He concluded:

19. In these circumstances, it seems to me that the just order to make in the present case is to direct that the costs of the receiver and Promontoria both of the hearing and application in the Circuit Court and the appeal to this court should be costs in the cause such that, if the receiver and Promontoria succeed in their defence to the counterclaim of the management company at trial, they will be entitled to their costs as against the management company but, on the other hand, if they fail to succeed in their defence, they will not be entitled to their costs of

the hearing in the Circuit Court or in this court in relation to the application for an interlocutory injunction.

In *Crowley v Promontoria (Oyster) DAC*[14] Sanfey J, when referring to Ord 99 r 2(3) of the RSC (Costs) 2019, stated that: **18–15**

4. The fundamental principles in relation to costs are that the award of costs is discretionary, and that generally costs will "follow the event". Section 169(1) of the Legal Services Regulation Act 2015 ("LSRA") sets out a non-exhaustive list of circumstances in which the court may depart from this rule "having regard to the particular nature and circumstances of the case, and the conduct of the proceedings by the parties …". Under O.99, r.2 (3) of the Rules of the Superior Courts, the court is required, "upon determining any interlocutory application", to make an award of costs "save where it is not possible justly to adjudicate upon liability for costs on the basis of the interlocutory application". The court is required by O.99, r.3(1) to have regard to the matters set out in s.169(1) of the [LSRA] where applicable.

5. O. 99, r.2(3) is in identical terms to the former O.99, r.1(4A). This latter rule was introduced in February 2008, and was addressed by Laffoy J. in her decision in *Tekenable Limited v Morrissey* [2012] IEHC 391, a decision which was expressly approved by the Supreme Court in *ACC Bank plc v Hanrahan* [2014] 1 IR 1.

When referring to the principles regarding interlocutory applications Sanfey J stated: **18–16**

There have been a number of further authorities considering the relevant principles regarding costs in interlocutory applications since *Tekenable*, and these authorities were addressed in a very helpful summary of the law by McDonald J. in the recent decision of *Paddy Burke (Builders) Limited (in liquidation and in receivership) v Tullyvaraga Management Company Limited* [2020] IEHC 199. In that case, McDonald J. cited with approval the approach of Barrett J. in *Glaxo Group Limited v Rowex Limited* [2015] 1 IR 185, in which Barrett J. commented as follows: "xi. A distinction falls to be drawn between (a) cases where the decision on an interlocutory injunction application turns on issues in respect of which a different picture may emerge at trial and (b) cases where the application turns on matters such as adequacy of damages or balance of convenience which will not be addressed again at the trial. In the former category of cases, a risk of injustice may arise in determining costs at the stage of the interlocutory injunction application; in the latter the same risk may not arise.

He went on to state: **18–17**

8. The "event" in the application therefore is the refusal of the plaintiff's challenge to the appointment of the Receiver and the consequential orders sought. The issue presently is whether there is any basis upon which I should not award the costs of the application to the defendants.

9. As s.169(1) of the LSRA makes clear, I am entitled to have regard, in deciding

[14] [2020] IEHC 365.

the issue of costs, to "the particular nature and circumstances of the case, and the conduct of the proceedings by the parties". The submissions of the plaintiff make complaints in relation to the conduct of the proceedings by the defendants. The plaintiff cites the late – albeit by one day – delivery of the submissions invited by the court. The plaintiff complains of late service of an appearance on behalf of the defendants, and the late filing of affidavits in the present application.

18–18 He concluded:

> 14. I am of the view that, notwithstanding that the conduct of the defence of the application was unsatisfactory in some respects – in this regard, see the comments at para. 24 of the judgment – the defendants are entitled to the costs of the application. The motion was without merit, and has caused considerable expense and delay in the receivership.
>
> 15. Accordingly, I will order that the application be refused, and that the defendant be entitled to the costs of the application, to be adjudicated in default of agreement.

INDEX